JURISPRUDENCE
THEORY AND CONTEXT

JURISPRUDENCE:
THEORY AND CONTEXT

BRIAN BIX

WestviewPress
A Division of HarperCollins*Publishers*

Copyright © in London, England by Sweet & Maxwell
Published in 1996 in London by Sweet & Maxwell
100 Avenue Road,
Swiss Cottage
London NW3 3PF.

Printed and bound in Great Britain

Published in 1996 in the
United States of America by
Westview Press,
5500 Central Avenue,
Boulder, Colorado, 80301—2877

Library of Congress
Cataloging-in-Publication Data available upon request.

ISBN 0–8133–3206–0

No natural forests were destroyed to make this product,
only farmed timber was used and re-planted

©
Sweet & Maxwell
1996

For Joseph Raz

Preface

This book derives from past efforts to teach jurisprudence: in particular, the struggle to explain some of the more difficult ideas in the area in a way that could be understood by those new to the field, without at the same time simplifying the ideas to the point of distortion. This text is grounded in a combination of frustrations: the frustration I sometimes felt as a teacher, when I was unable to get across the beauty and subtlety of the great writers in legal theory[1]; and the frustration my students sometimes felt, when they were unable to understand me, due to my inability to explain the material in terms they could comprehend.

I do not underestimate the difficulty of the task I have set myself, and I am sure that this text does not always achieve all that it sets out to do. At the least, I hope that I do not appear to be hiding my failures behind legal or philosophical jargon. H. L. A. Hart once wrote the following in the course of discussing an assertion made by the American judge and theorist Oliver Wendell Holmes:

> "To make this discovery with Holmes is to be with a guide whose words may leave you unconvinced, sometimes even repelled, but never mystified. Like our own [John] Austin, . . . Holmes was sometimes clearly wrong, but again like Austin he was always wrong clearly."[2]

I do not purport to be able to offer the powerful insights or the

---

[1] Unlike some writers (see, *e.g.* William Twining, "Academic Law and Legal Philosophy: The Significance of Herbert Hart" (1979) 95 *Law Quarterly Review* 557 at 565–580), I do not distinguish between "jurisprudence", "legal theory", and "legal philosophy", and I will use those terms interchangeably.

[2] H. L. A. Hart, "Positivism and the Separation of Law and Morals" (1958) 71 *Harvard Law Review* 593 at 593.

elegant prose of Holmes, but I do strive to emulate him in the more modest, but still difficult, task of expressing ideas in a sufficiently straightforward manner such that when I am wrong, I am "wrong clearly".

This book is part introductory text and part commentary. In the preface to his classic text, *The Concept of Law*, Hart stated his hope that his book would "discourage the belief that a book on legal theory is primarily a book from which one learns what other books contain."[3] My aims are less ambitious: the present text *is* a book meant to inform readers what other books contain—the idea being that the primary texts are not always as accessible as they might be. However, this book is distinctly *not* meant as a substitute for reading those primary texts: the hope and the assumption is that readers will go to the primary texts first, and will return to them again after obtaining whatever guidance is to be offered in these pages.

One can find entire books on many of the topics discussed in the present volume in sections. I have done my best to offer overviews that do not sacrifice the difficulty of the subjects, but I fear that some misreading is inevitable in any summary. In part to compensate for the necessarily abbreviated nature of what is offered, a "Suggested Further Readings" section is offered at the end of the book (and there are footnote citations to the primary texts throughout the book) for those who wish to locate longer and fuller discussions of certain topics.

A related problem is that, in the limited space available, I could not include all the topics that are associated with jurisprudence (a course whose content varies greatly from university to university). The variety of topics included in one source or another under the category of jurisprudence is vast, so inevitably there always seems to be more missing than present in any text. Through my silence (or brevity), I do not mean to imply that the topics not covered are not interesting, not important, or are not properly part of jurisprudence. Selection for inclusion and exclusion was partly arbitrary, and partly a reflection of which topics best fit the themes I wanted to consider.

---

[3] H. L. A. Hart, *The Concept of Law* (Oxford: Clarendon Press, 1961), p. vi. (Except where otherwise noted, references to *The Concept of Law* will be to the original edition; the posthumously published revised edition, which includes a reply to critics, has a slightly different pagination.)

One caveat I must offer is that references to legal practice offered in this book will be primarily to the practices in the American and English legal systems, as these are the systems with which I am most familiar. It is likely (although far from certain) that any comments based on those two legal systems would be roughly generalisable to cover all common law systems. The extent to which my lack of familiarity with Roman law/civil code systems biases my views about legal theory and about the nature of law I must leave to others to judge.

Work on this book often overlapped work I was doing for other smaller projects: sometimes work done for the book was borrowed for other projects, and sometimes I found that work done for other projects could be usefully incorporated in the book. An earlier version of parts of Chapter 4 appeared in "Conceptual Questions and Jurisprudence" (1995) 1 *Legal Theory* 415; earlier versions of parts of Chapters 7, 8, and 9 will appear in "Natural Law Theory" in *A Companion to the Philosophy of Law and Legal Theory* (forthcoming, D. Patterson ed., Oxford: Basil Blackwell, 1996); an earlier version of brief sections of Chapters 3 and 9 appeared in "Questions in Legal Interpretation" in *Law and Interpretation* (A. Marmor ed., Oxford: Clarendon press, 1995), pp. 137–154; and an earlier version of parts of Chapters 3 and 14 appeared in "Questions in Legal Interpretation" (1994) 18 *Tel Aviv Law Review* 463 (translated into Hebrew). I am grateful to the publishers for allowing me permission to use material from those articles.

I would like to thank the following for their helpful comments on earlier drafts of parts of the book: Mark Addis, Ian Ayres, Scott Brewer, Neal Feigenson, John Finnis, Stephen Gilles, Matthew Kramer, Brian Leiter, Andrei Marmor, Thomas Morawetz, Martha Nussbaum, Dennis Patterson, Stanley L. Paulson, Frederick Schauer, Scott Shapiro, M.B.E. Smith, Larry Solum, Scott Sturgeon, Lloyd Weinreb and Kenneth Winston.

BRIAN BIX

Contents

Table of Cases

PART A

Legal Theory: Problems and Possibilities

It is surprising how often one can go through entire jurisprudence books or courses without the most basic questions ever being raised, let alone resolved. The purpose of the opening chapters is to mention some of these basic questions:

(1) In what sense is a general theory of law possible?
(2) What is the point of conceptual claims, and how can one evaluate them?
(3) In which senses can one speak of the relative merits of different legal theorists or of different approaches to law?

Some of these questions, and the answers suggested for them, will be applicable primarily to the second section of this book, which covers a number of individual theories about the law. Other questions will have resonance that extends throughout all the book's topics.

Chapter One

Overview, Purpose and Methodology

Why study jurisprudence?

For many students, the question has a simple answer: for them, it is a required course which they must pass in order to graduate. For students in this situation, the questions about any jurisprudence book will be whether it can help them to learn enough of the material to pass the course (or to do sufficiently well in the course that their overall class standing is not adversely affected). However, even students who have such a "minimal survival" attitude towards the subject might want to know what further advantage they might obtain from whatever knowledge of the subject they happen to pick up.

At the practical level, reading and participating in jurisprudential discussions develops the ability to analyse and to think critically and creatively about the law. Such skills are always useful in legal practice, particularly when facing novel questions within the law or when trying to formulate and advocate novel approaches to legal problems. Thus, even those who need a "bottom line" justification for whatever they do should be able to find a reason to read legal theory.

At a professional level, jurisprudence is the way lawyers and judges reflect on what they do and what their role is within society. This truth is reflected by the way jurisprudence is taught as part of a *university* education in the law, where law is considered not merely as a trade to be learned (like carpentry or fixing automobiles) but as an intellectual pursuit. For those who believe that only

3

the reflective life is worth living, and who also spend most of their waking hours working within (or around) the legal system, there are strong reasons to want to think deeply about the nature of law.

Finally, for some (whether the blessed or the cursed one cannot say), jurisprudence is interesting and enjoyable on its own, whatever its other uses and benefits. There will always be some for whom learning is interesting and valuable in itself, even if it does not lead to greater wealth, greater self-awareness, or greater social progress.

NOTES ON METHOD

Part of the purpose in writing this book was to counter a tendency to treat jurisprudence as just another exercise in rote memorisation. It is often tempting for jurisprudence students, especially those whose background is in law rather than philosophy, to treat the major writers in the area as just a variation on black-letter, doctrinal law: that is, as points, positions and arguments to be memorised, in order that they can later be repeated in the final examination.

A second problem in the way that legal theory is presented and studied is the tendency to see different legal theorists as offering competing answers to simple questions. Thus, H. L. A. Hart and Lon Fuller are thought to be debating certain easily stateable propositions in their 1958 exchange in the *Harvard Law Review*. The only thing allegedly left for the student is to figure out which theorist was right and which one was wrong.

I believe that legal theory would be more clearly (and more deeply) understood if its issues and the writings of its theorists were approached through a focus on questions rather than answers. Once one sees that different theorists are answering different questions, one can see how these theorists are often describing different aspects of the same phenomenon rather than as disagreeing about certain simple claims about law. In this text, I will focus on the questions being answered (the problems to which the theories try to respond), and will frequently point out the extent to which apparently contradictory legal theories can be shown to be compatible.

The approach both derives from and helps to explain the under-discussed matter of how we can have descriptive theories of an ongoing social phenomenon such as law (questions of methodology). Legal systems, and people's experiences of them, are extremely complex. Inevitably, a theory about law can capture only a portion of the relevant facts (this claim is not new to legal theory; the claim and its implications are discussed insightfully and in detail by H. L. A. Hart and John Finnis,[1] among others). Once one accepts the importance of selection in constructing social theories, the focus then turns to the basis on which selection occurs.

It is not surprising that different theorists might have had different criteria for selection, which correspond to the different issues which were troubling them or to the differing topics that were their particular interests. It may be open to someone to claim that there is only one proper viewpoint for theory, or that one set of issues or values is clearly more significant than all alternatives, but I have not found such arguments convincing; therefore, this text will go forward on a different basis.

The possibility that claims in legal theory may sometimes be relative to a particular purpose or a particular viewpoint does not empty legal theory of all significance or interest: I think the opposite may be true. However, it does mean that arguments within a theory or about a theory must be more subtly and more carefully made.[2]

Not all arguments in legal theory can be so cleanly and peacefully resolved, nor am I claiming that legal theorists are all (or even mainly) people of limited vision who cannot appreciate the subleties of other theorists' arguments. Most of the crimes of unjust simplification and distortion can probably be blamed on those like myself who write about the subject and attempt to teach it, rather than on the writers whose work is being taught.

---

[1] Hart, *The Concept of Law*, pp. 79–88; John Finnis, *Natural Law and Natural Rights* (Oxford: Clarendon Press, 1980), pp. 1–11.

[2] Although the approach I advocate has some connections with the more sophisticated versions of relativism (*e.g.*, the perspectivism of Friedrich Nietzche, Peter Winch's *Verstehen* approach to the social sciences and the pragmatism of Richard Rorty), it is also compatible with a more traditional approach to truth. We need not say that there are many truths, only that the truth about a complex social or moral phenomenon is unlikely to be captured completely by any single theory alone.

In this text I will attempt to offer perspectives which may allow students to understand the significance of various ideas in jurisprudence. I hope to offer this assistance in a way which preserves the power or the complexity of the theories I am discussing, but in the end there can never be any adequate substitute for reading the theorists in their own words.

Another theme that will arise regularly throughout these discussions is that of the difficulties inherent in the project of legal theory. The problem is partly the difficulty of any type of social theory, a topic already touched upon. There are also problems in legal theory that come from the fact that many theorists appear to make "conceptual" claims, claims that purport to go to the nature of a concept (*e.g.* "law" or "rights") rather than to the working of a social process or institution. It is then important to know how to judge the success of such a project, and, even more fundamentally, to determine why such projects are worth attempting.

Many of these general questions will be explored in the early chapters of this text, but the same themes will be reflected upon in the later discussions of specific theorists and issues.

For those who have done some reading in jurisprudence, there is the strange phenomenon of some ideas that seem simultaneously familiar yet mysterious: one knows of Lon Fuller's ideas of the internal morality of law, Kelsen's concept of the basic norm, the law and economics notion of wealth maximisation, and the like, but one does not know why anyone would put forward arguments this unusual. In this book, I hope to identify sufficiently the context (the problems being considered, as well as the philosophical tradition in which the theorist was writing) in which such ideas arise, so that the reader might gain a better understanding of why such arguments might be needed (and why they might be persuasive).

Chapter Two

The Possibility of General Jurisprudence

Most theoretical discussions about the nature of law begin with a confidence which belies the problems lurking at the foundations of any such inquiry: on what basis can we even speak of a general theory of "law" at all?

To begin at the beginning, "law" is an English term which refers to a certain collection of institutions and practices.[1] Those institutions and practices will vary from country to country, and in each country over time. It is even more complicated when we go to other countries where English is not the primary language: those countries may have institutions which are similar to those we call "law" and there may be a term in the native language which seems to correspond roughly to our term "law" (although in, *e.g.* Germany, the word "*Recht*" has connotations quite different from those of its English equivalent, "law"[2]).

The problems obviously increase when we consider countries or societies which do not have institutions and procedures even remotely similar to our own[3] (this makes it all the more difficult to find a term in that culture's langauge which we could, with confidence, translate as "law"). These may be societies where there appear to be no legal rules promulgated and enforced by the

---

[1] Even to make the few simple comments I make in this and the following paragraphs, I have limited the word "law" to its application to municipal, institutional law. I have put to one side the use of the term to apply to international law, religious law, scientific law, the regulations of games and societies, and other uses of the term.

[2] See Stanley L. Paulson, "Lon L. Fuller, Gustav Radbruch, and the 'Positivist' Theses" (1994) 13 *Law and Philosophy* 313 at 329–330.

[3] See generally Laura Nader, "The Anthropological Study of Law" (1965) 67 *American Anthropologist* 3.

state, apart from what we would call the conventional morality of the society, or where social pressure and mediation fulfil the functions that adjudication carries out in our society. On what basis do we place such social systems within—or outside—our definition of "law"?

The question is one of inclusion and exclusion. What societies or systems does the theory about "law" purport to cover? If someone objects that a theory presented is not true for international law, or for French law, or for the rules used by an Aboriginal tribe in Australia, when can the theorist legitimately respond that the objection is irrelevant, since the counter-examples are "not really law"? This, in turn, leads to the inquiry as to how the theorist comes by his or her conclusions regarding which systems are and are not "legal".

The theorist discussing "the nature of law" will probably have some initial notion of which institutions and processes fit into the category that he or she is trying to examine. However, one can wonder whether there are any reasons for dividing up the social world and placing the "law"/"non-law" border in one place rather than another.[4] Looking at the same question in another way, one might wonder whether it makes sense to speak of "law" as a self-defined or unitary category at all. Perhaps there are only a large number of vaguely similar social institutions and practices, and there is no more sense in theorising about them as a group as there would be in creating a theory about the similarities of all countries whose name (in English) began with the letter "C". (One could also make the point in a slightly different way: stating that law is in some sense a "class", but not one about which anything of (philosophical) interest can be said.[5]

As noted above, most legal theorists do not explore these fundamental questions at all; furthermore, those who have considered them have come to different conclusions. For example, Michael Moore, who devoted an entire article to the problem,[6] denied that different legal systems share the same nature in the

---

[4] Establishing a dividing line between "law" and "not law" has its purposes within a legal theory, as will be discussed in Chap. 11.

[5] See Frederick Schauer, "Critical Notice" (1994) 24 *Canadian Journal of Philosophy* 495 at 508.

[6] Michael Moore, "Law as a Functional Kind" in *Natural Law Theories* (R. George, ed., Oxford: Oxford University Press, 1992), pp. 188–242.

sense of sharing the same structure, institutions or processes. However, he thought that there is an existing categorisation of social systems which might apply in this case: one could say that all the systems *which served the same function* within their communities or countries shared the same nature (*e.g.* one might argue that what is common to "law" everywhere is the function of resolving disputes or the function of establishing public norms of behaviour).

Ronald Dworkin rejected the value of (although not the possibility of) a general theory of law on the basis that any such theory (in his terms, any such "interpretation") that was valid for all the systems we would like it to cover would be at such a high level of generality that it would not tell us anything interesting.[7] His alternative was to offer a theory which is primarily an interpretation of a single legal system.

A third option,[8] one that I favour, combines elements of the above approaches. Within this option, legal theory is both a discussion of law in general and a focus on a particular legal system. We look at a group of social systems, but as a means of understanding better our own legal system. We therefore have an obvious, non-arbitrary basis for justifying discussing some countries' and communities' social systems while ignoring those of others: we choose the social systems which appear to us to be like our own legal system in significant ways. This approach does not require any prior claims about "law" or "legal systems" constituting a unitary, self-defined group. By losing the ambition to say something "necessarily true" about all legal systems, existing, historical or imaginary, one also loses the need to enter the murky world of metaphysical and social abstractions.

The above set of questions leads to a related line of inquiry: what is the status of the claims made within theories of law? Are these claims of sociology, anthropology or psychology, discussing how people naturally or inevitably act in large groups? Are they metaphysical claims, about the "essence" or "nature" of law?[9] Or

---

[7] See Ronald Dworkin, "Legal Theory and the Problem of Sense" in *Issues in Contemporary Legal Philosophy* (R. Gavison ed., Oxford: Clarendon Press, 1987), p. 16.

[8] It is based on comments made by Joseph Raz.

[9] See, *e.g.* Ernest Weinrib, *The Idea of Private Law* (Cambridge, Mass.: Harvard University Press, 1995) (discussing the essence or nature of (private) law).

are they (merely) claims about the way we use language (*e.g.* the way we use the terms "law" or "legal")?

The short answer to the above is that different theories seem to be responding to different types of inquiries and make different kinds of claims. Where convenient, these differences will be noted in the course of discussing the various theories in later chapters.

Chapter Three

Transforming the Question

In the first chapter of *The Concept of Law*, H. L. A. Hart considered the standard question of legal theory, "what is law?"[1] Past theorists had given various answers to this question, from the mundane but unsatisfactory to the bizarre (among the responses quoted are "what officials do about disputes", and "the prophecies of what the courts will do"[2]). What may be most remarkable about Hart's discussion is that he never directly answered the question he was considering. Instead, the chapter achieved something far more subtle. The question is not so much answered (or avoided or circumvented) as transformed. Hart's argument is that when one question is asked, we are actually seeking the solution to an entirely different question, and it is because we have been asking (or trying to answer) the wrong question that the answers given have been so unsatisfactory.

Hart proposed that the question "what is law?" is usually best seen as an attempt to consider one of three issues: "How does law differ from and how is it related to orders backed by threats? How does legal obligation differ from, and how is it related to moral obligation? What are rules and to what extent is law an affair of rules?"[3] Whether one agrees with Hart's analysis or not, one can

---

[1] Hart, *The Concept of Law*, pp. 1–6.
[2] *ibid.* p. 1. The second quotation is taken from Oliver Wendell Holmes, "The Path of the Law" (1897) 10 *Harvard Law Review* 457 at 461 ("The prophecies of what the courts will do in fact, and nothing more pretentious, are what I mean by the law"). This quotation, and the attitude towards law it represents, will be discussed in greater detail in Chap. 4 (under the heading "American Legal Realism").
[3] Hart, *The Concept of Law*, p. 13.

see how he has succeeded in diverting attention from definitional obsessions to more mundane and manageable (although not simple) questions. Hart's response to the question "what is law?" was basically to counter "why do you ask?" This is an attempt to simplify, or dissolve, a seemingly difficult or metaphysical question by trying to convert it or reduce it to questions relating to the proper descriptions of our practices. As Ludwig Wittgenstein described philosophy in general,[4] legal philosophy under a Hartian approach sees its primary purpose as a kind of therapy: a way of overcoming the temptation to ask metaphysical questions ("what is law?" or "do norms exist?"), and a method of transforming such questions into (re-)descriptions of the way we actually act.[5]

The way Ronald Dworkin dissolved the "debate" about whether the Nazi regime had law or not could be seen as a variation of the type of analysis I have in mind. He wrote that when we look at matters closely, we may see that there is no real disagreement between those who say that the Nazis did have "law" and those who say that they did not. On one hand, we understand what people mean when they say that the Nazis *did* have law: that the Nazi institutions resemble our own and share the same history and original purposes. On the other hand, we also understand what people are trying to say when they insist that the Nazi regime did not have law: that what went on was so evil and procedurally flawed that the rules of that regime did not create moral obligations to obey them, in the way such rules do in just regimes.[6] The two claims are both reasonable, and they are also compatible. Seen in this way, the "debate" disappears, and we can turn our attention to other, perhaps more substantial, disputes.

---

[4] See, *e.g.* Ludwig Wittgenstein, *Philosophical Investigations* (New York: Macmillan, 1968), §§ 133, 255.

[5] *ibid.* § 109:
   "We must do away with all *explanation*, and description alone must take its place. And this description gets its light, that is to say its purpose, from the philosophical problems. These are, of course, not empirical problems; they are solved, rather, by looking into the workings of our language, and that in such a way as to make us recognize those workings of our language: *in despite of* an urge to misunderstand them. The problems are solved, not by giving new information, but by arranging what we have always known. Philosophy is a battle against the bewitchment of our intelligence by means of language."

[6] Dworkin, "Legal Theory and the Problem of Sense", pp. 15–17.

One should not expect all debates to dissolve, clarify, or become less heated by being "transformed"—recharacterised or seen from a new perspective. Many debates in jurisprudence, as elsewhere, reflect basic moral or political issues, and no amount of transformation will relieve us of the obligations to make choices in these areas.[7] The trick is to separate true problems and true questions from muddles that we have been enticed into by our own somewhat confused and confusing ways of thinking and speaking. Unfortunately, there is no easy or foolproof method of effecting this separation; one can only offer analyses and await affirmation or rebuttal by one's peers.

Finally, there is another way in which one can "transform the question" in jurisprudence: as discussed earlier in this chapter, one can move the focus from the claims the theorists are making, and consider those theories in the contexts of the type of questions that the theorist was trying to answer and the type of problems that he or she was trying to solve. (As Raymond Aron noted in another context, the interest of a theory depends largely on whether the theorist has asked, and attempted to answer, interesting questions.[8]) The basis for this type of transformation, and how it might affect our thinking about jurisprudential claims, is discussed in detail in the next chapter.

---

[7] Elsewhere I have criticised theories that appear to be trying to elide difficult political and moral decisions by offering complicated theories of language or metaphysical theories. See Brian Bix, *Law, Language, and Legal Determinacy* (Oxford: Clarendon Press, 1993), pp. 45–49, 153–154, 176–177.

[8] Raymond Aron, *Main Currents in Sociological Thought* (R. Howard and H. Weaver, trans., New York: Anchor Books 1970), Vol. II, p. 232.

Chapter Four

Conceptual Questions and Jurisprudence

Conceptual analysis is an integral part of jurisprudence,[1] but the nature and purpose of such inquiries are often not clearly stated. In this chapter, I attempt to elaborate some of the differing reasons for conceptual analysis, and what consequences may follow from choosing one objective rather than another. By showing that divergent purposes are often present in competing analyses of the same concept, I also hope to indicate why some "debates" in the jurisprudential literature are best understood as theorists talking past one another. (While I will be discussing problems that are inherent in many types of conceptual analysis, my primary focus will be on conceptual analysis within jurisprudence.)

I begin this chapter by discussing how conceptual theories differ from other types of theories in the physical and social sciences, indicating some connections between the problem of conceptual theories and other, better-known problems in philosophy. I then proceed to outline alternative ways of understanding conceptual claims. Finally, I consider the claim that conceptual analysis of jurisprudence should be replaced by naturalist analysis.

---

[1] For example, arguably the two most important and influential books in the area in the last half of this century have been H. L. A. Hart, *The Concept of Law* (Oxford: Clarendon Press, 1961), and John Rawls, *A Theory of Justice* (Cambridge, Mass.: Harvard University Press, 1972), both of which could be characterised as being primarily works in conceptual theory (although some differences follow from the fact that the focus of the former book was a social institutional practice, while the focus of the latter was a moral–political concept).

How Conceptual Theories Differ

Conceptual claims, conceptual theories and conceptual questions are assertions or inquiries about labels (labels which often also serve as categories): for example, "law", "art" and "democracy". The point of conceptual questions is often obscure to students, and there are times when even the theorists involved in the exercise seem to lack a clear notion of their objectives.[2] Students sometimes react to long debates about "what is law?" or about "the nature of rights", by asking "who cares?" and "why does this matter?", while practitioners often assume that such questions are purely matters of definition and are therefore uninteresting. While I by no means want to encourage a dismissive or cynical approach to legal theory, I do believe that the sceptical questions—"what is the point?" and the like—should always be kept in mind, and that it is only by keeping such questions in mind that the issues (and the theorists) can be understood clearly and in depth.

Conceptual questions should be seen in contrast to other questions theorists ask. Theories in the physical and social sciences usually attempt to describe the world in such a way that we can better understand why past events occurred or predict how future events will unfold.[3] Examples of conceptual questions include: How is light distorted by travel through water? How do animals react to changes in amounts of daylight? What effect did Protestant thought have on the rise of capitalism?[4] These are questions of cause and effect which are in principle testable, through controlled experiments, careful observations or the analysis of past events. These theories are useful, and, perhaps equally important,

---

[2] This is by no means universal. Among the more articulate discussions of purpose are those in Hart, *The Concept of Law*, Chap. 1; Jules Coleman, "Negative and Positive Positivism" (1982) 11 *Journal of Legal Studies* 139 reprinted in Coleman, *Market, Morals and the Law* (Cambridge: Cambridge University Press, 1988), pp. 3–27; and Joseph Raz, *Ethics in the Public Domain* (Oxford: Clarendon Press, 1994), pp. 179–193.

[3] One should also distinguish philosophical explanations that try to respond to problems of the form "how is X possible, given Y and Z?" *e.g.* "How is it possible that we know anything, given the facts the skeptic enumerates . . . ? [and] How is it possible that motion occurs, given Zeno's arguments?" Robert Nozick, *Philosophical Explanations* (Cambridge, Mass.: Harvard University Press, 1981), p. 8.

[4] See Max Weber, *The Protestant Ethic and the Spirit of Capitalism* (T. Parsons, trans., New York: Scribner, 1976).

they are falsifiable (or, if "falsifiable" is too strong a word for some tastes, one might be able to use "rebuttable" as a substitute). If the data we collect in the future do not fit the predictions made according to the theory, we should at least begin to suspect that the theory might be wrong.

I am thereby contrasting purely conceptual theories with two different kinds of theories: (non-conceptual) theories in the natural sciences, and non-conceptual theories in the social sciences. Theories in the natural sciences

> "consider[ ] the general characteristics of phenomena and establish[ ] regular or necessary relations between them. This elaboration tends toward the construction of a system of laws or relations that are increasingly general and, insofar as possible, of a mathematical nature."[5]

Non-conceptual theories in the social sciences also tend toward conclusions about causation and causal regularities, but (in contrast to non-conceptual theories in the physical sciences) the selection of relevant data tends to turn at least in part on complicated (and contested) value judgments.[6]

Matters are necessarily different with questions and theories whose only purpose appears to be to offer definitions or to delimit categories: for example, "what is law?" and "what is art?" Consider, by way of example, all the different reasons someone might give for a claim that some artefact is not "art": it does not have sufficient quality, it was not created with the requisite intention, it is too functional or practical, or it is tied closely into daily life or religious belief.[7] If I believe that certain works by Man Ray are "not really art" while you disagree, or if I think that the old apartheid legal system in South Africa deserved to be call "law" and you do not, what is the nature of our disagreement?[8] What are we

---

[5] Aron, *Main Currents in Sociological Thought*, Vol. II, pp. 230–231.

[6] *ibid.* pp. 231–238.

[7] As to the latter, see Patricia Nelson Limerick, "More than Just Beads and Feathers", *New York Times Book Review*, January 8, 1995. (In the context of reviewing two books about Native American artefacts, discussing the argument that Native American culture, unlike "Western" culture, does not "quarantine" aesthetic experience).

[8] Colin McGinn once argued that it did not make sense to speak of people disagreeing about concepts; they could only be characterised as talking about different concepts: Colin McGinn, *Wittgenstein on Meaning* (Oxford: Basil Blackwell, 1984), pp. 146–147.

disagreeing about, and is it important? And how can we determine who is right?

A conceptual claim, as opposed to a claim that is meant to be predictive or explanatory, is not falsifiable (rebuttable).[9] However, as will be explained, I do not mean to imply that purely conceptual theories are immune to criticisms. As will be argued, one can criticise conceptual theories for having greater or lesser success relative to their stated (or implied) purposes, and one can also criticise the theory's purpose (*e.g.* on the basis that it is not ambitious enough).

Conceptual claims often define terms by necessary and sufficient conditions. Conceptual claims are claims that cannot be directly verified or rebutted by empirical observation (although such theories are not entirely cut off from the empirical world). Consider the differences between the conceptual claim "swans are white" and the empirical claim "all swans are white". The latter assumes that we have already defined the category "swan" to our satisfaction, and it is a matter of discovering whether all members of that category are coloured white. A conceptual claim about swans, by contrast, could survive a discovery of a swan-like creature that was not white. That creature would simply, by definition, not be a swan. As Jay Rosenberg states (when discussing the contrast between philosophy and other forms of inquiry), the results of conceptual theory are not (immediately or primarily) about discovering new facts, "but rather a new clarity about what are and what aren't the old facts."[10]

The contrast is with scientific (and social scientific) theories that posit an empirical, causal connection between events. The contrast is also with historical theories that speak in terms of causation (*e.g.* "the development of religious toleration leads to democracy"). However, within scientific and historical theories, there may be elements of the theory which assume, or tacitly make, a conceptual

---

[9] I recognise that, at least in the opinion of some historians and theorists who take a hermeneutic approach to social theory, the reference to falsifiability may seem blunt or perhaps naive. However, the term does work as a useful shorthand in summarising the differing criteria for success of conceptual theories as contrasted with other types of theories in the social sciences.

[10] Jay Rosenberg, *The Practice of Philosophy* (2nd ed., Englewood Cliffs, N.J.: Prentice-Hall, 1984), p. 8.

claim. (When someone says "the development of religious toleration leads to democracy", how are "religious toleration" and
"democracy" being defined?)

The merit of a conceptual claim can only be evaluated once it is
clear what the purpose of the claim is. The thesis defended in this
chapter is that (descriptively or historically speaking) different
conceptual claims have different purposes. Further, theorists often
do not clearly state what purpose underlies their particular
conceptual claims, which is what makes it difficult to evaluate the
merit of such claims, or to compare two different claims.

It may be helpful to begin by placing the problem of conceptual
theories in context. Most conceptual theories in law are odd not
only for not being predictive or falsifiable, but also for being
descriptive. There is something basically paradoxical about putting
forward a descriptive theory about a social institution or a social
phenomenon. Social practices change, and therefore it is often
inappropriate (or at least premature) to use the regularities of the
past to justify grand theoretical claims about a practice.

For example, a theorist might, after careful observation of past
practices within a given society (or even a number of societies),
conclude that all legislation begins with a statement of purpose.
The declaration is then made, that "all legislation contains a
statement of purpose" or "a statement of purpose is one of the
essential or defining elements of legislation". However, when the
next enactment does not carry a statement of purpose, how can
one argue against a person who states that the enactment nonetheless still warrants the label "legislation"? Is this the same or
different from generalities in the physical sciences (as the discovery of a creature that seemed clearly to be a swan but was black
rebutted the contention "all swans are white")?

This inquiry appears to be much like the old philosophical
inquiry regarding which properties of some object or class are
accidental and which essential (similar questions are also raised in
the modern philosophical topic of natural kinds theory[11]). Does
the fact that legislation always seems to have a statement of

---

[11] See, e.g. Hilary Putnam, "The Meaning of 'Meaning'" in *Mind, Language and
Reality* (New York: Cambridge University Press, 1975), pp. 215–271.

purpose make that statement of purpose part of what makes a declaration "legislation", an aspect of how we can tell "legislation" from other types of documents? The problem is that talk about "essences" and the "nature" of items does not fit as comfortably with human artefacts and social institutions as it does (say) with biological species or chemical elements.[12] The difference is in the way that categories that refer to human artefacts and social institutions do not figure in lawful explanations; that is, we neither expect nor find evidence of necessary relationships among those categories or between those categories and other phenomena. With human artefacts and social institutions, the categories themselves can be difficult to delimit; the basically fluid and contested nature of conceptual definitions can be seen to derive from the fact that the sets of items understood to be named by concepts like "art", "law" or "rights" are themselves contested. (This fluidity and contestedness of boundaries is central to understanding the problems and possibilities of conceptual analysis, and the theme will come up again later in this chapter.)

If the problem regarding conceptual theories appears to have some similarities with the notion of accidental versus essential properties, it also seems related to the more modern rubric of "rule-following": how can we tell the difference between a variation within a practice and a change to a different practice?[13] For example, can one change one of the rules of chess and still be playing "chess", or is it a different game that is only related to chess? Similarly, is it still "legislation" without a statement of purpose, and is it still "law" if it does not serve the common good? As practices change, and the label some conceptual/descriptive theory placed on the practice no longer fits the practice, are we to say that the original label was "wrong" (whatever that might mean here), or that the old practice is gone and a new practice has begun?

As noted at the beginning of the chapter, one basic reaction to all of these kinds of inquiries is to wonder why or under what

---

[12] See, e.g. John Dupré, "Natural Kinds and Biological Taxa" (1981) 90 *Philosophical Review* 66; Bix, *Law, Language, and Legal Determinacy*, pp. 162–171.
[13] See, e.g. Wittgenstein, *Philosophical Investigations*, §§ 143–242.

circumstances these types of questions are worth asking. Why does it matter if we call the slightly changed game "chess" or not, or call the unjust system of dispute resolution "law" or not? This chapter aims to articulate the possible reasons for having such debates.

One ground-level reason for conceptual inquiries is to maintain a structure within which meaningful discussion can occur. The question of identity is important, in this sense, for we want to know whether two people who appear to be discussing the same subject are in fact doing so. The idea is that without some agreed subject underlying our disagreements about "justice", "democracy", "law" and so on, the great debates on these subjects would collapse into an uninteresting exchange of parties talking past one another.[14] To disagree is to disagree *about* something.

The common category grounding the discussion may be delimited by a proffered definition (for example, "when I talk about 'legal systems', I mean the following: x, y, and z; and for all systems that fit that description, I believe the following is true: . . . "). The question then becomes on what basis one selects one proffered definition over an alternative. I will return to that question later in this chapter.

An alternative approach is sometimes helpful in understanding conceptual claims. Many of the misunderstandings regarding conceptual debates arise because while conceptual claims purport (by their form if not by some more express statement) to be merely descriptive, they almost always have evaluative or prescriptive elements. Some of the disagreements present within conceptual "debates" might be better understood as disagreements regarding the best answer to a particular question or problem. For example, the various theories of "justice" could be seen as competing answers to the question "what are the morally best set of rules, criteria or procedures for the distribution of goods in society?"

However, while seeing some disagreements about concepts as really being disagreements about the best answer to set (moral) questions may work in a few cases, it is unlikely to succeed as a

---

[14] See, *e.g.* Susan Hurley, *Natural Reasons* (Oxford: Oxford University Press, 1989), pp. 30–32.

general method of understanding conceptual theories. For example, we are still left with the problem of how to explain disagreements about terms like "law" and "democracy". Those who disagree about whether a particular governmental system was "democratic" or not might still agree about any normative question put to them—for example, whether that governmental system was the best one for the country which used it.

In summary, conceptual theories and conceptual claims set the boundaries of categories. The drawing of such boundaries can be helpful in establishing a common ground for investigation and discussion, but the placement of the boundaries is often contested. The question remains: on what basis can it be asserted that one conceptual theory is better than another? That question will be focused on next.

ALTERNATIVE PURPOSES

If most conceptual debates are not straightforward descriptions and they are not alternative answers to simple normative questions, can these debates be understood in a way that does not dismiss them as pointless? I believe that they can be, if one starts by trying to understand the (various) purposes of conceptual definitions. One possible "purpose" is what I would call a default option: definition as arbitrary stipulation. (Although some might say that arbitrary stipulations are theories "without purpose", or perhaps "no theory at all", for the present analysis it is convenient to consider them as an alternative to the other "purpose-driven" approaches.)

Some might argue that conceptual definitions can *only* be arbitrary, because there cannot be any one right way to divide up social reality. For example, one might argue that, when considering questions such as whether we describe the rules of wicked governments as "law", or whether we consider international law as really being "law", any answer is as true or as legitimate as any other. Under this analysis, there cannot be a "right" or "wrong" conceptual definition, only a "more or less convenient" one, and all that we can ask is that theorists be as clear as possible about the reasons behind their boundary lines (if there are any such reasons), and that they be consistent in their application of these boundaries.

Under this approach, a disagreement between two definitions of "law" or "democracy" would not be important; it would just be evidence of contrasting conventions. There would be no particular reason why you should not adopt my convention, or I yours, for the purpose of discussing some issue of mutual interest. However, if most conceptual definitions were merely arbitrary, it would be hard to explain the often vigorous disagreements over which definition of "law" or "democracy" or the like was to be adopted; surely these arguments are driven by more than pride that one's own arbitrary suggestion be accepted rather than another person's. On the other hand, if the definitions are not arbitrary stipulations, there needs to be some basis for claiming that one definition is better than another, and this is where one needs reference to the purpose of the definition.[15]

(In conceptual debates, theorists rarely claim simply that their definitions of "law" or "democracy" "are true" or "better describe reality" compared to the alternatives, for too many questions would be begged by such a claim.[16] What could it mean, for example, to say that one's conceptual analysis was "true"? Social reality simply does not come so cleanly marked off.)

Once past the default option of arbitrary stipulation, conceptual definitions usually have broadly one of three objectives:

(1) they can be an attempt to track and explain linguistic usage;

---

[15] As discussed earlier, even with "arbitrary" stipulations, it is open to theorists to say that one stipulation is "better" because it is more useful or more convenient for a particular purpose.

[16] This is reminiscent of Lon Fuller's criticism of (pre-H. L. A. Hart) legal positivism:

" . . . [W]e encounter a series of definitional fiats. A rule of law is—that is to say, it really and simply and always is—the command of a sovereign, a rule laid down by a judge, a prediction of the future incidence of state force, a pattern of official behaviour, etc. When we ask what purpose these definitions serve, we receive the answer, 'Why, no purpose, except to describe accurately the social reality that corresponds to the word "law."' When we reply, 'But it doesn't look like that to me,' the answer comes back, 'Well, it does to me.' There the matter has to rest."

Lon Fuller, "Positivism and Fidelity to Law—A Reply to Professor Hart" (1958) 71 *Harvard Law Review* 630 at 631.

(2)   they can be an attempt to discover the "significance" of a
      concept, hidden in our practices and intuitions regarding
      usage; or
(3)   they can impose moral or qualitative criteria which must be
      met before the label should be applied (perhaps on the
      basis that such criteria are deeply embedded in our
      usage).

(The distinction between the second and the third category may
be arbitrary or unnecessary, and I do not think anything turns on
there being three rather than two categories. That said, I think
that there is some basis for distinguishing the second category,
evaluations of "significance" that at least purport to be morally
neutral (as with Hart's discussion of the significance of legal rights,
discussed below), and the third category, definitions which openly
use and encourage moral judgments (as in the works of natural law
theorists, also discussed below).)

One possible basis for claiming that one conceptual theory was
superior to another would be that the definition proffered better
reflects the way we actually use the term. Occasionally one comes
across a conceptual theory whose ambition is no greater than to
track usage,[17] but this is unusual. Conceptual analysis is often tied
to usage, but the tie is usually a loose one. This tie sometimes
encourages the confusion that discussions about such questions as
"what is law?" and "what are rights?" are merely linguistic
investigations.[18] However, conceptual discussions are rarely only
about proper dictionary entries. Theorists who pay attention to
usage usually do so because they believe that usage reflects some
deeper, more interesting truth.

This leads us to consider the second justification for conceptual
definitions: that a particular way of dividing up a subject-matter is
justified on the basis that this way better displays certain interesting or important aspects of the practice (aspects which may be
hinted at by our linguistic practices).[19]

---

[17] See Raz, *Ethics in the Public Domain*, pp. 179–182 (discussing linguistic approaches
to the nature of law).
[18] See, *e.g.* Ronald Dworkin, *Law's Empire* (Cambridge, Mass.: Harvard University
Press, 1986), pp. 31–44 (arguing against "semantic theories" of law).
[19] See, *e.g.* Finnis, *Natural Law and Natural Rights*, pp. 3–11; Raz, *Ethics in the Public
Domain*, pp. 216–218.

One example of this second approach can be seen in H. L. A. Hart's position in the debate about the best (conceptual) understanding of legal rights.[20] Hart defended his "claim theory" of legal rights, even against an alternative definition that Hart conceded better fit the way we use the relevant legal terms, on the basis that his definition captured an important aspect of the way people perceive and experience legal rights.[21] The "claim theory" asserts that what is most significant or most interesting about legal rights is the role played by the right-holder's power and ability to choose. For most rights, the holder can waive the corresponding duty or, if the duty is violated, waive enforcement, or waive compensation for the violation, if it comes to that.

The alternative position is the "interest" or "benefit" theory of rights, often represented by Jeremy Bentham or Neil MacCormick.[22] Advocates of this position point out that there are a number of situations where we speak of rights where the putative right-holder has no such power: at one end, inalienable rights and, at the other end, rights ascribed to children, legally incompetent adults and animals. Therefore, they argue, it is better to define rights in terms of a certain kind of legally protected interests. There are some skirmishes on the boundaries; for instance, to what extent the example of third party beneficiaries to contracts (which in some jurisdictions have no power to enforce the contract) offers "evidence" for either side. However, mostly there is agreement about the overall situation: that "interest theories" of legal rights can better track usage, but at the cost of a somewhat awkward definition and no grand conclusion; by contrast, "will theories" make an interesting claim, but at the cost of a less than optimal fit with how we use the term. If conceptual claims are about disclosing what is "important" or "significant" about a concept, then Hart's theory of rights is tenable, despite its less then perfect fit with usage.

---

[20] Some other aspects of the jurisprudential debates about rights will be discussed later, in Chap. 10.

[21] See H. L. A. Hart, "Legal Rights" in *Essays on Bentham* (Oxford: Clarendon Press, 1982); pp. 161–193.

[22] See Hart, "Legal Rights", pp. 164–170 (summarising Bentham's "benefit theory of rights"); Neil MacCormick, "Rights in Legislation" in *Law, Morality and Society* (P.M.S. Hacker and J. Raz eds., Oxford: Clarendon Press, 1977), pp. 189–209.

The problem with this second approach, conceptual definitions as being about what is "interesting" or "important" regarding some practice or attitude, is that these underlying judgments may be insufficiently objective ("objective" here meaning sufficiently independent of individual interests and perspectives that there would likely be a consensus on the matter in question). Importance may be best seen as a statement of utility—an appropriate answer to the question "why is X important?" is "because it helps to obtain Y"—however, we might then be left without any consensus about proper ends (whether "Y" is worth pursuing, and, even if so, whether "Z" might not be the more important objective here). If we disagree about the purposes of a practice, we are also likely to disagree about which aspects of the practice are "important" or "significant" (and why they are so). The result is a certain kind of theoretical stalemate: for example, it would be difficult for a theorist, basing his concept of "law" on a particular view of which ends law does or should pursue, to persuade a second theorist, with a different view about law's objectives and (thus) a different theory, that the first theory was superior to the second. (Arguably this kind of unresolvable disagreement is part of what is going in the debates between the supporters of legal positivism and its critics.[23])

The third approach to conceptual questions is to set standards: a test the object or activity must pass before the relevant label has been earned. For example, one might believe that something should only be called "literature" if it has "passed the term of time", that is, if its high critical standing has not been significantly diminished over many years. Similarly, some might believe that a created object should only be called "art" if it reaches a certain quality or significance.

One may wonder what sense there is to giving normative tests for concepts in the social sciences. It is one thing to say that "literature" is very good fiction, where here the label becomes a shorthand for an evaluative judgment ("her books are fiction, to be sure, but I would hardly call them 'literature'"). However, when

---

[23] See, e.g. H. L. A. Hart, "Postcript" in *The Concept of Law*, (2nd ed. Oxford: Clarendon Press, 1994), pp. 248–249 (contrasting his view that the primary purpose of law is to guide human behaviour with Ronald Dworkin's view that the primary purpose of law is to offer a moral justification for state coercion).

the term in question is one of general use, like "law", one could argue that it only invites confusion to use a term of general description as also implying a statement of worth.[24]

Although the justification for this approach to conceptual definitions is often not articulated, one possible argument for it often hinted at is as follows: terms like "art", "democracy", and "law", although they have a strong descriptive element, are rarely simply descriptive: there is a residual (positive) normative element that philosophers seeking analytical clarity cannot simply wish away.[25] In many circles, it would be considered insulting to be told that one's society did not really have "law" or that its government was not really "democratic". When we say, "we would not call what Nazi Germany had 'law'", or "we would not speak of 'a right' to be punished for something we had done", the theorist is trading on our linguistic intuitions—when we think a label is appropriate and when inappropriate—and these intuitions sometimes contain judgmental elements. It is as if the intuitions reflect some truth about social phenomena, some truth we understand at the intuitive level but not yet or not yet clearly at an articulate level.

It may be helpful at this point to consider an example from the jurisprudential literature that cuts across different approaches to conceptual definitions. Simon Roberts criticised H. L. A. Hart's analysis of legal systems,[26] arguing that under Hart's analysis many communities (in particular, small tribes and so-called "primitive"

---

[24] See Hart, *The Concept of Law*, pp. 203–207.
  There are ethical concepts, described in the literature as "thick concepts", in which description and evaluation (or, to put the same point another way, description and reasons for action) are inextricably entwined (*e.g.* "rude", "cowardly", "brutal"). See, *e.g.* Bernard Williams, *Ethics and the Limits of Philosophy* (Cambridge, Mass.: Harvard University, Press, 1985), pp. 140–152; Philippa Foot, "Moral Arguments" (1958) 67 *Mind* 502 at 507–509. However, how best to understand thick concepts, and what implications they have for moral theory, is beyond the scope of this book.

[25] Kenneth Winston, in summarising the ideas of Morris Cohen and Lon Fuller, described a comparable notion in different terms. As I understand Winston's summary, a (teleological) "ideal element" is required for the intelligibility of all social institutions, including law (the ideal being the "principle of order, a limiting conception", which creates the conceptual structure within which actual subjects are perceived), and therefore any definition which does not incorporate such an element would be defective. Kenneth Winston, "The Ideal Element in a Definition of Law" (1986) 5 *Law and Philosophy* 89 at 98, 105–106.

[26] From Hart, *The Concept of Law*.

societies) would be held not to have "law", as many such communities do not have the centralised legislative and adjudicative
bodies Roberts believed to be assumed by Hart's model.[27] However, it is not clear why Hart could not simply reply to this
challenge, that for his own purposes he has chosen an analysis and
definition of law and of legal systems that only covers certain
Western societies. He could have said: definitions are arbitrary; if
other theorists want a wider definition, they are welcome to set
one. (I do not claim that this was in fact Hart's position, only that
a position of this sort is tenable.)

It appears that there are two unstated premises in Roberts'
criticism: first, that the conceptual definition of "law" is not (or
should not be) an arbitrary matter and, secondly, that all (or
almost all) societies should be held to have legal systems. As
regards the second point, the argument might be that saying that
a community has a legal system is implicitly to state that this
community is advanced, mature and sophisticated, and that to say
that a community does not have one is to say that it is "primitive"
and unimportant. This type of argument fits into my third
category, discussed earlier. However, the point remains that until a
theorist offers grounds for judging conceptual definitions and the
reasons for adopting one over another, arguments about the
"truth" or "correctness" of a conceptual definition are ungroun-
ded and thus pointless.

Given all of the considerations discussed during the course of
this chapter, it is not surprising that often the different participants in the conceptual "debates" in legal theory—debates about
how the concepts are best defined—are often best understood as
talking past one another. One example may be the famous
jurisprudential "debate" between H. L. A. Hart and Lon Fuller.[28]
This is not the place to argue the matter in detail,[29] but the debate
can be summarised as follows. Hart offered an analysis of law with
the purpose of maximising clarity in discussing law in general and
particularly in the moral evaluation of legal rules, while Fuller

---

[27] Simon Roberts, *Order and Dispute* (Middlesex, England: Penguin, 1979),
pp. 23–25.
[28] H. L. A. Hart, "Positivism and the Separation of Law and Morals" (1958) 71
Harvard Law Review 593; Lon Fuller, "Positivism and Fidelity to Law—A Reply to
Professor Hart" (1958) 71 *Harvard Law Review* 630.
[29] There will be much more on Hart and Fuller in Chaps. 5 and 8.

offered a moral test for applying the term "law", based partly on usage and partly on viewing law as a form of social ordering, to be contrasted with other forms of social ordering.[30] The two positions are incompatible in the sense that a particular legal system might fail to be "law" under Fuller's analysis while it would be under Hart's analysis. However, the two analyses are not inconsistent, in the sense that one can argue, without contradiction, that both are valuable and useful.

There is one further practical question to consider. I have argued that conceptual theories and claims can only be evaluated in the light of their underlying purposes, but I have also noted that many (and perhaps most) such theories and claims fail to articulate their purposes. How then can any evaluation be done, if the reader must provide the standard against which the test will be tested?

I suggest that the best approach is the following: where a theorist has not articulated a purpose, one should seek a purpose against which the theory would have some claim to success, without making the theory trivial.[31] Thus, to interpret a theory as merely tracking linguistic usage may make the theory largely successful, but (in the area of jurisprudence anyway) this is a relatively unambitious purpose, and a reader should see if the theory might also achieve some more substantial purpose.

CONCEPTUAL ANALYSIS AND NATURALISM

Some writers have begun to question how much of traditional jurisprudence *has been* conceptual analysis, and, a related matter, how much of jurisprudence *should be* conceptual analysis.

---

[30] In conversation, Frederick Schauer has offered the interesting suggestion that Hart and Fuller could be seen to have had a common purpose in that both were trying to put forward theories which would make it more likely that officials and citizens would resist unjust laws. However, analysing theories in this way, in terms of intended but indirect effects on readers' practical reasoning, is beyond the scope of this book.

[31] This type of analysis is related to Donald Davidson's discussion of "charity" in interpretation. See Donald Davidson, *Inquiries into Truth and Interpretation* (Oxford: Clarendon Press, 1984), pp. 196–197, 200–201.

For example, in a forthcoming article on American legal realism, Brian Leiter argues that this school of thought has been misunderstood because commentators have assumed wrongly that the realists, like most legal theorists this century, were offering conceptual analyses.[32] Leiter argues that the legal realists, at least in their theorising about judicial decision-making, were in fact philosophical naturalists.[33]

"Naturalism" is the belief that there is no area of philosophical inquiry to which the sciences (broadly understood) are not applicable; in Leiter's terms, it is the belief that "philosophical theorizing ought to be continuous with and dependent upon empirical inquiry in the natural and social sciences."[34] Examples of such "naturalist" approaches are certain modern approaches to epistemology, which hold that considerations of how people actually arrive at their beliefs are relevant to the inquiry of how we ought to arrive at our beliefs.[35] Also relevant is the natural kinds theory of reference, which holds (roughly speaking) that the nature of things in the world (independent of our beliefs about those things) helps to determine the meaning of terms.[36]

Leiter's observations about American legal realism are almost certainly right, and a helpful corrective to the way those theorists are often perceived. However, Leiter also seems to hint at a more general, and more controversial, claim about legal theory, when he comments at one point that jurisprudence in general is decades behind other areas of philosophy in abandoning pure conceptual analysis for naturalist analysis.[37]

---

[32] Brian Leiter, "Legal Realism" in *A Companion to the Philosophy of Law and Legal Theory*, (forthcoming, D. Patterson ed., Oxford: Basil Blackwell, 1996). American legal realism will be discussed in the present text in Chap. 4.
[33] *ibid.*
   Leiter does not claim that naturalist methodology competely supplanted conceptual analysis for the legal realists. He argues that, in conceptual matters, the legal realists are best understood as having been "tacit legal positivists". *ibid.*
[34] *ibid.* For the consequences this approach has for a wide variety of different philosophical inquiries, see David Papineau, *Philosophical Naturalism* (Oxford: Basil Blackwell, 1993).
[35] See, *e.g.* the papers collected in Hilary Kornblith, *Naturalizing Epistemology* (2nd ed., Cambridge, Mass.: MIT Press, 1994).
[36] See, *e.g.* Putnam, "The Meaning of 'Meaning' ".
[37] Leiter, "Legal Realism".

My initial response is that it may be unwise to evaluate as a group all conceptual theories, even all conceptual theories in jurisprudence. One might argue that epistemology and judicial reasoning are to be distinguished from the type of conceptual questions that are often raised in jurisprudence. When considering how we know things or how judges can/should decide legal questions, there is an immediate attraction to the position that how people in fact do these activities should play an integral part in the analysis of how they *should* do them.

However, questions like "what is law?" (or "what is art?") and "what is the nature of 'rights'?" are of a different type altogether, for it is less clear how empirical claims *could* offer clear answers to the questions being asked. It is not that empirical facts—what people actually do, or what there actually is—have no place at all in the analysis (as noted earlier, many theorists see a role for actual linguistic usage in constructing a conceptual theory). Rather, the problem is that the scope of the category ("law", "rights", "art") is as contested as the best way of understanding the items that fit within the category.[38] Empirical observation is not likely to settle these contests, as the role of empirical facts (*e.g.* how important linguistic usage should be in constructing or evaluating the theories) is itself highly contested.

For all the reasons that make conceptual analysis in legal and political philosophy muddled, confused and confusing—the lack of articulation of underlying purposes, the varying and contrary purposes, and the contested nature of conceptual boundaries—I doubt that these discussions will (or should) soon be conquered by naturalism.

CONCLUSION

In summary, conceptual debates in jurisprudence (and elsewhere) are often confusing because a central element in the discussion is left unstated. In proposing a conceptual claim, or in evaluating

---

[38] While one might argue that the scope of categories central to other disputes, *e.g.* the category of "warranted assertion" in epistemology, is also sometimes contested, I would argue that for such categories the disputes, if they exist at all, are very much at the margins, as contrasted with conceptual disputes in legal and political theory, where the disputes are pervasive and central.

such a claim, it is critical to determine the purpose with which the claim is put forward. When the purpose is not articulated, there is the danger that the participants in conceptual debates will misunderstand one another, and offer arguments that do not meet.

In this chapter, I have offered four options for conceptual claims:

(1) they are arbitrary stipulations;
(2) they track linguistic usage;
(3) they try to explain what is "important" or "interesting" about something; and
(4) they establish an evaluative test for the label.

My impression is that most conceptual claims in legal theory belong to the third or fourth categories.

Within the approach suggested in this chapter, one might not be able to say that a particular conceptual analysis was "right" or "true" (at least not in the sense that there would be only one unique "right" or "true" answer for all conceptual questions), but I do not see this as a significant loss. It should be sufficient that one can affirm (or deny) that an analysis is good (or better than an alternative) for a particular purpose.

PART B

Individual Theories about the Nature of Law

The heart of many jurisprudence courses is the discussion of the approaches to law of various well-known individual theorists. The following chapters offer an overview of five of the most highly regarded legal theorists, locating some of the issues to which their theories were responses, and placing the theories within the context of larger movements in jurisprudence.

Chapter Five

H. L. A. Hart and Legal Positivism

Legal positivism is based on the simple assertion that the proper description of law is a worthy objective, and a task that need be kept separate from moral judgments (regarding the value of the present law, and regarding how the law should be developed or changed). Early advocates of legal positivism included Jeremy Bentham (1748–1832), John Austin (1790–1859) and (in a quite different way) Hans Kelsen (1881–1973) (whose views will be discussed separately in Chapter 6). One could just as easily dig deeper, and place the roots of modern legal positivism with the philosophers and political theorists Thomas Hobbes (1588–1679) and David Hume (1711–1716).[1]

In simple terms, legal positivism is built around the belief, the assumption or the dogma that the question of what is the law is separate from (and must be kept separate from) the question of what the law should be. The position can be summarised in the words of John Austin (1790–1859):

---

[1] As the editors do in George Christie and Patrick Martin eds., *Jurisprudence: Text and Readings on the Philosophy of Law* (2nd ed., St. Paul, Minn.: West Publishing, 1995), Chap. 5. John Finnis goes a few steps further, and states that the groundwork for legal positivism (the establishment of human-posited law as a separate subject-matter) was laid by medieval writers, in particular St Thomas Aquinas: John Finnis, "The Truth in Legal Positivism" in *The Autonomy of Law* (R. George ed., Oxford: Clarendon Press, 1996) pp. 195–203. I discuss the connections and differences between Aquinas' view and modern legal positivism in Chapter 7.

"The existence of law is one thing; its merit or demerit is another. Whether it be or be not is one enquiry; whether it be or be not conformable to an assumed standard, is a different enquiry. A law, which actually exists, is a law, though we happen to dislike it, or though it vary from the text, by which we regulate our approbation and disapprobation."[2]

Legal positivism seeks from the study of law nothing more and nothing less than what is considered the foundation of modern social theory: that social institutions can be studied in an objective fashion, free from bias or ideology.[3] Such separation does not deny—in fact, theorists advocating legal positivism usually strenuously assert—that something identified as "a valid law" or "a valid legal system" may sometimes be sufficiently evil or unjust that it should not be obeyed.[4]

The notion that the description of a practice or an institution should be prior to and separate from its evaluation seems to modern audiences too obvious to need declaration, let alone justification.[5] However, the controversial nature of legal positivism becomes clearer when we keep in mind both the history of writing about law and the type of institution law is.

As to the first point, historically, much of the writing about law in general (as contrasted with writing about specific legal systems, which discuss what rules are in force or should be in force) involved moral and political inquiries regarding under what conditions government was legitimate and (the apparently related question) under what conditions citizens have a moral obligation to obey the law.

---

[2] John Austin, *The Province of Jurisprudence Determined* (H. L. A. Hart ed., London: Weidenfeld & Nicolson, 1955; 5th ed., R. Campbell, 1885), Lecture V.

[3] This approach to social theory has been challenged in various ways, not least by those who believe that social practices can only be understood in a "hermeneutic" way. These matters are beyond the scope of the present work, except to the extent that they overlap the writings of modern legal theorists.

[4] See, *e.g.* Hart, "Positivism and the Separation of Law and Morals", pp. 615–621.

[5] This is also the reason why I discuss legal positivism prior to natural law theory in this book. Although the latter has a longer history, to many people's way of thinking legal positivism, separating description and evaluation, would seem the usual or default view, while natural law theory would seem the unusual position that needs to be explained or justified. As recently as the nineteenth century, exactly the opposite was the case.

As to the second point, law is a practice so infused with moral-sounding claims (*e.g.* that citizens "ought to do X", where "X" is some action required by the legal rules) and moral-sounding terminology (*e.g.* legal"rights" and "obligations") that a strictly descriptive theory of law seems either difficult or inappropriate (for the same reason that a "descriptive theory of morality" or a "descriptive theory of justice" sound strange).

The attempt to place the study of law on a "scientific" foundation—objective and pure[6] of bias—led many of the early legal positivists to try to create a strictly empirical way of understanding legal actions and legal concepts, thus understanding them as functions of past, current or future facts. This search in legal theory can be seen as deriving from the broader search for a "scientific" approach to the social sciences that could match the approach used in the "hard sciences" (*e.g.* physics and chemistry), whereby theories would be based only on "objective" observations of events that could be easily reproduced or confirmed by other theorists (in somewhat more technical language, the "normative" in law was reduced to the "empirical"). Thus, legal rules were analysed in terms of citizens' past tendencies to obey, the use by legislators of particular kinds of language, the future likelihood of the imposition of sanctions, predictions of what judges were likely to do, and so on.

H. L. A. Hart's significance comes in part from the way he moved legal positivism in a different direction. While he continued to insist on the importance of the conceptual separation of law from morality (the separation of describing what law is from advocating how law should be), he criticised attempts to analyse law in strictly empirical (factual) terms. (In this, he was following a growing and influential view that the social sciences require an approach distinctly different from that used in the hard sciences, an approach based on understanding not merely the actions that occur, but also the meaning those actions have to the participants in the practices or institutions being studied.[7])

---

[6] Kelsen referred to his theory as "*Reine Rechtslehre*", the "Pure Theory of Law". His view is discussed in Chap. 6.

[7] See generally Max Weber, *Max Weber on the Methodology of the Social Sciences* (E. Shils and H. Finch eds., New York: Free Press, 1949); Peter Winch, *The Idea of a Social Science* (London: Routledge, 1958).

SUMMARY OF HART'S POSITION

At the time that H. L. A. Hart (1907–1992) began forming his legal theory, an influential view within the legal theory literature was that law was best understood as the command of a sovereign to its subjects.[8] Hart's approach to legal theory can be seen as a reaction to the command theory, and he presented his theory in that way on a number of occasions, as will become evident in the course of the following summary.[9]

The "command theory" offered a picture of law as a matter of commands (orders backed by threats) by a sovereign (one who is habitually obeyed by others, but who does not habitually obey anyone else) to citizens. Hart found weaknesses at almost every point. First, it was hard to speak of there being a sovereign—a person or entity that is habitually obeyed, but has no habit of obedience to any other person or entity—in many (if not most) modern governments, where even the highest governmental roles and institutions are subject to legal restraints. Secondly, the concept of a sovereign creates difficulty in explaining the continuity of law: for when someone new takes over, that person has no history of habitual obedience. Thirdly, there is much that is significant within legal systems that is lost if one looks only to the commands backed by threats (or if one treats all aspects of the law as variations of commands backed by threats).

In summary, from Hart's perspective, the problem with the Command Theory's on approach to law, and indeed with most purely empirical approaches, was that they were unable to distinguish pure power from institutions considered just or accepted as valid, unable to distinguish the orders of terrorists from a legal system.

Hart's alternative view of law is grounded on his views of rules, in particular on a view of the difference between rules and habits.

---

[8] This position is ascribed by Hart, and by many others, to John Austin. See, *e.g.* Hart, *The Concept of Law*, pp. 18–25. Some have argued that this misstates Austin's position, or at least that it misses many of the subtleties of his argument. See *e.g.* W. L. Morrison, *John Austin* (London: Edward Arnold, 1982), pp. 178–205; Roger Cotterrell, *The Politics of Jurisprudence* (London: Butterworths, 1989) pp. 64–65, 74. However, the question of the correct interpretation of Austin's work is beyond the scope of the present work.

[9] Hart, "The Separation of Law and Morality", pp. 600–606; Hart, *The Concept of Law*, pp. 18–120.

To an outside observer, there may be no way to distinguish someone acting in a particular way out of habit from her acting the same way in compliance with a rule. I may go to the cinema every Saturday, but that is not because I think that there is some legal, moral or social/conventional rule that states that I should.

According to Hart, the difference between these two kinds of regularities of behaviour can be seen through the participants' attitudes. With habits, the statement of the behaviour is nothing more than a description: I go to the cinema every Saturday. With a rule, however, the statement can take on additional roles: as an explanation, a justification and a basis for criticising deviation: the statement has a normative role.[10] Many, and perhaps most, citizens are not merely "in the habit" of obeying the authorities; they have internalised the rules as reasons for acting in certain ways (and for criticising others when they do not act as required).

Hart's theory, here as elsewhere, is responding to the idea that when analysing social institutions or social practices, a theory which takes into account, or helps to explain, the way participants understand those institutions or practices is, by that fact alone, significantly better than one which does not do so. Hart described his own work as "an easy in descriptive sociology",[11] in that he often relied on distinctions that were rooted in linguistic practice, and in turn based on differences in behaviour and attitude.

As for seeing law as being orders backed by threats, this view seems to elide what had long seemed a basic distinction: that a legal system was something different from (and presumably something better than) the rule over a frightened populace by gangsters. Hart captured the core of this distinction in his discussion of the difference between feeling obliged and having an obligation. We feel obliged to act in the way ordered by a gunman, because we fear the consequences if we do not act in that way; however, the moment the fear of possible consequences is removed, we would see no reason to act as demanded. Having an obligation under some valid normative system (whether the rules of a game we are playing, the canons of one's religion, or society's legal rules) is

---

[10] Hart, *The Concept of Law,* pp. 9–10, 54–57.
[11] *ibid.* p. v.

psychologically more complex. One acts because one believes that one ought to do so, not because (or not merely because) one fears the consequences of acting in a contrary way.[12]

Against a view that reduced all legal rules to variations on some single type, as (one reading of) John Austin's theory seemed to reduce all legal rules to commands, Hart emphasised the multiplicity of law. He contrasted rules that imposed duties with those that conferred powers (whether power conferred on officials within the legal system, or the delegation of certain legal powers to citizens, as can be said to occur through the operation of rules for contracts, wills, trusts, etc.), and he contrasted rules that applied directly to citizens ("primary rules") and rules that governed the operation of the rule system itself ("secondary rules": involving rules of change, adjudication and recognition; the rule of recognition is, discussed below).[13]

(Later commentators have pointed out that Hart was probably mistaken in his further implication that the distinction between primary and secondary rules matches that between duty-conferring and power-imposing rules; additionally, there are questions regarding whether the rule of recognition is best understood as a duty-imposing or power-conferring rule (or neither).[14] However, for present purposes these are matters of detail as against the general point that there is a variety of types of law, and that our understanding of this type of social system would be distorted by any attempt to analyse all of the law in terms of a single type of rule.)

There is no room here to discuss all aspects of Hart's legal theory in detail[15]; instead, I will offer brief discussions on four of the more telling topics in Hart's work: the rule of recognition, the internal aspect of rules, the "open texture" of rules and the "minimum content of natural law".

---

[12] *ibid.* pp. 79–84.

[13] *ibid.* pp. 89–96.

[14] See, *e.g.* Joseph Raz, *The Concept of a Legal System* (2nd ed., Oxford: Clarendon Press, 1979), p. 199.

[15] The two best sources for such an extended discussion are probably Neil MacCormick, *H. L. A. Hart* (Stanford: Stanford University Press, 1981) and Michael Bayles, *Hart's Legal Philosophy: An Examination* (Dordrecht: Kluwer Academic Publishers, 1992).

THE RULE OF RECOGNITION

Central to Hart's theory is the concept of a rule of recognition: a set of criteria by which the officials determine which rules are (and which rules are not) part of the legal system. The standards applied are referred to as justifications for the actions of the officials, although to some extent the standards are also created by those actions. To explain: sometimes the standards applied are written down in an official text (*e.g.* a written constitution) or at the least are clearly expressed in criteria that the officials state that they are following (*e.g.* "to become valid law, proposed legislation must be passed by a majority of each House of the Congress and then signed by the President"). At other times, the standards the officials are following can only be determined after the fact by reference to the decisions they have made.

A number of issues have been raised by later commentators regarding the rule of recognition: for example, whether it is best understood as a duty-imposing or power-conferring rule; and whether there can be more than one rule of recognition within a given legal system.[16] However, what should be kept centrally in mind is what the concept of a rule of recognition indicates; what it stands for. The rule of recognition expresses, or symbolises, the basic tenet of legal positivism: the fact that there are (in principle) criteria, largely agreed upon by officials, for determining (in the vast majority of cases) which rules are and which are not part of the legal system, points to the separation of the identification of the law from its moral evaluation, and the separation of statements about what the law is and what it should be.

THE INTERNAL ASPECT OF RULES (AND OF LAW)

The "internal aspect" of rules[17] is central to Hart's approach to law. It can best be understood within the context of (and it has repercussions for) certain general problems of constructing general social theories (a subject touched upon in earlier chapters and in an earlier section of this chapter). There are two related problems to consider:

---

[16] Joseph Raz, *The Authority of Law* (Oxford: Clarendon Press, 1979), pp. 95–96.
[17] See Hart, *The Concept of Law,* pp. 54–57, 79–88.

(1)   How must social theories be different from theories in other areas?

(2)   To what extent can a social theory be "scientific"?

One factor which must be considered prominently in constructing a theory of law, which would not be relevant to the construction of theories about atomic composition, chemical interaction, photosynthesis and the like, is that law is a human creation to serve human purposes and it is an institution that requires human participation. Because of these aspects, understanding any social process, including law, will be different in kind from understanding processes which are purely physical, chemical or biological.

This is the context for understanding Hart's concept of the internal aspect of rules. The idea is that one cannot understand a social system unless one understands how the people who created the system or who participate in the system perceive it. This "hermeneutic" approach—that is, giving priority to trying to understand how other people perceive their situation—is always in tension with those who want social theory to be more scientific.[18]

The "scientific" approach to social theory would rely only on data that were "objective", data on which different observers would always agree. The "scientific" approach to legal theory might be exemplified in various theorists' writings: for example, Christopher Columbus Langdell's view of legal theory as the search for the system of basic principles within the law,[19] and the American legal realists (to some extent reacting against Langdell's view[20]) emphasising what judges "actually do" as contrasted with what they are saying that they are doing. (Hart also specifically mentioned the work of the Scandinavian legal realist Alf Ross, who (according to Hart) "claimed that the only method of representation of the law fit to figure in a modern rational science of law was

---

[18] The foundational work advocating a hermeneutic approach to social theory is probably Max Weber, " 'Objectivity' in Social Science and Social Policy" in *The Methodology of the Social Sciences* (E. Shils and H. Finch eds., New York: Free Press, 1949), pp. 50–112. Hart's immediate influence (and a source almost as important as Weber on this topic) was Winch, *The Idea of a Social Science*; see Hart, *The Concept of Law*, p. 242.

[19] See William Twining, *Karl Llewellyn and the Realist Movement* (Norman, Oklahoma: University of Oklahoma Press, 1985), pp. 10–11.

[20] See the discussion of American legal realism in Chap. 17.

one which shared the structure and logic of statements of empirical science".[21])

Hart's argument is that whatever advantage a "scientific" approach might have, it simply is not adequate for a full understanding of law.[22] One can only understand normative—rule-following—behaviour if one leaves one's spectator's perspective and tries to understand the perceptions of the participants in the system (that is, the perceptions of the people who are following the rules, and who perceive themselves as doing so). In Hart's terms, to understand "any form of normative social structure", "the methodology of the empirical sciences is useless; what is needed is a 'hermeneutic' method which involves portraying rule-governed behavior as it appears to its participants".[23]

The attack on a purely scientific approach can be seen in Hart's distinction between habitual behaviour and rule-following, mentioned earlier.[24] As noted, Hart emphasised the difference between rules and habits, a difference that resided primarily in the participants' perceptions of what they were doing, and in their reactions to and attitudes towards the actions about them. When an action was done "as a rule", rather than "as a habit", the rule is given as a justification for the action, and the rule is also the basis for any criticisms (including self-criticism) for any divergence from the prescribed actions.[25] By contrast, we tend to have no justifications at hand (and sometimes we lack explanations of any kind) for our habits, and we certainly do not criticise or expect criticisms

---

[21] H. L. A. Hart, "Introduction" in *Essays in Jurisprudence and Philosophy* (Oxford: Clarendon Press, 1983), p. 13.

[22] For an excellent discussion of the problems of methodology in jurisprudence, with particular attention to Hart's work, see Stephen Perry, "Interpretation and Methodology in Legal Theory" in *Law and Interpretation* (A. Marmor ed., Oxford: Clarendon Press, 1995), pp. 97–135.

[23] Hart, "Introduction", p. 13.

[24] Similarly, to a "scientific" observer, someone who obeyed the law merely out of fear of sanctions would look the same as someone who obeyed the law because he or she believed that the legal system was legitimate—although a legal positivist (with that position's dogmatic separation of description and moral evaluation) might be foreclosed from referring to that conflation as a basis for rejecting a purely external viewpoint.

[25] For the suggestion that one needs to distinguish the "emotional" and "volitional" aspects of the "internal point of view", see Neil MacCormick, *Legal Reasoning and Legal Theory* (Oxford: Clarendon Press, 1978), pp. 288–292; Neil MacCormick, *H. L. A. Hart*, pp. 33–34.

when there are deviations from those habits. Because a scientific, purely "external", approach to law would conflate habitual actions and rule-following, according to Hart it would inevitably miss some matters which are at the essence of law.

However, to say that one is going to take the perspective of a participant in the social practice is at best a first step. After all, most social practices have a large number of participants, all of whom do not share the same view of, or attitude towards, the practice. One prominent legal theorist, John Finnis (whose views are discussed at greater length in Chapter 7) argues that the perspective chosen should be that of a (hypothetical) practically reasonable person, who applies appropriate moral reasoning to conclude (if true) that the legal system creates binding (prima facie) moral obligations.[26] A second prominent legal theorist, Ronald Dworkin (whose views are examined in Chapter 9), argues that one should theorise as if one were a participant in the social practice, offering an interpretation of that practice that makes it the (morally) best practice it can be.[27] Both of these perspectives are, from Hart's perspective, too extreme: he wants a legal theory which would be free from moral evaluations or moral commitments (unlike Finnis' approach), while remaining a descriptive theory of the practice rather than a participation in it (unlike Dworkin's approach).[28]

Hart was trying to keep a difficult middle position.[29] He argued that a legal theory should be constructed around the perspective of someone who accepted the legal system, but the theory itself (or, to put the matter differently, the theorist herself) need not, and should not, endorse the system (as one which is generally just or which creates binding moral obligations). In other words, the theory simultaneously:

(1)   attempts to take into account the participant's perspective; and

---

[26] See Finnis, *Natural Law and Natural Rights*, pp. 3–18.

[27] See generally Dworkin, *Law's Empire*.

[28] See Hart, "Introduction", pp. 8–12; Hart, "Postscript", pp. 240–244; Hart, "Comment" in *Issues in Contemporary Legal Philosophy* (R. Gavison ed., Oxford: Clarendon Press, 1987), p. 39.

[29] An analysis similar to what follows, although in greater detail, was offered in H. H. Hill, "H. L. A. Hart's Hermeneutic Positivism: On Some Methodological Difficulties in *The Concept of Law*" (January 1990) 3 *Canadian Journal of Law and Jurisprudence* 113.

(2)   manages to choose among possible participants' perspec-
      tives without having to make moral judgments; while
(3)   keeping sufficient distance from the participants' per-
      spective to allow for moral criticism of the whole system/
      enterprise.

The danger is of Hart's position sliding towards an Austin-like
command theory, on one side, and a position closer to Finnis' or
Dworkin's, on the other.

To put the matter a different way, the question is how to take
seriously the need to accept the perspective of a participant in a
practice while still maintaining a sufficient distance to be able to
criticise the practice (and the participants). In social theory (or
perhaps, more accurately, "social sciences meta-theory"), this has
led to an ongoing debate regarding whether an attempt to
"explain each culture or society in its own terms . . . rules out an
account which shows them up as wrong, confused or deluded".[30]
(One can say: if you claim to understand the perspective of the
believing participant of a particular practice, but you think the
practice is irrational and cruel, then you have not really understood or properly incorporated the perspective of the believer,
because that is not how it looks to him or her.[31]) An additional
complication, one whose implications are hard to tease out, is that
in the social sciences one must consider the role of an internal
point of view, both in the evaluation of data gathered and in the
actual gathering of that data nor to evaluating it.[32] This additional
point is unclear in its implications because it ties into the debate
on what it would mean to "gather evidence" for a general theory
of law (and what kind of evidence one would want), a debate
alluded to earlier in this book.

One attempt at a defensible middle position between external
points of view and fully committed internal points of view was
articulated by Joseph Raz, in a position called "statements from a

---

[30] Charles Taylor, *Philosophy and the Human Sciences* (Cambridge: Cambridge University Press, 1985), p. 123. Taylor defends the view that one can have an
"interpretative" or "*Verstehen*" approach while still retaining the ability to
criticise what is being explained.

[31] This position, derived from Peter Winch and Jürgen Habermas, is well summarised in Hill, "H. L. A. Hart's Hermeneutic Positivism", pp. 116–117.

[32] Hill, "H. L. A. Hart's Hermeneutic Positivism", pp. 123, 124–125.

point of view" or "detached statements".[33] These are statements which accept a particular normative position for the purpose of making a limited claim, but without endorsing that normative position. Thus, one can tell a vegetarian friend at a restaurant, "given your beliefs, you should not order that dish", even if one is not a vegetarian. In a similar way, "[l]egal scholars—and this includes ordinary practising lawyers—can use normative language when describing the law and make legal statements without thereby endorsing the law's moral authority".[34] A lawyer can say to a client: if you accept the law as valid (as imposing moral obligations), then you should do X or should avoid doing X.

Whether Hart's analysis (with or without the help of Raz's addition) can maintain its precarious middle position is a difficult and provocative question to which I offer no (allegedly) conclusive answer.

OPEN TEXTURE

The problem of gaps in the law has been known for a long time. Aristotle wrote:

> "When the law speaks universally, then, and a case arises on it which is not covered by the universal statement, then it is right, when the legislator fails us and has erred by over simplicity, to correct the omission—to say what the legislator himself would have said had he been present, and would have put into his law if he had known."[35]

There are a number of different ways in which legal rules might fail to cover (unusual) factual situations that arise. Hart introduced the idea of "open texture" to discuss one such way.[36] If the legislators introduce a rule to deal with a particular set of circumstances, how is a judge to apply the rule to an entirely different type of situation? Hart's example is the rule

---

[33] See Raz, *The Authority of Law*, pp. 153–157; see also Hart, "Introduction", pp. 14–15.

[34] Raz, *The Authority of Law*, p. 156.

[35] Aristotle, *Nicomachean Ethics*, V, 10:1137b20–24.

[36] Hart, *The Concept of Law*, pp. 119–132. Hart's concept was related to and derived from an idea in Friedrich Waismann's philosophy of language. I discuss the connections and differences in greater detail in Bix, *Law, Language, and Legal Determinacy*, pp. 7–25.

"No vehicles in the park", introduced to remove automobiles from the area, but then asking whether the rule should apply to motorcycles or roller skates or other objects which may or may not be "vehicles".

Part of the argument is that legislative purpose is incomplete or imprecise: the legislators have not considered all possible situations, so that legislative intent (even if clearly known) will not answer all possible problems in applying rules. Another part of the argument is that language is imprecise: there will be many occasions when it will be uncertain whether a general term (*e.g.* "vehicle") applies to the particular object in question (*e.g.* roller skates).

From these premises, Hart concluded that judges must inevitably use their discretion to make new law, on occasions where the legal rules have "open texture". He also noted that judicial law-making at the margins was a good thing, giving necessary flexibility to the application of legal rules.[37]

Upon reflection, it is not a surprising conclusion that language is generally clear, but there are occasions when it is not. How to obey or comply with an order or request is usually obvious, but there are times when circumstances make the matter uncertain. A directive that may seem straightforward in one set of circumstances may seem confused or absurd when applied after a significant change of circumstances. There are aspects of the "open texture" debate that derived from the nature of language, aspects that derive from the nature of rules and rule-following, and aspects that derive from suggestions about the best way to construct a system for applying rules.[38]

Hart's discussion derives from concerns about the ability of rules to guide behaviour, and also about the need for, and advantages of, judicial law-making at the margins. The same set of considerations raises other problems that Hart did not consider at such length: for example, problems about the nature of legislative intention and how it can be discovered or derived, and problems about when it is legitimate for a judge to interpret a rule contrary to the rule's clear meaning or contrary to legislative intentions. For a variety of reasons, English jurisprudence (at least at the time

---

[37] Hart, *The Concept of Law*, pp. 126–127.
[38] See Bix, *Law, Language, and Legal Determinacy*, pp. 22–25.

Hart was writing) was not as focused on the legitimacy of judicial action as American jurisprudence has been in recent decades.[39]

In many ways, Hart's discussion of "open texture" was preliminary: there is much work that must still be done in disentangling arguments based on the nature of language and arguments based on the nature of rules, and it is probably too quick to conclude immediately from the existence of "open texture" that judges do (or should) have discretion in deciding hard cases.[40] However, Hart's primary purpose in putting forward the notion of "open texture" was to counter the argument trying to tie legal positivism to a naive view of judicial decision-making.[41] To the point that rules by themselves do not always determine the results of cases, Hart's response was that this is true (and is caused by "open texture"); however, this does not mean that law is intertwined with morality, but only that judges sometimes legislate. This interstitial legislation may be based in part on moral standards, but it does not follow that those standards are then best seen as having been "in the legal rules" all along.[42]

The Minimum Content of Natural Law

Some commentators have made a great deal of Hart's discussion of "the minimum content of natural law",[43] seeing it as a great concession that undermines all that Hart had tried to claim earlier, regarding the separation of law and morality. This view, I would argue, is a clear misunderstanding of Hart's discussion, although it may be that a certain lack of clarity in the text invited the misreading.

The text occurs in the context of a general discussion of the ways that law and morality can be said to overlap (for example, the way

---

[39] Among the factors that create this more intense focus in the United States is the ability and willingness of American courts to invalidate legislation (under federal and state constitutional provisions), the controversial nature of some of those decisions, and the tension between such decisions and the strong democratic ethos in American political thought.

[40] These matters are discussed in greater detail in Bix, *Law, Language, and Legal Determinacy*, pp. 7–10, 17–35.

[41] See, *e.g.* Hart, "Positivism and the Separation of Law and Morals", pp. 606–615.

[42] See *ibid.* pp. 614–615.

[43] Hart, *The Concept of Law*, pp. 189–195.

that conventional moral beliefs obviously affect the way that the law develops and the fact that ideas about how law and society ought to be affect how statutes—in particular, ambiguous statutes —are interpreted[44]), in order to show what is *not* claimed by the legal positivist position that there is no necessary connection between law and morality (or, to put the point a different way, what is not excluded by that position). The "minimum content of natural law" is just one more exploration along this borderline, a border that Hart believes separates legal positivism from natural law theory.

The particular argument is that there are certain contingent facts of the human situation in this century (and all past centuries): that we are all mortal and vulnerable, that resources are limited, and that we are all dependent to some extent on other people. These facts are contingent, in that it is not impossible (however unlikely it may be) that future scientific developments might change these facts (for example, some series of discoveries might make us physically invulnerable). However, given these facts, certain consequences are likely to follow. Among these, Hart speculated, is that any legal or moral[45] system that did not offer certain minimal protections (against murder, serious assault and theft) to at least a significant minority of the population would not—could not—survive for very long.

This is not a conceptual point, merely a prediction, and a reasonable one. Even if one were to take it as a concession to the natural law theorists, it is a trivial one, for two reasons. First, we are not likely ever to come across such a society; and if we did find a society which flouted these minimal requirements and survived, the correct response would be to change Hart's series of criteria, not to conclude that either legal positivism or natural law theory had been proven wrong. Secondly, this "minimum content" test does not reflect the usual lines of disagreement between legal positivists and natural law theorists. Advocates of natural law theory argue for a moral test for legal validity that sets far higher standards, not just the Hobbesian moral minimum that Hart discussed.[46] Most natural law theorists would want the right to

---

[44] *ibid.* pp. 199–210.
[45] Here, Hart meant "moral" in the sense of the conventional morality which is accepted within a society (or a sub-culture), restrains the actions of its members, and is enforced by peer pressure of various kinds.
[46] Hart, "The Separation of Law and Morality", p. 623.

declare as "not law" legal systems, or certain rules of legal systems, that otherwise easily pass the minimal standards of Hart's discussion.

LATER DEVELOPMENTS

A number of theorists have worked to carry on Hart's project: among these have been David Lyons, Neil MacCormick, Jules Coleman and Wil Waluchow.[47] The most influential writer in this tradition has probably been Joseph Raz (1939–).[48] This section will offer a brief summary of some of the ideas of Coleman and Raz, to give a sample of the directions in which legal positivism has developed.

Jules Coleman's "Negative and Positive Positivism"[49] offered a version of Hartian legal positivism that seemed less vulnerable to the criticisms raised by Ronald Dworkin (which will be discussed in Chapter 9). Under this approach, the rule of recognition is a rule conventionally agreed among officials which could (but need not) incorporate a community's moral standards.[50] This friendly amendment to Hart's approach creates "a form of positivism which accepts the controversial [moral] nature of some legal reasoning, while denying that this is incompatible with the essential, affirmative claim of the theory that law is everywhere conventional in nature."[51]

Raz's approach to law is subtle and multifaceted, and not easily summarised in a few sentences. Some of the key positions are as follows: first, Raz offers the "social thesis" as the core of legal

---

[47] See, *e.g.* David Lyons, *Ethics and the Rule of Law* (Cambridge: Cambridge University Press, 1984); Neil MacCormick, *Legal Reasoning and Legal Theory* (Oxford: Clarendon Press, 1978); Jules Coleman, *Markets, Morals and the Law* (Cambridge: Cambridge University Press, 1988); Wil Waluchow, *Inclusive Legal Positivism* (Oxford: Clarendon Press, 1994).

[48] See, *e.g.* Raz, *The Authority of Law* (Oxford: Clarendon Press, 1979); Raz, *Ethics in the Public Domain* (Oxford: Clarendon Press, 1994).

[49] Jules Coleman, "Negative and Positive Positivism" (1982) 11 *Journal of Legal Studies* 139, reprinted in Coleman, *Market, Morals and the Law* (Cambridge: Cambridge University Press, 1988), pp. 3–27.

[50] See Jules Coleman, "Authority and Reason" in *The Autonomy of Law* (R. George ed., Oxford: Oxford University Press, 1996), pp. 287–319.

[51] Coleman, "Negative and Positive Positivism" in *Markets, Morals and the Law*, p. 27. Hart later seemed to adopt or affirm a position close to Coleman's: see Hart, "Postscript", pp. 250–254.

positivism: that what is law and what is not are matters of social fact (Raz favours a strong version of the social thesis that he dubs the "sources thesis"—that the existence and content of every law are fully determined by social sources).[52] This restatement of the legal positivist's separation between law and morality is tied to, and supported by, a distinction between deliberating as part of the process of coming to a decision, and the execution of the decision once made.[53] When judges are merely applying decisions already reached (by the legislature or by prior court decisions), they are applying existing law (determining what the law *is*); when judges consider moral factors in the creating a new rule, or in considering possible changes to an existing rule, they are determining what the law *should be*. (This view takes no position on whether it is a good thing or a bad thing that judges legislate, or whether they should do so more often then they currently do. The point rather is that it is both analytically clearer, and in line with the way we usually think and talk about the law, to maintain a distinction between applying the law and making new law).

Secondly, it is in the nature of law (of a legal system) that it has or claims legitimate authority.[54] This means that legal rules purport to be "exclusionary reasons": "reasons to exclude a consideration from being the ground for a . . . decision".[55] Raz's analysis links law, authority and practical reasoning. For Raz, the connection between authority and practical reasoning is a general one: authorities and authoritative reasons affect our moral deliberations; where there is an authority (which we recognise as such), our decision is based at least in part on what the authority (whether that authority is the law, a sacred text, a religious leader, an army commander, etc.) states we should do; we incorporate the authority's weighing of the relevant factors rather than simply weighing all the relevant considerations for ourselves. In Raz's terms:

"The authority's directives become our reasons. While the acceptance of the authority is based on belief that its directives are well-founded in

---

[52] See Raz, *The Authority of Law*, pp. 37–52.
[53] See Raz, *Ethics in the Public Domain*, pp. 190–192.
[54] See *ibid.* pp. 194–221.
[55] Joseph Raz, "Facing Up" (1989) 62 *Southern California Law Review* 1153 at 1158.

reason, they are understood to yield the benefits they are meant to bring only if we do rely on them rather than on our own independent judgment of the merits of each case to which they apply."[56]

Raz's analysis of rules thus differs in basic ways from Hart's analysis. Hart was offering a "practice theory" of rules in that his analysis was such that one could only speak of something being a rule if our society had an internal attitude towards it (that is, they used the rule as a basis for justifying behaviour and criticising deviation from behaviour). Raz's objections to the practice theory of norms were summarised as follows: "It does not explain rules which are not practices; it fails to distinguish between social rules and widely accepted reasons; and it deprives rules of their normative character."[57] (Raz allows that an analysis of legal rules must make reference to a social practice, but that is because they are *legal* rules—tied to a certain kind of social institution—rather than just because they are *rules*.[58]) As noted, Raz's alternative is to define rules in terms of their role in practical reasoning (moral deliberation): rules are "protected reasons" or "exclusionary reasons".[59]

NON-NORMATIVE APPROACHES

In his book *Norm and Nature*,[60] Roger Shiner argued that legal positivism inevitably develops, as it becomes more sophisticated and responds to criticisms, towards positions close to those of natural law theory (he also argued that, in turn, natural law theory, in its more sophisticated forms, develops in the direction of legal positivism). The basis of that argument can be seen in outline

---

[56] Joseph Raz, *Practical Reason and Norms* (2nd ed., Princeton: Princeton University Press, 1990), p. 193. The phrase "the benefits they are meant to bring" refers to the argument that one treats a source as authoritative if, in following the directives of that source, one is more likely to get things right than if one deliberated and decided for oneself. See *ibid.*

[57] *ibid.* p. 53 (footnote omitted). These criticisms are elaborated at *ibid.* pp. 50–58. Ronald Dworkin also offers a sharp criticism of Hart's practice theory of rules in *Taking Rights Seriously* (London: Duckworth, 1977), pp. 48–58. Hart accepts some of these criticisms in Hart, "Postscript", pp. 254–259.

[58] Raz, *Practical Reason and Norms*, p. 53.

[59] *ibid.* pp. 49–84.

[60] Roger Shiner, *Norm and Nature* (Oxford: Clarendon Press, 1992).

from issues discussed above. For example, an empirically based theory of law like John Austin's (in Shiner's terminology, an example of "simple positivism") has a number of obvious defects, which appear to be remedied in H. L. A. Hart's theory (in Shiner's terms, an example of "sophisticated positivism"), with its use of an "internal point of view". However, as discussed earlier in this section, we are already approaching natural law theory, in that the line seems quite thin between viewing law through the perspective of citizens or officials who accept the law as creating (prima facie moral) obligations (Hart's "internal point of view") and constructing one's theory around the conditions when law in fact imposes valid (prima facie) moral obligations.

In a review of *Norm and Nature*,[61] Frederick Schauer agreed with Shiner's basic analysis, but held that Shiner's view of "sophisticated legal positivism" was not the inevitable path that this approach to law need take. Schauer offered as an alternative an empirical, non-hermeneutic version of legal positivism, arguing that, in relation to the Hartian version of legal positivism discussed above, his alternative was as tenable but lacked the dangers of sliding into natural law theory. In other words, Schauer was offering a kind of "return to Austin".

Schauer's basic argument is that one can construct a version of the "internal point of view", where citizens' actions in conformity with the law, and officials' enforcement of the law, are all explained adequately in prudential terms (for example, the citizens fearing legal sanctions, and the officials fearing reprimand or removal from office, and hoping for appointment to a higher office).[62] The point of this transformed "internal point of view" is that the aspect of "normativity" (the fact that citizens or officials accept the law as creating moral obligations, as offering (additional) reasons to act in compliance with what the law prescribes) is removed, and that it is that aspect of sophisticated legal positivism that sends it sliding towards natural law theory.[63]

We are then returned to Hart (and his many and various followers) to discover why a theory based on such a "bad man's

---

[61] Frederick Schauer, "Critical Notice "[reviewing R. Shiner, *Norm and Nature* (1992)], (1994) 24 *Canadian Journal of Philosophy* 495.

[62] *ibid.* pp. 500–501.

[63] *ibid.* pp. 498–501.

view of the law"[64] is considered inadequate. The answer is because it fails to take into account the perspective of people who accept the law, those who follow its prescriptions for non-prudential reasons.[65] One argument is that this is the "central" or "focal" sense of law, which any theory should try to explain, while obeying the law for fear or favour is a "lesser" or "attenuated" sense of law.[66] Schauer's response is that centring one's theory on citizens or officials who believe that law imposes moral obligations is dubious when theorists themselves are far from united on law's moral status (see Chapter 16), with a number of legal positivists like Joseph Raz arguing strongly against the proposition that law creates prima facie moral obligations. The better approach, Schauer argues, is to leave the question completely open at the definitional level and argue the issue out from there.[67]

As against the conventional view (which, for what it is worth, is also this author's view) that Hart's use of a (quasi-)hermeneutic approach in legal theory constituted a significant advance in legal positivism in particular and legal theory in general, Schauer's analysis may provide a radical challenge.

---

[64] See Holmes, "The Path of the Law", pp. 460–461.

[65] Hart was not entirely clear on whether prudential interests could be a sufficient basis for an "internal point of view". See Hart, *The Concept of Law,* pp. 198 (including within an internal view those who accept the law because of "calculations of long-term interest").

[66] See Finnis, *Natural Law and Natural Rights*, pp. 6–18. One could also argue that those who accept the law (on non-prudential grounds) constitute a majority (or at least a significant minority) of the population. This, however, is an empirical claim, with little evidence available either in support or in opposition: see Schauer, "Critical Notice", p. 502.

[67] Schauer, "Critical Notice", p. 503.

Chapter Six

Hans Kelsen's Pure Theory of Law

Hans Kelsen (1881–1973) was a prolific and influential Austrian legal theorist, who spent the last decades of a long, productive life in the United States, having escaped Europe at the time of Hitler's rise to power. His work was influential in international law as well as jurisprudence, and he was a central figure in the drafting of the Austrian Federal Constitution after the First World War.

Over the course of four decades of jurisprudential writing, Kelsen published dozens of books and articles,[1] with his position on various matters changing in subtle but important ways.[2] This presents a difficulty for any attempt at a summary of Kelsen's view, a task already complicated by the sophistication of Kelsen's theory and the unfamiliarity (to American and English audiences at least) of the philosophical tradition within which Kelsen was working (in particular neo-Kantianism, a school of thought that attempted to

---

[1] "Dozens" is actually a bit of an understatement. By one count, Kelsen published 387 separate works (approximately 100 of which dealt exclusively with legal theory). Of those 387 works, 18 books and 121 articles are available in English: Michael Hartney, "Appendix: Bibliography of Kelsen's Publications in English" in Hans Kelsen, *General Theory of Norms* (M. Hartney trans. and ed., Oxford: Clarendon Press, 1991), pp. 440–454.

[2] Especially if one takes into account Kelsen's very last writings, which were unpublished during his lifetime, some of his changes in ideas and attitude were actually quite dramatic, at times appearing to support just the set of views he had most vigorously opposed 60 years earlier: see Stanley L. Paulson, "Kelsen's Legal Theory: The Final Round" (1992) 12 *Oxford Journal of Legal Studies* 265 at 265–266. On the different "phases" of Kelsen's work, see Michael Hartney, "Introduction" in Hans Kelsen, *General Theory of Norms*, pp. xx–liii; Stanley L. Paulson, "Towards a Periodization of the Pure Theory of Law" in *Hans Kelsen's Legal Theory* (L. Gianformaggio ed., Torino: G. Giappichelli, 1990), pp. 11–47.

apply Immanuel Kant's ideas more broadly to questions of social and ethical theory).[3] Though Kelsen is not as well known as he should be in England and the United States, internationally he is one of the most influential legal theorists of this century. The picture of Kelsen's theory I will be presenting will attempt to contain the general themes that continued throughout most of his writings, while there will be little attention paid to the ways in which Kelsen's view changed.

THE PURE THEORY OF LAW

Kelsen referred to his theory as "*Reine Rechtslehre*", a "Pure Theory of Law". In Kelsen's words, the theory was "pure" "because it only describes the law and attempts to eliminate from the object of this description everything that is not strictly 'law'".[4] Moral judgments, political biases and sociological conclusions were all to be pushed aside as improper for a "scientific" description of the social institution of law.[5]

The previous chapter noted the importance of the normative aspect of law in H. L. A. Hart's legal theory (it is central to the "internal aspect of rules", which in turn is central to Hart's theory and the way it differs from empirical theories like that of John Austin). With Kelsen's theory, the normativity of law is, if anything, an even more central and dominating factor. One could even say, with only slight exaggeration, that explaining the normative nature of law is the *sole* purpose of Kelsen's theory (as contrasted, say, with Hart, who is also interested in the difference between

---

[3] Because Kelsen wrote much of his important work in German (and until recently was poorly served by his English translators) and because he wrote out of a different philosophical tradition (a Continental tradition strongly influenced by Kant), his work has not been as central to the development of English-language legal theory as might have been warranted. For the above reasons, I used Hart rather than Kelsen to introduce the topic of modern legal positivism, even though most of Kelsen's works were published prior to Hart's most important works.

[4] Hans Kelsen, *The Pure Theory of Law* (M. Knight trans., Berkeley, Calif.: University of California Press, 1967), p. 1.

[5] One should not over-read Kelsen's talks about a "science" of law. Here, "science" is the translation of the German *Wissenschaft*, whose meaning and application generally is broader than the English "science". For example, it is usual and uncontroversial to use the term *Wissenschaft* even when referring to literacy theory.

primary and secondary rules, the difference between duty-imposing and power-conferring rules, the open texture of rules, etc.).
Most of what is puzzling to readers of Kelsen's legal theory can be
better understood if one keeps in mind the theory's focus on
normativity.

There are two basic starting points for understanding Kelsen's
approach to legal theory. First, normative claims—arguments for
how one ought to act or for how things ought to be—can be
grounded only on (justified by) other normative claims.[6] This is
the argument, usually attributed to David Hume, that one cannot
derive a normative conclusion from purely factual premises: "one
cannot derive an 'ought' from an 'is' ". In other words, a purely
factual description of a situation will never be sufficient, by itself,
to justify a conclusion that something ought (morally) to be done.
One can only justify such a conclusion by first accepting or
inserting a moral premise.[7]

Secondly, such lines of justification must necessarily come to an
end at some point.[8] In day-to-day discussions each (normative)
argument put forward is based on or justified by some more
general or more basic argument. We tend to forget that if we look
closely enough at the chain of arguments in favour of a particular
position, we will eventually come to an argument that is not
justified by some other argument, and the validity of this final
argument can only be based on its being tacitly or explicitly
accepted (accepted "on faith", as it were).

Consider the following example: a religious person tells you that
it is wrong to commit adultery. When you ask her why, she says
"because that is what is said in the Bible". Being in an obstinate
mood, you say "so what?", to which her response is that the Bible
is the word of God. To a second "so what?", her patient response
would be that we should all do as God tells us to do. However, if at
this point you ask why that is so, you are likely to get no more than

---

[6] See Kelsen, *The Pure Theory of Law*, pp. 4–10.

[7] Which is not to say that the moral premise will not be "obvious" or something
"everyone agrees with".

While there are some philosophers who contest the general view that one cannot
derive an "ought" proposition from an "is" proposition, a discussion of these
dissenting views is well outside the scope of this book. For present purposes, one
need note only that Kelsen's approach to law is grounded on the majority view
that such a derivation is not possible.

[8] See Kelsen, *The Pure Theory of Law*, pp. 193–195.

a puzzled (or angry) look. This line of argument has come to an end; either one accepts that one ought to what God says or one does not.[9] There is also a sense in which the foundational argument "we ought to do what God says" is entailed by or implied by the religious person's initial assertion that "one should not commit adultery". (This is not to say that one could not reach the same normative conclusion using other starting points, but only that for this particular person, *this* conclusion derives from or implies *that* starting point.)

Kelsen's argument was that there is a fundamental argument implied ("presupposed") by legal statements, just as there is a fundamental argument implied by religious statements. (In more technical language, Kelsen applied a "neo-Kantian" approach to legal theory, an approach based on aspects of Kant's theory of knowledge, in particular Kant's transcendental argument.[10])

The best way to understand Kelsen's project may be to think of him as asking this question: "what follows from the fact that someone treats legal rules as valid norms?"[11] Like many great philosophers, Kelsen tried to show us what is interesting or paradoxical about matters which seem to us ordinary and unremarkable. For Kelsen, the ordinary and unremarkable fact to be considered is that while looking at a simple collection of actions, we sometimes see those actions as normative. Whenever one looks at people putting slips of paper into a box, and sees "voting", or looks at a group of people raising and lowering their hands in various sequences, and sees "the passage of valid legislation", this gives empirical actions into normative meanings.[12] The transformation is clearer on the occasions when someone says that since

---

[9] That the argument could be stretched a step or two further does not alter the basic analysis; *e.g.* the religious person could say, "one ought to do what God says because He created humanity and all the world", with the implied claim that one ought to obey whoever (whatever) created us. However, there is no particular reason why everyone must accept that normative position.

[10] See, *e.g.* Kelsen, *The Pure Theory of Law*, pp. 201–205; Stanley L. Paulson, "The Neo-Kantian Dimension of Kelsen's Pure Theory of Law" (1992) 12 *Oxford Journal of Legal Studies* 311.

[11] See Paulson, "The Neo-Kantian Dimension of Kelsen's Pure Theory of Law", p. 324.

[12] See, *e.g.* Hans Kelsen, *Introduction to the Problems of Legal Theory* (B. L. Paulson and S. L. Paulson trans., Oxford: Clarendon Press, 1992), pp. 6–12.

those certain actions have been done (the group of people raising and lowering their hands), one now "ought" to do something (*e.g.* pay a certain tax). The border between 'is" and "ought" has been crossed, and the question is what can be derived from that.

Here we need to return to the idea of the normative chain of justification. One starts with some simple legal normative statement: for example, "one cannot park here (it is illegal to do so)". If the person making this statement was asked why it was so, she would probably note that this regulation was validly promulgated by some city council, judge or administrator. If the questioner pushes further, the chain could be followed back: for example, that the administrator was authorised to act in this area by an act of the legislature, and the act of the legislature was passed according to the procedures set down in the constitution.[13] Things get slightly trickier when one gets to the constitution itself. The document might itself have been a modification of an earlier basic law, or it might have been drawn up under the authorisation of an earlier basic law. However, again, we will eventually come to a point either so fundamental or so early in the society's legal history that one cannot go any further back, and no further justification can be offered.

Following the whole chain through then leads to the following implication: to assert the (normative) validity of the individual legal rule ("one cannot park on this street") is implicitly to affirm the validity of the fundamental link in the chain (*e.g.* "one ought to do whatever is authorised by the historically first constitution"), for the same reason that affirming an individual religious belief implicitly affirms the fundamental norm of the religion. To put the matter differently, the affirmation of the fundamental norm is "presupposed" by any express or implied affirmation of individual legal rules. This affirmation of the fundamental norm is what Kelsen calls the "*Grundnorm*" or "Basic Norm".[14]

---

[13] There are complications for Kelsen's argument when an official acts within his or her area of authorisation, but acts in an unauthorised (illegal) way: see, *e.g.* Stanley L. Paulson, "Material and Formal Authorisation in Kelsen's Pure Theory" (1980) 39 *Cambridge Law Journal* 172.

[14] See, *e.g.* Kelsen, *Introduction to the Problems of Legal Theory*, pp. 56–60.

REDUCTION AND LEGAL THEORY

Hans Kelsen believed that all legal norms could and should be understood in terms of an authorisation to an official to impose sanctions: if A (citizen) does X (wrong action), then B (an official) has the authority to impose Y (a sanction).[15]

Thus, Kelsen would want us to translate "you shall not murder", into the following instruction to an official: if any citizen murders, you (the official) have the authority to impose a sanction upon that person. (If the instruction to the official is only an authorisation, one might wonder how Kelsen can explain the fact that officials are bound to impose sanctions; it is not usually just a matter within their discretion. Kelsen would say that where officials have an obligation to act, this only means that there is another norm, instructing a higher official to this effect: "if the lower official does not impose a sanction in this situation, you are authorised to impose a sanction on that official"—and so it would go up the hierarchy.)

This is a slightly awkward formalisation of criminal laws as it stands, but its awkwardness becomes far greater when we try to put civil laws, in particular laws which confer powers, into the same form. For example, a statute authorising the creation of wills might read: if A creates a valid will (by following certain procedural and substantive requirements), and then dies, and A's executor refuses to follow the instructions of the will, then B (an official) has the authority to impose a sanction on A's executor.

Reduction (analysis of complicated phenomena into a small number of factors or variables) is the natural tendency whenever one posits a theory or a model of behaviour: in some ways, it is the essence of the activity. To the extent that one can discuss a complex social phenomenon, like law, in terms of one or two concepts, the process of theorising seems to be a success. There is no point in a theory merely replicating the complexity of the phenomena about us: that gives us nothing. An explanation is

---

[15] Kelsen's actual terminology is that the official "ought" to impose the sanction, but Kelsen uses the word "ought" broadly, in a sense which is best summarised as "authorised to" rather than "should perform": see Hans Kelsen, "On the Basis of Legal Validity" (1981) 26 *American Journal of Jurisprudence* 178 at 178–179, note b (trans. by Stanley L. Paulson) (translator's note on Kelsen's use of "*bestimmen*" and "*sollen*").

necessarily a sifting of the important from the unimportant, the essential from the accidental. There is something satisfying about being able to say something like "law is basically or essentially . . . " (where the blank might be filled in by "orders backed by threats" or "authorisations to officials to impose sanctions"). To understand the essence of something has always been considered a component of wisdom, so we tend to welcome the opportunity, when a theorist tells us that she has "discovered" what the essence of law (or government or community or marriage) is.

On the other hand, simplification is often distortion. The more one tries to recharacterise the variety of experience as though it was homogeneous, the more awkward and inaccurate the description will be. All social theorists (economists and anthropologists as well as legal and political theorists) must consider the proper balance between descriptive accuracy and explanatory power. (It is a problem that is particularly significant in understanding the limitations of the law and economics movement, which will be discussed in Chapter 18). Kelsen's theory lies towards an extreme in reduction: an attempt to reduce all laws to a particular form.[16] However, as H. L. A. Hart pointed out when discussing John Austin's approach to law,[17] while such reductions seem to have the benefit of simplicity, this benefit is largely a surface matter, as the effect of trying to force the various legal norms into a single structure is awkwardness, poor fit and a risk of misleading the reader.

HART V. KELSEN

Perhaps because of the limited dialogue between (or overlap in) H. L. A. Hart scholars and Hans Kelsen scholars, the differences between Hart and Kelsen are often poorly understood. Often, Kelsen is seen as an imperfect stopping point between Austin's mistaken views and Hart's solutions (a position that does not stand up long under close examination). One text actually

---

[16] Kelsen is neither the first nor the last theorist to make such an attempt. More recently, J. W. Harris has attempted to analysis all laws in terms of duties: see J. W. Harris, *Law and Legal Science* (Oxford: Clarendon Press 1979).

[17] Hart, *The Concept of Law*, pp. 27–41.

states that Hart is merely Kelsen in clearer prose.[18] Even if this is meant to be complimentary to Kelsen, it does a disservice to both sides.[19] In this section, I will briefly discuss some of the things which join and separate the two writers.

There is a particular question that theorists who focus on the normativity of law—and Hart as well as Kelsen would fit into this category—could be said to be trying to answer: how is a legal system to be distinguished from the orders of gangsters?[20] For Hart, this question led to an investigation of the differences in action and attitude between how we act when we are following a rule and how we act when we are being compelled to do the same action. This in turn led to Hart's discussion of the "internal aspect" of rules and of law, which is basic to his approach to legal theory.

Kelsen's response to the gangster/law question would be simple: those who see the actions of the people in power in a normative way (and thus presuppose the Basic Norm in dealing with the official's promulgations) see the people in power as legitimate authorities; those who do not see the actions this way will see the people in power as gangsters or their equivalent. In a sense, Kelsen's response is comparable to Hart's: the difference between the commands of valid law and the orders of gangsters is determined by, indeed is constituted by, the attitudes of the citizens or officials.

Here, we also see how legal positivism links Hart and Kelsen: both analyse the difference between gangsters and legitimate government by focusing on the more or less "neutral" question of citizens' or officials reaction. Hart and Kelsen's positions avoid making moral judgments. They pass by the more obvious answer to the gangster/law question, which would be quickly given by a natural law theorist: that the difference between legitimate leaders

---

[18] Jeffrie Murphy and Jules Coleman, *Philosophy of Law* (revised ed., Westview Press, 1990), p. 27.

[19] One can find Hart's comments on Kelsen in H. L. A. Hart, *Essays in Jurisprudence and Philosophy* (Oxford: Clarendon Press, 1983), pp. 286–342. However, one often gets the impression that Hart did not entirely understand Kelsen's work, a misunderstanding probably caused by Kelsen's starting point being so different from the Anglo-American tradition within which Hart wrote.

[20] See Hart, *The Concept of Law*, pp. 6–7, 20–24, 79–81.

and gangsters is that the former act justly and for the common good and the latter do not.

The differences between Hart and Kelsen are equally interesting and significant. While both Hart and Kelsen emphasised the normative aspect of law in response to and in criticism of fact-based approaches, their notion of the "normative" differed.[21] Hart's view of the normative reduced to certain types of social facts, while Kelsen resisted any reduction of "normative" to facts.[22] While Hart's theory tried to track and explain actual social practices (with labelling of the work as "descriptive sociology", and the careful distinctions, *e.g.* feeling obliged versus having an obligation, acting out of habit versus following a rule, and the different kinds of rules), Kelsen's theory tended to be more abstract—appropriate for what purported to be a "pure theory" and a neo-Kantian analysis.

The most obvious differences may be ones of methodology, which have been hinted at in passing over the course of this chapter and the previous one: on the one hand, Hart's analysis builds on close attention to actual practices (and how they are perceived by their participants) and linguistic usage; on the other, Kelsen is offering a kind of logical analysis of law and of normative thinking in general.

ON THE NATURE OF NORMS

Especially in his later works, Kelsen became caught up in the question of what is the nature of norms. Analysis in (metaphorical) terms of one norm "justifying" or "generating" another, and inquiries regarding whether a legal system can contain norms with contradictory contents, seemed to create a confusion in Kelsen "between a norm as a kind of sentence or sentence-meaning and as a contingent entity created and repealed by certain social events".[23] Arguably, this line of inquiry was what was behind many of the changes in his theory over time, as well as some of the

---

[21] Stanley L. Paulson, "Continental Normativism and Its British Counterpart: How Different Are They?" (1993) 6 *Ratio Juris* 227.

[22] *ibid.* p. 236.

[23] Hartney, "Introduction", pp. xlii–xliii.

stranger (or more absurd) notions of the later work (which have not been discussed in this chapter).[24]

At times, some members associated with "Scandinavian legal realism"[25] appear to make the converse mistake. The Scandinavian legal realists were opposed to anything in legal theory that had the flavour of metaphysics. When they looked for some object to correspond with legal concepts like "norm" and "right", they rejected any explanation that seemed to posit unworldly entities: instead, these theorists offered psychological and anthropological explanations to fill the vacuum. Consider the following discussion by Karl Olivecrona about rights:

> "[T]he word 'right', as used in jurisprudence as well as common discourse, lacks semantic reference.
>
>   . . .
>
> We have, however, the illusion that the word 'right' signifies a power over [an] object, though a power that we can never grasp. The illusion stems from the emotional background. Under certain circumstances, especially in situations of conflict, the idea of possessing a right gives rise to a feeling of strength. When I am convinced of having a right, I am in some way more powerful than my opponent, even if he be actually stronger."[26]

Both the perceived need to posit abstract entities for explanation and the perceived need to avoid anything that has any outward appearance of being an abstract entity are likely to lead theorists and theories astray. One can avoid such problems by reacting to apparently abstract terms, like "norm" and "right", by asking merely for the rules that govern the use of those terms within the legal system in question.[27]

(This is not to deny that important philosophical work can be done on an analytical theory of norms.[28] For the moment, it is

---

[24] See, e.g. Hartney, "Introduction", pp. xlii–liii.

[25] See, e.g. Lord Lloyd and M. D. A. Freeman, *Lloyd's Introduction to Jurisprudence* (6th ed., London: Sweet & Maxwell, 1995), pp. 731–782 ("The Scandinavian Realists").

[26] Karl Olivecrona, *Law as Fact* (London: Stevens & Sons, 1971), p. 184.

[27] This type of metaphysics-avoiding analysis has roots in the writings of both H. L. A. Hart and Ludwig Wittgenstein. I discussed the approach in greater detail in Bix, "Questions in Legal Interpretation", pp. 137–141.

[28] See, e.g. Georg Henrik von Wright, *Norm and Action* (London: Routledge & Kegan Paul, 1963).

sufficient to note that most legal theorists are not well equipped to do this sort of work. Such inquiries tend to lead legal theorists far astray, and asking these sorts of questions is almost always irrelevant to what the legal theorists wish to know.[29])

---

[29] See Bix, "Questions in Legal Interpretation", pp. 137–141.

Chapter Seven

Natural Law Theory and John Finnis

We take it for granted that the laws and legal system under which we live can be criticised on moral grounds: that there are standards against which legal norms can be compared and sometimes found wanting. The standards against which law is judged have sometimes been described as "a [the] higher law". For some, this is meant literally: that there are law-like standards that have been stated in or can be derived from divine revelation, religious texts, a careful study of human nature or consideration of nature. For others, the reference to "higher law" is meant metaphorically, in which case it at least reflects our mixed intuitions about the moral status of law: on one hand, that not everything properly enacted as law is binding morally; on the other hand, that the law, as law, does have moral weight—it should not be simply ignored in determining what is the right thing to do. (If the law had no intrinsic moral weight, why would we need to point to a "higher law" as a justification for ignoring the requirements of our society's laws?)

TRADITIONAL NATURAL LAW THEORY

The approach traditionally associated with the title "natural law" was connected with arguments for the existence of a "higher law", elaborations of its content, and analyses of what should follow from the existence of a "higher law" (in particular, what response citizens should have to situations where the positive law—the law enacted within particular societies—conflicts with the "higher law").[1]

While one can locate a number of passages in the classical Greek writers that express what appear to be natural law positions,[2] the best-known ancient formulation of a natural law position was offered by the Roman orator Cicero.

Cicero (106–43 BC) was strongly influenced (as were many Roman writers on law) by the works of the Greek Stoic philosophers (some would go so far as to say that Cicero merely offered an elegant restatement of already established Stoic views). Cicero offered the following characterisation of "natural law":

> "True law is right reason in agreement with nature; it is of universal application, unchanging and everlasting; it summons to duty by its commands, and averts from wrongdoing by its prohibitions. And it does not lay its commands or prohibitions upon good men in vain, though neither have any effect on the wicked. It is a sin to try to alter this law, nor is it allowable to attempt to repeal any part of it, and it is impossible to abolish it entirely. We cannot be freed from its obligations by senate or people, and we need not look outside ourselves for an expounder or interpreter of it. And there will not be different laws at Rome and at Athens, or different laws now and in the future, but one eternal and unchangeable law will be valid for all nations and all times, and there will be one master and ruler, that is, God, over us all, for he is the author of this law, its promulgator, and its enforcing judge. Whoever is disobedient is fleeing from himself and denying his human nature, and by reason of this very fact he will suffer the worst penalties, even if he escapes what is commonly considered punishment."[3]

In Cicero's discussions of law, we come across most of the themes traditionally associated with natural law theory (although, as might be expected in the first major treatment of a subject, some of the analysis is not always as systematic or as precise as one might want): natural law is unchanging over time and does not

---

[1] Some of the modern writers who are sometimes associated with natural law, like Lon Fuller and Ronald Dworkin, have approaches far outside the tradition described in this chapter. Both Fuller and Dworkin are discussed in later chapters.

[2] These include passages in Plato, *Laws*, IV, 715b ("enactments, so far as they are not for the common interest of the whole community, are no true laws") and Aristotle, *Nicomachean Ethics*, V, 7:1134b18–1135a5, as well as Sophocles, "Antigone", 450–460.

[3] Cicero, *Republic*, III.xxii.33.

differ in different societies; every person has access to the standards of this higher law by use of reason; and only just laws "really deserve [the] name" law, and "in the very definition of the term 'law' there inheres the idea and principle of choosing what is just and true."[4]

Within Cicero's work, and the related remarks of earlier Greek and Roman writers, there was often a certain ambiguity regarding the reference to "natural" in "natural law": it was not always clear whether the standards were "natural" because they derived from "human nature" (our "essence" or "purpose"), because they were accessible by our natural faculties (that is, by human reason or the human conscience), because they derived from or were expressed in nature, that is, in the physical world about us, or some combination of all three.

As one moves from the classical writers on natural law to the early Christian writers, aspects of the theory necessarily change and therefore raise different issues within this approach to morality and law. For example, with classical writers, the source of the higher standards is said to be (or implied as being) inherent in the nature of things, while with the early Christian writers, there is a divine being who actively intervenes in human affairs and lays down express commands for all mankind—although this contrast overstates matters somewhat, as the classical writers referred to a (relatively passive) God, and the early Christian writers would sometimes refer to the rules of nature as expressing divine will. To the extent that the natural law theorists of the early Church continued to speak of higher standards inherent in human nature or in the nature of things, they also had to face the question of the connection between these standards and divine commands: for example, whether God can change natural law or order something which is contrary to it, a question considered by St Ambrose and St Augustine (among others) in the time of the early Church and by Francisco Suarez hundreds of years later.

The most influential writer within the traditional approach to natural law is undoubtedly St Thomas Aquinas (1224–1274). However, the context of Aquinas' approach to law (its occurrence within a larger theological project that offered a systematic moral

---

[4] Cicero, *Law*, II.v.11–12.

system) should be kept in mind when comparing his work with more recent theorists.

Aquinas identified four different kinds of law: the eternal law, the natural law, the divine law, and human (positive) law.[5] For present purposes, the important categories are natural law and positive law.

According to Aquinas, positive law is derived from natural law. This derivation has different aspects. On some occasions the natural law dictates what the positive law should be: for example, natural law requires that there be a prohibition on murder. At other times, the natural law leaves room for human choice (based on local customs or policy choices)[6]: thus while natural law would probably require regulation of automobile traffic for the safety of others, the choice of whether driving should be on the left or the right side of the road, and whether the speed limit should be set at 55 or 65 miles per hour, are probably matters in which either choice would be compatible with the requirements of natural law. The first form of derivation is like logical deduction; the second, Aquinas refers to as the "determination" of general principles (*determinatio*).[7]

As for citizens, the question is what their obligations are regarding just and unjust laws. Positive laws which are just "have the power of binding in conscience".[8] A just law is one which is consistent with the requirements of natural law—that is, it is "ordered to the common good", the law-giver has not exceeded its authority, and the law's burdens are imposed on citizens fairly. Failure with respect to any of those three criteria, Aquinas asserts, makes a law unjust[9]; but what is the citizen's obligation in regard to an unjust law? The short answer is that there is no obligation to obey that law. However, a longer answer is warranted, given the amount of attention this question usually gets in discussions of natural law theory in general, and of Aquinas in particular.

The phrase *lex iniusta non est lex* ("an unjust law is not law") is often ascribed to Aquinas, and is given as a summation of his

---

[5] St Thomas Aquinas, *Summa Theologiae* in *The Treatise on Law* (R. J. Henle trans. and ed., Notre Dame: University of Notre Dame Press, 1993), Question 91.

[6] Aquinas, *Summa Theologiae*, Question 95, art. 2, corpus.

[7] *ibid.* A similar distinction is drawn in Aristotle, *Nicomachean Ethics*, V, 7:1134b18–1135a5.

[8] Aquinas, *Summa Theologiae*, Question 94, art. 4, corpus.

[9] *ibid.* Question 96, art. 4, corpus.

position and the natural law position in general.[10] This view is at least somewhat misleading on several counts. Aquinas never used the exact phrase above, although one can find similar expressions: "every human positive law has the nature of law to the extent that it is derived from the Natural Law. If, however, in some point it conflicts with the law of nature it will no longer be law but rather a perversion of law"[11]; and "[unjust laws] are acts of violence rather than laws; as Augustine says, 'A law that is unjust seems not to be a law' ".[12] (One also finds similar statements by Plato, Aristotle, Cicero, and St Augustine—although, with the exception of Cicero's, these statements are not part of a systematic discussion of the nature of law.)

Another question goes to the significance of the phrase. What does it mean to say that an apparently valid law is "not law", "a perversion of law" or "an act of violence rather than a law"? Statements of this form have been offered and interpreted in one of two ways. First, one can mean that an immoral law is not valid law at all. John Austin interpreted statements by the English commentator Sir William Blackstone (*e.g.* "no human laws are of any validity, if contrary to [the law of nature]"[13]) in this manner, and pointed out that such analyses of validity are of little value. Austin wrote:

> "Suppose an act innocuous, or positively beneficial, be prohibited by the sovereign under the penalty of death; if I commit this act, I shall be tried and condemned, and if I object to the sentence, that it is contrary to the law of God . . . the Court of Justice will demonstrate the inconclusiveness of my reasoning by hanging me up, in pursuance of the law of which I have impugned the validity."[14]

Although one must add that we should not conflate questions of power with questions of validity—for a corrupt legal system might

---

[10] A good discussion on "*lex iniusta non est lex*", its meaning in general and its significance in Aquinas' work can be found in Norman Kretzmann, "*Lex Iniusta Non Est Lex*: Laws on Trial in Aquinas' Court of Conscience' (1988) 33 *American Journal of Jurisprudence* 99.

[11] Aquinas, *Summa Theologiae*, Question 95, art. 2, corpus.

[12] *ibid.* Question 94, art. 4, corpus.

[13] William Blackstone, *Commentaries on the Laws of England* (Oxford: Clarendon Press, 1765–1769), I.41.

[14] Austin, *The Province of Jurisprudence Determined*, p. 185, quoted in Hart, "Positivism and the Separation of Law and Morals", 616.

punish someone even if shown that the putative law was invalid under the system's own procedural requirements—we understand the distinction between validity under the system's rules and the moral worth of the enactment in question.

A more reasonable interpretation of statements like "an unjust law is no law at all" is that unjust laws are not laws "in the fullest sense".[15] As we might say of some professional, who had the necessary degrees and credentials, but seemed nonetheless to lack the necessary ability or judgment: "she's no lawyer" or "he's no doctor". This only indicates that we do not think that the title in this case carries with it all the laudatory implications it usually does. (It may well be that, for our purposes, knowing that this doctor is not competent is the most important fact; however, the fact that he does have the required certification is not thereby negated or made entirely irrelevant.) Similarly, to say that unjust laws are "not really laws" may only be to point out that they do not carry the same moral force or offer the same reasons for action that come from laws consistent with "higher law". This is almost certainly the sense in which Aquinas made his remarks,[16] and the probable interpretation for nearly all proponents of the position.

However, this interpretation leaves the statement as clearly right as the prior interpretation was clearly wrong. One wonders what the source of controversy was.

To say that an unjust law is not law in the fullest sense is usually intended not as a simple declaration, but as the first step of a further argument. For example: "this law is unjust; it is not law in the fullest sense, and therefore citizens can in good conscience act as if it was never enacted; that is, they should feel free to disobey it." This is a common understanding of the idea that an unjust law is no law at all, but it expresses a conclusion that is controversial.

---

[15] Finnis traces the notion to Aristotle's notion of "focal meaning" and Max Weber's concept of "ideal types": see Weber, *The Methodology of the Social Sciences*, pp. 90–106; Aristotle, *Eudemian Ethics*, VII, 2:1236a16–30; *Nicomachean Ethics*, VIII, 4:1157a30–1157b3; *Politics*, III, 1:1275a33–1276b4.

[16] Elsewhere, Aquinas wrote: 'But even an unjust law retains some semblance of the nature of law, since it was made by one in power and in this respect it is derived from the Eternal Law": Aquinas, *Summa Theologiae*, Question 93, art. 2.

There are often moral reasons for obeying even an unjust law: for example, if the law is part of a generally just legal system, and public disobedience of the law might undermine the system, there is a moral reason for at least minimal public compliance with the unjust law. There is a hint of this position in Aquinas (he stated that a citizen is not bound to obey "a law which imposes an unjust burden on its subjects" if the law "can be resisted without scandal or greater harm"), and it has been articulated at greater length by later natural law theorists (most recently by John Finnis,[17] as discussed below).

Aquinas' theory is in some ways more the structure of an ethical system than the full ethical system itself. For most of us, little practical guidance for difficult moral questions can be found from the advice, "good should be done and sought and evil is to be avoided".[18] However, Aquinas offers few prescriptions on particular moral issues more specific than that. The assumption may have been that the teachings of the Church and the holy books, combined with the reflections of a wise person,[19] would be sufficient to fill in the content of the moral system.

In the period of the Renaissance and beyond, discussions about natural law were tied in with other issues: assertions about natural law were often the basis of or part of the argument for individual rights and limitations on government; and such discussions were also often the groundwork offered for principles of international law.

In overview: it is normally a mistake to try to evaluate the discussions of writers from distant times with the perspective of modern analytical jurisprudence. Cicero and Aquinas were not concerned with a social scientific analysis of law, as many modern advocates of legal positivism could be said to be. The early natural law theorists were concerned with what legislators and citizens and governments ought to do, or could do in good conscience. It is not that these writers (and their followers) never asked questions like "what is law?" However, they were asking the questions as a starting point for an ethical inquiry, and therefore

---

[17] Finnis, *Natural Law and Natural Rights*, pp. 359–362.

[18] Aquinas, *Summa Theologiae*, Question 94, art. 2, corpus.

[19] Cf. *ibid.* where Aquinas distinguishes propositions which are self-evident to all and those that are self-evident only to the wise.

one should not be too quick in comparing their answers with those in similar-sounding discussions by recent writers, who see themselves as participating in a conceptual or sociological task.

JOHN FINNIS

John Finnis' work is an explication and application of Aquinas' views (at least, of one reading of Aquinas, a reading advocated by Germain Grisez, among others): an application to ethical questions, but with special attention to the problems of social theory in general and analytical jurisprudence in particular.

For Finnis, the basic questions are the ethical one, "how should one live?", and the meta-ethical one, "how (by what procedure or analysis) can we discover the answer to ethical questions?" These ethical and meta-ethical questions are primary; legal theory for Finnis is best understood as a small if integral part of the larger scheme of things.

Finnis' response to these basis questions involves, among other things, the claim that there are a number of separate but equally valuable intrinsic goods (that is, things one values for their own sake), which he called "basic goods". In *Natural Law and Natural Rights*, Finnis lists the following as basic goods: life (and health), knowledge, play, aesthetic experience, sociability (friendship), practical reasonableness and religion (Finnis' list of basic goods changed somewhat in later writings). These are "intrinsic" goods in the following sense: one can value, for example, health for its own sake, but medicine only as a means to health. If someone stated that she was buying medicine, not because she or someone she knew was sick or might become sick, and not because it was part of some study or some business, but simply because she liked having a lot of medicine around, one might rightly begin to question her sanity.

At this level, we can only distinguish the intelligible from the unintelligible. We *understand* the person who is materialistic and greedy, however much we disapprove of that approach to life. The greedy person is seeking the same basic goods we are. Much of what is conventionally considered morality occurs in Finnis' theory at the second level of discussion: the principles for how we should deal with and combine the quest for various intrinsic goods.

Finnis describes the list of basic goods, and other aspects of his moral theory, as "self-evident", but he does not mean this in the sense that the truth of these propositions would be immediately obvious to all competent thinkers. Part of what makes a proposition self-evident is that it cannot be derived from some more fundamental proposition; thus, self-evident is here the opposite of provable.[20] (However, while self-evident propositions cannot be proven, they can be supported by consistent observational data and by dialectical arguments.) Also, it is not the case that everyone will be equally adept at reaching these "self-evident" conclusions: those of substantial experience, who are able and willing to inquire deeply, may be better able to discover the self-evident truths than would others (Aquinas at one point wrote of propositions which are only self-evident to the wise[21]).

Because there are a variety of basic goods, with no hierarchy or priority among them, there must be principles on how to choose when the alternatives promote different goods. (This is one basis for contrasting Finnis' position with utilitarian moral theories, under which all goods can be compared according to their value in a single unit, *e.g.* promoting happiness.) On a simple level, we face such choices when we consider whether to spend the afternoon playing soccer (the value of play) or studying history (the value of knowledge). The choice is presented in a sharper form when we must choose whether to lie (choosing against the value of knowledge), in a situation where we believe that lying would lead to some significant benefit or avoid a greater evil. Morality offers a basis for rejecting certain available choices, but there will often remain more than one equally legitimate choice (again there is a contrast with utilitarian theories, under which there would always be a "best" choice).

For Finnis, the move from the basic goods to moral choices occurs through a series of intermediate principles, which Finnis calls "the basic requirements of practical reasonableness". Among the most significant, and most controversial, is the prescription that one may never act directly against a basic good (as lying is an

---

[20] See Robert George, "Recent Criticism of Natural Law Theory" (1988) 55 *University of Chicago Law Review* 1371 at 1386–1393 (explaining and defending this aspect of Finnis' argument).

[21] Aquinas, *Summa Theologiae*, Question 94, art. 2, corpus.

action against knowledge or torture an action against life (and health)), regardless of the benefit one believes will come from taking that path.[22] In other words, the ends never justify the means where the chosen means entail a harming of a basic good.

Other intermediate principles listed in *Natural Law and Natural Rights* (the list changed somewhat in Finnis' later writings) include that one should form a rational plan of life, have no arbitrary preferences among persons, foster the common good of the community and have no arbitrary preferences among the basic goods.[23]

Law enters the picture as a way of effecting some goods (social goods which require the co-ordination of many people) that could not be effected (easily or at all) without it, and as a way of making it easier to obtain other goods.[24] Thus, the suggestions Finnis makes about law and about legal theory are in a sense derived from his primary concern with ethics. As to questions regarding the obligation to obey the law, Finnis follows Aquinas: one has an obligation to obey just laws; laws which are unjust are not "law" in the fullest sense of the term and one has an obligation to comply with their requirements only to the extent that this is necessary to uphold otherwise just institutions.[25]

Given that Finnis' starting point is so different from that of the legal positivists, it is surprising to discover some similarities in their theories.[26] These similarities occur because even though Finnis' theory might be seen as primarily a prescriptive account—a theory of how we should live our lives—certain descriptive elements are necessarily assumed.[27] First, if one if going to ask what implications

---

[22] Predictably, within this approach, much turns on characterisation of an action. Harming another person in self-defence would likely be justified on the ground that the purpose of the action is to defend one's own life (the basic good of "life/health"); the harm to one's attacker is but a side-effect, even if one that is foreseeable or inevitable.

[23] Finnis, *Natural Law and Natural Rights*, pp. 100–127.

[24] *ibid.*, pp. 260–264.

[25] *ibid.*, pp. 354–362.

[26] Finnis elsewhere discussed the ways in which a natural law theorist can affirm, more or less on the terms offered, nearly every "dogma" associated with modern legal positivism. See Finnis, "The Truth in Legal Positivism", pp. 203–205.

[27] One could also offer historical reasons for the similarities. Finnis was H. L. A. Hart's student at Oxford, and Joseph Raz was first a classmate and has more recently been a colleague of many years.

morality has for law, one must first understand what "law" is. Secondly, it is part of Finnis' project to consider which proposals within various aspects of legal regulation are foreclosed and which allowed by our general ethical theory.[28] Further, Finnis believes that a proper ethical theory is necessary for doing descriptive theory well, as valuation is a necessary and integral part of theory construction.[29]

Like Hart, Finnis emphasised the need to use an "internal point of view" in analysing a legal system[30] and, like Joseph Raz, Finnis believes that our understanding of legal systems should centre on the fact that law affects our reasons for action.[31] As noted earlier, regarding the "internal point of view", Finnis makes an important amendment to Hart's approach. He argues that, in deriving legal theory, one should not take the perspective of those who merely accept the law as valid (Hart appears to include even those who accept the law as valid for prudential reasons); the theory should assume the perspective of those who accept the law as binding *because* they—correctly—believe that valid legal rules create (prima facie) moral obligations. The difference may seem minor, but it means crossing a theoretically significant dividing line: between the legal positivist's insistence on deriving theory in a morally neutral way and the natural law theorist's assertion that moral evaluation is an integral part of proper description and analysis. Finnis' approach to descriptive theory, unlike Hart's, requires the theorist to judge the moral merits of the legal system(s) being described, and it is just the propriety or necessity of such moral evaluations in the process of descriptive theory which has been the dividing line in recent times between legal positivism and natural law theory.

---

[28] See, *e.g.* Finnis, *Natural Law and Natural Rights*, pp. 169–173 (property law), 188–192 (bankruptcy).

[29] *ibid.* pp. 6–18.

[30] *ibid.* pp. 3–13.

[31] *ibid.* pp. 12–13. Also like Raz, Finnis believes that values (and value choices) are incommensurable, and that this has important consequences for legal theory and moral theory. See Joseph Raz, *The Morality of Freedom* (Oxford: Clarendon Press, 1986), pp. 321–366; John Finnis, "On Reason and Authority in *Law's Empire*" (1987) 6 *Law and Philosophy* 357 at 370–376; "Natural Law and Legal Reasoning" (1990) 38 *Cleveland State Law Review* 1 at 7–9; "Concluding Reflections" (1990) 38 *Cleveland State Law Review* 231 at 234–241.

A similar difference or change can be seen in comparing Raz's practical reasoning approach to law and Finnis' approach. For Raz, what is central is that law *purports to* create moral reasons for action; for Finnis, what is central is that, under certain conditions, law *does* create moral reasons for action. The difference may seem slight, but it is also significant.

Chapter Eight

Understanding Lon Fuller

A SECOND KIND OF NATURAL LAW THEORY

At the beginning of the last chapter, I offered an overview of natural law theory. To be more exact, I offered an overview of *one type* of natural law theory, which I would describe as "traditional natural law theory". One could divide most of the theorists who have been labelled—or who have labelled themselves—as "natural law theorists" into two groups. The first group would include the theorists discussed in the earlier chapter; Cicero, Aquinas and Finnis, among many others, who discuss the implications for law and legal theory of a more general moral system. The second group reflects debates of a different kind and a more recent origin; its approach focuses more narrowly on the proper under-standing of law as a social institution or a social practice. (The two types of approaches are by no means contradictory or inconsistent, but they reflect sets of theoretical concerns sufficiently different that it is rare to find writers contributing to both.)

The second (or "modern") set of approaches to natural law arises as a response to legal positivism, and the way legal positivists portrayed (and sometimes caricatured) traditional natural law positions. While attacks on the merits of natural law theory can be found in the works of John Austin, Oliver Wendell Holmes and Hans Kelsen, most recent discussions of "natural law theory" derive from the 1958 "Hart–Fuller debate" in the *Harvard Law Review*.[1] In this exchange, H. L. A. Hart set the groundwork for a

---

[1] H. L. A. Hart, "Positivism and the Separation of Law and Morals" (1958) 71 *Harvard Law Review* 593; Lon Fuller, "Positivism and Fidelity to Law—A Response to Professor Hart" (1958) 71 *Harvard Law Review* 630.

restatement of legal positivism. Part of his defense and restatement involved demarcating legal positivism for natural law theory, and the demarcation point offered was the conceptual separation of law and morality. Lon Fuller (1902–1978) argued against a sharp separation of law and morality, but the position he defended under the rubric of natural law theory was quite different from the traditional natural law theories of Cicero and Aquinas (as will be discussed in detail below).

In part because of responses to legal positivists like Hart, a category of natural law theory has arisen which is best understood by its contrast to legal positivism, rather than by its connection with the traditional natural law theories of Cicero and Aquinas. While the traditional theories were generally taking a particular position on the status of morality (that true moral beliefs are based in or derived from human nature or the natural world, that they are not relative, that they are accessible to human reason, etc.), a position which then had some implications for how legislators, judges and citizens should act (as well as for all other aspects of living a good life), the second category of "natural law theory" contains are theories specifically about law, which hold that moral evaluation of some sort is required in describing law in general, particular legal systems, or the legal validity of individual laws.

The two most prominent members of this second group are Lon Fuller, who referred to his approach as a "natural law" approach, and who is the subject of this chapter, and Ronald Dworkin, who only occasionally and with some reluctance takes on that title, and who is the subject of the next chapter.

Fuller's Approach

Lon Fuller rejected what he saw as legal positivism's distorted view of law as a "one-way projection of authority": the sovereign gives orders and the citizens obey. Fuller believed that this approach missed the need for co-operation and reciprocal obligations[2] between officials and citizens for a legal system to work.

---

[2] See, *e.g.* Lon Fuller, *The Morality of Law* (revised ed., New Haven: Yale University Press, 1969), p. 39 ("There is a kind of reciprocity between government and the citizen with respect to the observance of rules").

Additionally, Fuller criticised legal positivists for misunderstanding the centrality of the ideal of law (which he alternatively described as "order", "good order" and "justice") in any understanding of law itself. To exclude the ideal from a theory of law on the basis of a "separation of description and evaluation" is to miss the point entirely: the social practice and social institution of law is by its nature a striving towards such ideals.[3]

Fuller characterised law as "the enterprise of subjecting human conduct to the governance of rules".[4] Law is a way of governing people, to be contrasted with other forms of governance, for example, managerial direction.[5] Law is a particular means to an end; a particular kind of tool, if you will.[6] With that in mind, one can better understand the claim that rules must meet certain criteria relating to that means, to that function, if they are to warrant the title "law". If we defined "knife" as something that cuts, something which failed to cut would not warrant the label, however much it might superficially resemble true knives. Similarly, if we define law as a particular way of guiding and co-ordinating human behaviour, if a system's rules are so badly constructed that they cannot succeed in effectively guiding behaviour, then we are justified in withholding the label "law" from them.[7]

Another way to view the same analysis is to point out that those in authority are not entirely free when they create law. They must respond to and adapt to the external order, factors beyond their

---

[3] See Winston, "The Ideal Element in a Definition of Law", pp. 98, 103–104, 109.

[4] Fuller, *The Morality of Law*, p. 96. Kenneth Winston argues that the quoted characterisation "is meant to define not law in general but only the process of legislation": Winston, "Introduction" in Lon Fuller, *The Principles of Social Order* (Durham, N.C.: Duke University Press, 1981), p. 30, n. 33.
I declined to call Fuller's characterisation a "definition" of law, as there is evidence that Fuller had little regard for the project of "defining law": see Winston, "The Ideal Element in a Definition of Law", p. 91 (quoting from a letter Fuller wrote in which he disccused this matter). However, I believe that Fuller's discussions are, like other "definitions of law", at least in part a conceptual claim about law. (On "conceptual claims", see Chap. 4.)

[5] Fuller, *The Morality of Law*, pp. 207–214.

[6] In many of the writings discussed, Fuller was speaking primarily, if not exclusively, of legislation. In other writings, Fuller focused on adjudication, mediation, contractual agreements, and managerial direction. See Fuller, *The Principles of Social Order* (a collection of published and unpublished works).

[7] Lloyd Weinreb, *Natural Law and Justice* (Cambridge, Mass.: Harvard University Press, 1987), pp. 102–103.

control: aspects of human nature (in particular how people interact, and how they react to various forms of guidance), the nature of society (which institutional structures work and which do not), and the resources available.[8]

Fuller offered, in place of legal positivism's analyses of law based on power, orders and obedience, an analysis based on the "internal morality" of law. Like traditional natural law theorists, he wrote of there being a threshold that must be met (or, to change the metaphor, a test that must be passed) before something could properly (or in the fullest sense) be called "law". Unlike traditional natural law theorists, however, the test Fuller applies is one of function and procedure rather than strictly one of moral content.

The internal morality of law consists of a series of requirements which Fuller asserted that a system of rules must meet—or at least substantially meet—if that system is to be called "law". (At the same time, Fuller wrote of systems being "legal" to different extents, and he held that a system which partly but not fully met his requirements would be "partly legal" and could be said to have "displayed a greater respect for the principles of legality" than systems which did not meet the requirements at all.[9])

The eight requirements were:

(1)   laws should be general;
(2)   laws should be promulgated, that citizens might know the standards to which they are being held;
(3)   retroactive rule-making and application should be minimised;
(4)   laws should be understandable;
(5)   laws should not be contradictory;
(6)   laws should not require conduct beyond the abilities of those affected;
(7)   laws should remain relatively constant through time; and
(8)   there should be a congruence between the laws as announced and their actual administration.[10]

---

[8] See Kenneth Winston, "Introduction", pp. 13–14.
[9] Fuller, *The Morality of Law*, pp. 122–123.
[10] *ibid.* pp. 33–91.

Fuller's approach is often contrasted with that of traditional natural law positions. Fuller at one point tried to show a connection, writing that "Aquinas in some measure recognized and dealt with all eight of the principles of legality". On the other hand, Fuller also realised that there were significant differences: he once referred to his theory as "a procedural, as distinguished from a substantive natural law". However, he chafed at the dismissal of his set of requirements as "merely procedural": an argument frequently made by critics that his "principles of legality" were amoral solutions to problems of efficiency, such that one could just as easily speak of "the internal morality of poisoning".[11] Such criticisms misunderstand the extent to which our perceptions of justice incorporate procedural matters. This is a matter Fuller himself brought up through an example from the (then) Soviet Union. In that system, there was once an attempt to increase the sentence for robbery, an increase also to be applied retroactively to those convicted of that crime in the past. Even in the Soviet legal system, not known for its adherence to the Rule of Law, there was a strong reaction by lawyers against this attempt to increase sentences retroactively. It is a matter of procedure only, but still it seemed to them—and it would seem to us—a matter of justice.[12] Following the rules laid down (just as one example of procedural justice) is a good thing, and it is not stretching matters to characterise it as a moral matter and a matter of justice.

On the other hand, there were times when Fuller overstated the importance of his "principles of legality". When critics argued that a regime could follow those principles and still enact wicked laws, Fuller stated that he could not believe that adherence to the internal requirements of law were as consistent with a bad legal system as they were with a good legal system.[13] There are various ways that this "faith" can be understood. One argument could be that a government which is just will be likely to be good on procedural matters as well. It is also worth noting that when proper procedures are followed (*e.g.* the requirement that reasons publicly be given for judicial decisions), some officials might be

---

[11] *ibid.* pp. 200–202.

[12] *ibid.* pp. 202–204. Lloyd Weinreb analyses our concept of justice as having two aspects, which are sometimes in tension: people getting what they deserve, and following the rules laid down: Weinreb, *Natural Law and Justice*, pp. 184–223.

[13] See Fuller, "Positivism and Fidelity to Law", p. 636.

less willing to act in corrupt ways.[14] The contrary claim, that governments which are evil will be likely to ignore the procedural requirements, also has some initial plausibility. There have been regimes so evil that they have not even bothered with any of the legal niceties, with establishing even the pretence of legality, and to some extent Nazi Germany is an example. However, there have also been regimes, generally condemned as evil, which have at least at times been quite meticulous about legal procedures (South Africa before the fall of apartheid or East Germany before the fall of communism may be examples). Since the principles of legality can be understood as guidelines for making the legal system more effective in guiding citizens' behaviour, wicked regimes would have reason to follow them.

Thus, while following the principles of legality is itself a moral good, may indicate a government committed to morally good actions and may hinder base actions, it is probably claiming too much for those principles to say that following them would guarantee a substantively just system. However, one should not conclude, as some critics have, that the evaluation of Fuller's entire approach to law should turn on the empirical question of whether there have ever been (or ever could be) wicked governments which, for whatever reason, followed the rules of procedural justice. (Like the question of whether there can ever be, over the long term, "honour among thieves", the ability to maintain procedural fairness amidst significant iniquities is an interesting topic for speculation, but little more.) The main points of Fuller's position—that a value judgment about the system described is part of the way we use the word "law" and that there is analytical value to seeing law as a particular kind of social guidance, which is to be contrasted with other forms of social guidance, and which can be more or less effective according to how well it meets certain guidelines—are not undermined by pointing out (if true) that some legal systems which are substantively unjust seem to do well on questions of procedural justice.

Those who approach natural law through the Hart–Fuller debate sometimes overemphasise the question of when a rule or a system of social guidance merits the label "law" or "legal". There is a danger with such a focus, in that debates about proper

---

[14] See *ibid.*; Fuller, *The Morality of Law*, pp. 157–159.

labelling (not just whether something is "law" or not, but also whether an object is "art" or not, whether a particular form of government is "democratic' or not, etc.) often lose real moral, sociological or conceptual arguments beneath line-drawing exercises. As mentioned earlier, it is always open to theorists to stipulate the meaning of the terms they use, even for the limited purpose of one discussion only. To say that it is important to determine whether the products of a wicked regime ought to be called "law" or not indicates that there is something further at stake (for example, whether and when citizens have a moral obligation to obey the law), but the burden must be on the advocate to clarify what the further point is. It may often be preferable to bypass questions of labelling and line-drawing, to face directly whatever further substantive issues may be present.

FULLER AND LEGAL PROCESS

Lon Fuller was a significant influence on the "legal process" approach to law, an approach that was important in American legal thought in the 1950s and 1960s. The legal process approach focused on the question of *how* and *by whom* decisions should be made: what is the best procedure for finding the answer to this sort of question, and which institution would be best placed to resolve a problem of this sort?[15]

> "By emphasizing reason as well as fiat in law, by demonstrating the essential irrationality of non-purposive legal interpretation, by reinforcing the interconnection of reason and principle and, most importantly of all, by arguing that adjudication is an institutionally discrete,

---

[15] See Henry M. Hart, Jr., and Albert M. Sacks, *The Legal Process: Basic Problems in the Making and Application of Law* (W. Eskridge & P. Frickey eds., Westbury, N.Y.: Foundation Press, 1994). The influential basic text of the legal process school was completed in 1958, and widely circulated, but never formally published until 1994. For a detailed discussion of the context, development, and subsequent criticisms of "legal process" (both the book and the movement), see William Eskridge, Jr. and Philip Frickey's "Historical and Critical Introduction" to the 1994 edition of the book.

rationalistic, rights-oriented and hence principle-based process of decision-making, Fuller contributed significantly to the construction of a distinctive post-realist 'process jurisprudence'."[16]

The legal process approach combined Fuller's emphasis on the functions of law with detailed attention to the relative institutional competences of various institutions within the law, and how these institutions interact.

Especially at times when there is pervasive doubt of achieving certainty or consensus in resolving basic social questions, it is proper to focus on the question of who should decide and how. There is a sense, however, in which the way that the legal process approach developed led to questions of process and institutional competence being over-emphasised, resulting in an indifference to the justice of results reached and a mistaken and extreme version of judicial restraint.[17]

Legal process was an intermediate movement in recent American jurisprudential thought. It can be seen as a kind of mainstream response to the challenges raised by legal realism (a movement discussed in Chapter 17).[18] In turn, critical legal studies, discussed in Chapter 19, developed in large part in reaction to legal process.[19]

---

[16] Neil Duxbury, *Patterns of American Jurisprudence* (Oxford: Clarendon Press, 1995), p. 232.

[17] *ibid.* pp. 233–241.

[18] See, *e.g.* Morton Horwitz, *The Transformation of American Law 1870–1960* (Oxford: Oxford University Press, 1992), pp. 254–255.

[19] See, *e.g.* Mark Kelman, *A Guide to Critical Legal Studies* (Cambridge, Mass.: Harvard University Press, 1987), pp. 186–212.

Chapter Nine

Ronald Dworkin's Interpretative Approach

Ronald Dworkin (1931–) is probably the most influential English-language legal theorist of his generation. Over the course of 30 years, he has developed a sophisticated alternative to legal positivism. Although his theory has little resemblance to the traditional natural law theories of Aquinas and his followers, Dworkin has occasionally referred to his approach as a natural law theory, and it does fall on the natural law side of the theoretical divide set by the Hart–Fuller debate.

In Dworkin's early writings (collected in *Taking Rights Seriously* (1977)), he challenged a particular version of legal positivism, a view which saw law as being comprised entirely of rules, and judges as having discretion in their decision-making where the dispute before them was not covered by any existing rule. Dworkin offered an alternative vision of law, in which the resources for resolving disputes "according to law" were more numerous and varied, and the process of determining what the law required in a particular case more subtle.

Dworkin argued that, along with rules, legal systems also contain principles. Legal principles are moral propositions that are stated in or implied by past official acts (statutes, judicial decisions and constitutional provisions). In contrast with rules, principles do not act in an all-or-nothing fashion: that is, they can apply to a case without being dispositive. Principles (*e.g.* "one should not be able to profit from one's own wrong" and "one is held to intend all the foreseeable consequences of one's actions") have "weight" favouring one result; there can be—and often are—principles favouring contrary results on a single legal question.

There is still a legal positivist-like separation of law and morality in this view of law, in that judges are told to decide cases based not on whatever principles (critical) morality might require, but rather based on a different and perhaps inconsistent set of principles: those relied upon, or implicit in, past official actions.

Dworkin argued for the existence of legal principles (principles which are part of the legal system, which judges are bound to consider where appropriate) by reference to legal practice (in the United States and England). Particularly telling for Dworkin's argument are those "landmark" judicial decisions where the outcome appears to be contrary to the relevant precedent, but the court still held that it was following the "real meaning" or "true spirit" of the law; and also more mundane cases where judges have cited principles as the justification for modifying, creating exceptions in, or overturning legal rules.

Because there are (numerous) principles as well as rules, there will be few if any occasions where the law "runs out" and judges must decide the case without legal guidance; but at first glance, legal determinacy might seem to be undermined by the abundance of sometimes contrary material. However, Dworkin had a response to that problem. Under his approach, judges consider a variety of theories regarding what the law requires in the area in question, rejecting those which do not adequately "fit" past official actions. Among the theories that adequately "fit", the judge chooses the one which best combines "fit" and moral value, making the law the best it can be. Two tenets of Dworkin's early writings were thus indirectly related: that law contains principles as well as rules; and that, for nearly all legal questions, there are unique right answers.

While there are reasons to conclude that Dworkin had overstated the differences between his view of the law and that of H.L.A. Hart, and also that he made out the line between rules and principles to be clearer than it (sometimes) is in practice,[1] what

---

[1] See, *e.g.* Hart, "Postscript", pp. 259–263; Joseph Raz, "Legal Principles and the Limits of Law" in *Ronald Dworkin and Contemporary Jurisprudence* (M. Cohen ed., London: Duckworth, 1984), pp. 73–87.

remains is the insight that a purely rule-based approach to the nature of law or the nature of judicial reasoning (whether such a view could ever fairly have been attributed to Hart or not) would be problematic. There is always the sense of moral standards qualifying the rules (*e.g.* that a rule should not apply as written if it would lead to an absurd result, or if one of the parties had acted inequitably, etc.) as somehow already having been present in the law, even before the standards are articulated or decisions based upon them are announced.[2]

CONSTRUCTIVE INTERPRETATION

In his later works, Dworkin offered what he called "an interpretive approach" to law.[3] (While Dworkin has said little about the relationship between his earlier writings and his later work, the later work is probably best seen as a reworking of earlier themes within a philosophically more sophisticated framework. However, Jules Coleman has offered the interesting view that there are basic differences between Dworkin's earlier and later writings, grounded on the fact that the political philosophy of the earlier writings was "rights-based liberalism", while the political philosophy of the later writings was "liberal community".[4])

In *Law's Empire*, Dworkin argued that "legal claims are interpretive judgments and therefore combine backward- and forward-looking elements; they interpret contemporary legal practice as an unfolding narrative".[5] According to Dworkin, every time a judge is confronted with a legal problem, he or she should construct a theory of what the law is. That theory must adequately fit the relevant past governmental actions (legislative enactments and judicial decisions),[6] while making the law the best it can be[7]:

---

[2] See Nigel Simmonds, *Central Issues in Jurisprudence* (London: Sweet & Maxwell, 1986), pp. 2–4.

[3] Dworkin, *Law's Empire*, pp. 46–48.

[4] Jules Coleman, "Truth and Objectivity in Law" (1995) 1 *Legal Theory* 33 at 48–54.

[5] Dworkin, *Law's Empire*, p. 225.

[6] *ibid.* pp. 227–228, 245–258.

[7] *ibid.* pp. 52, 143.

"Judges who accept the interpretive ideal of integrity decide hard cases by trying to find, in some coherent set of principles about people's rights and duties, the best constructive interpretation of the political structure and legal doctrine of their community."[8]

According to Dworkin, both law (as a practice) and legal theory are best understood as processes of "constructive interpretation", interpretation that makes its object the best it can be (in Dworkin's words, an interpretation which makes it "the best possible example of the form or genre to which it is taken to belong"[9]). Constructive interpretation is both an imposition of form upon the object being interpreted (in the sense that the form is not immediately apparent in the object) and a derivation of form from it (in the sense that the interpreter is constrained by the object of interpretation, and not free to impose any form the interpreter might choose). One can think of constructive interpretation as being similar to the way people have looked at collections of stars and seen there pictures of mythic figures, or the way modern statistical methods can analyse points on a graph (representing data), and determine what line (representing a mathematical equation, and thus a correlation of some form between variables) best explains that data.

(Dworkin believes that constructive interpretation is also the proper approach to artistic and literary interpretation, and his writings frequently compare the role of a judge with that of a literary critic. Both the applicability of constructive interpretation to artistic interpretation and the treatment of legal interpretation and artistic interpretation as analogous are controversial claims.[10])

Constructive interpretation depends upon being able to assign a distinctive value or purpose to the object of interpretation, whether that object is a work of art or a social practice. It is that value or purpose which serves as the criterion for determining whether one interpretation of the object is better or worse than an

---

[8] *ibid.* p. 255.

[9] *ibid.* p. 52.

[10] For contrary views, see, *e.g.* Andrei Marmor, *Interpretation and Legal Theory* (Oxford: Clarendon Press, 1992) pp. 35–60; Richard Posner, *Law and Literature: A Misunderstood Relation* (Cambridge, Mass.: Harvard University Press, 1988), pp. 209–268.

alternative. For the constructive interpretation of law, Dworkin states that the purpose of law is to constrain or justify the exercise of government power.[11]

The past actions of officials, whether judges deciding cases and giving reasons for their decisions or legislators passing statutes, are the data to be interpreted constructively. In making the law, or an area of the law, the best it can be, the criteria Dworkin mentions most often are, as before, "fit" and moral value. For some legal questions, the answer may seem easy because only one theory shows adequate "fit". However, where the law is unsettled or inconsistent, or where the legal question is novel, there will be alternative theories with adequate "fit". Among these, some will do better on "fit", others better on moral value. In making comparisons among alternative theories, the relative weighting of "fit" and moral value will itself be an interpretative question, and will vary from one legal area to another (*e.g.* protecting expectations may be more important regarding estate or property law, while moral value may be more important for civil liberties questions).[12]

Dworkin also writes of "Integrity": the belief that judges should decide cases in a way which makes the law more coherent, preferring interpretations which make the law more like the product of a single moral vision. The interpretation of the law should, to the extent possible (given the relevant interpretative constraints) "express ... a coherent conception of justice and fairness."[13-14] In some ways, the development of an interpretative theory around the concept of "Integrity" can be seen as a somewhat grander, somewhat more sophisticated version of the spirit underlying common law reasoning: a form of

---

[11] Dworkin, *Law's Empire*, pp. 93, 109, 127.
[12] See *ibid.* pp. 228–258.
[13-14] *ibid.* p. 225.

decision-making based in part on consistency, although a consistency sensitive to principle, and in part on a belief that past decisions were rough approximations of intuitions about justice and fairness.[15]

Dworkin's writings (both earlier and later) can be seen as attempts to come to terms with aspects of legal practice that are not easily explained within the context of legal positivism. For example:

(1)   the fact that participants in the legal system argue over even the most basic aspects of the way the system works (*e.g.* arguments over the correct way to interpret ambiguous statutes, and over how one should apply constitutional provisions to new legal questions), not just over peripheral matters or the application of rules to borderline cases;

(2)   even in the hardest of hard cases, the lawyers and judges in the case speak as if there were a unique correct answer which the judge has a duty to discover; and

(3)   in landmark cases, where the law seems on the surface to have changed radically, both the judges and commentators often speak of the new rule having "already been present" or the law "working itself pure".[16]

A standard response to Dworkin's work (both to his early writings and to the later "interpretive" approach) is that judges and legal theorists should not look at law through "rose-colored glasses", making it "the best it can be"; rather, they should describe law "as it is". The key to understanding Dworkin, in particular his later work, is to understand his response to this kind of comment: that there is no simple description of law "as it is"; or, more accurately, describing law "as it is" necessarily involves an interpretative process, which in turn requires determining what is the best interpretation of past official actions.[17] Law "as it is", law as objective or non-controversial, is only the collection of past official decisions by judges and legislators (which Dworkin refers to as the "pre-interpretive data", that which is subject to the

---

[15] See Simmonds, *Central Issues in Jurisprudence*, p. 89.

[16] *Omychund v. Barker* (1744) 26 E.R. 15 at 23.

[17] The first three chapters of *Law's Empire* contain the arguments underlying this conclusion: see Dworkin, *Law's Empire*, pp. 1–113.

process of constructive interpretation). However, even collectively, these individual decisions and actions cannot offer an answer to a current legal question until some order is imposed upon them, and that order is the choice, the moral and political choice, between tenable interpretations of those past decisions and actions.

If one asks, say, "what is the law regarding economic recovery for nervous distress?", it is quite possible that the lawyer one asks will not be able to offer any authoritative source which goes directly to the specific problem posed (that is, the question may be unsettled in the laws of that jurisdiction). It may be that the lawyer can point to certain statutes that have been passed that are relevant, and to certain decisions that have been made by courts at various levels on related matters, and perhaps even to the writings of commentators suggesting that future decisions on this question come out one way rather than another, but none of these items directly and conclusively answers the question posed. To get that answer, the lawyer must go through a certain kind of reasoning process, deriving an answer from the various materials. For Dworkin, this is an act of "interpretation".

What of the example where there do seem to be authoritative legal sources directly on point? For example, the lawyer might triumphantly announce that the appellate court had rendered a decision on the very issue just a few weeks earlier. Is that the end of the matter; is there then no need for "interpretation"? Even putting aside possible questions of whether the appellate court decision might not be subject to a different interpretation (its language perhaps having been ambiguous), Dworkin might point out that a skilled advocate could still argue, looking at all the relevant past legal decisions, that the appellate court decision was mistaken and should be overturned, or that the decision was too broad and it will probably (by later decisions) be limited to a few situations.

The "interpretive approach" has the advantage of reflecting (and being able to account for) the way that law (or at least certain areas of the law) is regularly subject to change and recharacterisation. This strength may also be the approach's weakness: that it emphasises the possibility of revision too much and the likelihood of settledness too little and that it celebrates the notion of the great individual judge rethinking whole areas of law and thereby deflecting attention from the important roles of consensus and shared understandings.[18]

A related kind of challenge has been offered to Dworkin's approach to law: that it is legal theory for (or from the perspective of) judges, rather than the full theory of law it purports to be.[19] Making the best theory of law one can from the relevant past legal decisions may be the appropriate prescription if one is a judge within a legal system[20]; however, why would one take the same perspective if one were merely a citizen in the society?

For many citizens, the perspective wanted on the law is similar to that of Justice Holmes' "bad man"[21]: people want to know what they have to do avoid legal sanctions (or, to put the matter differently, what they can get away with without facing sanctions). From the perspective of the ordinary citizen, there are a number of reasons to think of law in terms of a prediction of how judges (and police officers) will interpret the rules. Not only is there the desire to avoid legal sanctions, but if law is going to succeed in co-ordinating behaviour, then it is important that different citizens view what the law requires in roughly the same way (for example, if they all have comparable ideas about what traffic laws or anti-pollution laws require). Arguably, this kind of consensus is unlikely to come about—or at least less likely to come about—if citizens were to take up Dworkin's interpretative approach to the law.

RIGHT ANSWERS

For a long time, the idea most closely associated with Dworkin's work in legal theory was the "right answer thesis", the claim that all (or almost all) legal decisions have a unique right answer. It is

---

[18] For a more detailed discussion of some of these themes, see Gerald Postema, " 'Protestant' Interpretation and Social Practices" (1987) 6 *Law and Philosophy* 283; see also Bix, *Law, Language, and Legal Determinacy*, pp. 111–116, 125–129.

[19] See, *e.g.* Raz, *Ethics in the Public Domain*, pp. 186–187; Bix, *Law, Language, and Legal Determinacy*, pp. 118–120.

[20] Though Dworkin recommended that if the legal system within which one is working was sufficiently wicked, the judge should not try to make the legal system "the best it can be"; he or she should just lie about what the law requires: Ronald Dworkin, "A Reply by Ronald Dworkin" in *Ronald Dworkin and Contemporary Jurisprudence* (M. Cohen ed., London: Duckworth, 1984), p. 258.

[21] Holmes, "The Path of the Law", pp. 460–461; see generally William Twining, "The Bad Man Revisited" (1973) 58 *Cornell Law Review* 275.

interesting to note some of the ways that the presentation of this view, and attacks on it, have changed over time.

There are three themes that persist throughout Dworkin's many discussions of his "right answer thesis". The first is that this claim reflects our practice: that even in difficult decision, judges and lawyers discussing, arguing and deciding cases act as if and talk as if there was a right answer to be found. This reference to practice often elicits responses along the lines that judicial "right answer" rhetoric is just a matter of show or a matter of convention, and that judges in more reflective moments endorse a contrary position.[22]

A second theme, which has become more prominent in Dworkin's later writings, is that there are right answers to legal questions for the simple reason that judges must reach an answer to the questions placed before them, and some answers are better than others.[23] Every other argument Dworkin raises, and he raises quite a few, could be considered just a variation on this point.

While a theorist like Joseph Raz is concerned with distinguishing among judicial decisions, differentiating those that are based on legal standards and those that are based on extra-legal standards, and between those which apply prior decisions ("apply existing law") and those that make fresh decisions ("make new law"),[24] Ronald Dworkin finds such distinctions to be beside the point. He sees no reason not be view every standard a judge is required to apply as a "legal" standard.[25] Arguments about which aspects of what judges decide are based on "legal" factors and which on "extra-legal" factors seem to him of little interest. Therefore, from Dworkin's perspective, if that is the basis on which some oppose the "right answer thesis", then that whole aspect of the question can be disregarded.

A third theme is that the best way—and perhaps the only way—to prove or disprove the existence of unique right answers in (all) legal cases is to consider individual, difficult cases, and construct an argument that a particular result is the unique,

---

[22] See, *e.g.* Hart, "Postscript", pp. 273–275. For a response to this kind of argument, see Ronald Dworkin, "Legal Theory and the Problem of Sense" in *Issues in Contemporary Legal Philosophy* (R. Gavison ed., Oxford: Clarendon Press, 1987), pp. 11–13.

[23] See, *e.g.* Dworkin, "A Reply by Ronald Dworkin", pp. 275–278.

[24] See, *e.g.* Raz, *Ethics in the Public Domain*, pp. 187–192.

[25] Dworkin, "A Reply by Ronald Dworkin", pp. 261–262.

correct one (or to argue that, in this case, no one answer is better than the alternatives).[26]

General challenges have been raised to the possibility of right answers under Dworkin's approach based on problems of incommensurability (one cannot meaningfully state that one theory is better than another when one alternative is better on one value, *e.g.* "fit", and the other alternative is better on a different value, *e.g.* "moral worth")[27] and demonstrability (that, given Dworkin's other premises, he cannot conclude both that there are unique right answers to all legal questions and that these right answers will not be demonstrable at least in principle under optimal conditions).[28]

Some of Dworkin's later interpretative discussions treated the issue of "right answers" only in passing or by implication. The most recent work seems to go even further, treating the issue as an irritating distraction:

> "We should now set aside, as a waste of important energy and resource, grand debates about . . . whether there are right or best or true or soundest answers or only useful or powerful or popular ones. We could then take up instead how the decisions that in any case will be made should be made, and which of the answers that will in any case be thought right or best or true or soundest really are."[29]

On the other hand, while the tone of this quotation is dismissive, it continues a theme mentioned earlier: there are at least "best answers" to legal questions, even if for some reason one hesitates before calling them "right answers".

Why might the discussion of the "right answer thesis" be worth the effort? One point is a psychological and sociological one directed at judges and advocates. If they believed that in difficult cases there was likely to be a unique correct answer, however

---

[26] See, *e.g.* Ronald Dworkin, "Pragmatism, Right Answers, and True Banality" in *Pragmatism in Law and Society* (M. Brint and W. Weaver eds., Boulder, Colo.: Westview Press, 1991), p. 365.

[27] The debate between Dworkin and various critics on the issue of incommensurability is summarised in Bix, *Law, Language, and Legal Determinacy*, pp. 96–106.

[28] See Michael Moore, "Metaphysics, Epistemology and Legal Theory" (book review) 60 *Southern California Law Review* 453 at 480–483.

[29] Dworkin, "Pragmatism, Right Answers, and True Banality", p. 360.

difficult it might be to discover, and however much competent lawyers might disagree about which answer was the correct answer, the efforts and arguments would be directed at the legal materials: trying to construct an argument for one answer or another being the right one. However, if it were thought that, because of, for example, the law running out, or incommensurability problems, or the indeterminacy of language, there was usually no single unique right answer for the more difficult legal questions, then the attention of advocates and judges in such cases might turn too quickly (however quickly that might be) to legislative questions of which proposed legal rule would be best.

DWORKIN V. HART

Dworkin's early work gained prominence for its attacks on legal positivism, in particular H. L. A. Hart's version of legal positivism. What little direct response there was from Hart tended to come late in his life, and a good portion of it was only published posthumously.[30]

The "debate" between Dworkin and Hart, like the "debate" between Hart and Fuller, may be best understood as not having been a debate at all, as the term is normally used. The differences between the two theorists are not so much contrary views on particular issues, but both more and less than that: differing ideas about which questions and which concerns in legal theory are most pressing.[31] This is not to say that there are not some overlapping issues about which one could accurately state that the theorists have contrary positions, only that to focus on these direct disagreements would tend to underestimate the extent to which the theorists are actually talking past one another.

In one of his responses to Dworkin, Hart began by contrasting theories about law in general versus theories about a particular legal system (or, as he read Dworkin's theory, theories about how

---

[30] I am thinking in particular of Hart, "Comment", published in 1987; and Hart, "Postscript", published posthumously in 1994. For completeness one should also note Hart, *Essays in Jurisprudence and Philosophy*, pp. 137–141 (reproducing material first published in 1977), which discussed aspects of Dworkin's work, but more by way of reporting than debate.

[31] This is a point Hart himself noted: see Hart, "Comment", pp. 36–40.

judges in a particular legal system should decide cases).[32] This claim brings up (among other things) the question about the possibility of general jurisprudence (an issue considered in Chapter 2) and the proper characterisation of Dworkin's theory.

Elsewhere in the same article, Hart offers a contrast between possible types of legal theory, a contrast based on images. One type of theory is to be used "within" the legal system: for example, in telling a judge how to decide disputes. Another type of theory involves looking at the system "from the outside". Basing the argument on the images, one would say that a theory cannot be simultaneously part of the legal system and a description of the system from the outside.[33] In some ways, this last argument is a strange one for Hart to have put forward, for one of the most significant aspects of Hart's approach to law was that it demanded that we look at the perspectives of citizens and officials within a legal system, the "internal point of view", in constructing a theory of law.

The main question for this exchange between Dworkin and Hart is how much we can rely on the images, on the metaphors, alone in evaluating or creating arguments. It does sound strange to say that a theory is simultaneously part of the system and the best explanation of the system. However, this type of argument, with all its hints of circularity, is actually relatively common in modern philosophy; examples include the hermeneutic circle in literary theory, and John Rawls' use of reflective equilibrium in moral and political theory.

To the extent that there is a true conflict between Dworkin and Hart, it is at those times when Dworkin states or implies that there is no room for a substantive, detailed and interesting descriptive theory of law (that is not interpretative). This struggle can be seen not only in Hart's insistence on the space for and need for a (non-interpretative) descriptive theory of law in general, but also in his disagreement with any attempt to recast legal positivism as being about justifying present or future coercion,[34] and his claim that even if the "sense" of legal propositions in most or all legal systems is interpretative or evaluative, it does not follow that a descriptive

---

[32] *ibid.* pp. 36–38.
[33] *ibid.* p. 40.
[34] Hart, "Postscript", pp. 241–242.

theory of such matters need also be interpretative or evaluative.[35]

DEBUNKING QUESTIONS

Commentators will sometimes query "the real reason" for or "the real motivation" behind some line of analysis. This type of challenge has its roots in American legal realism[36] and its most enthusiastic recent proponents are in the critical legal studies movement (topics to be discussed in Chapters 17 and 19); the topic is also raised here because such claims are rarely considered from the perspective of the theorist being "debunked", a perspective from which the claims may lose some of their force.

Critics sometimes claim that the terms used by practitioners or theorists are labels without content, which only serve to mislead. If we look at the actual practice, the argument goes, we would find only an attempt to rationalise particular results. Additionally (as conclusion if not as premise), these arguments usually hold that it is all but nonsensical to say that one theory is better than another at explaining law. All that is going on in descriptive legal theory, this approach states, is an attempt to legitimise particular judicial decisions or methods.

Such analyses can be provocative, although there are times when one is concerned with how easily they seem to be produced. There are many such arguments about: for example, the early American theorists, like Christopher Columbus Langdell, who tried to portray legal reasoning and the judicial process as scientific, were said to be trying to defend unpopular conservative judicial decisions as "objective", as required by deductive reasoning that the judges could not legitimately sidestep. The American legal realists who debunked this formalistic approach could themselves be debunked: their positive programme legitimised legal reform and justified the use of policy arguments in the courts.[37] Similarly, H. L. A. Hart, with his arguments based on the "open texture" of language, could be seen as justifying limited judicial legislation in

---

[35] *ibid.* p. 244.
[36] See, *e.g.* Felix Cohen, "Transcendental Nonsense and the Functional Response" (1935) 35 *Columbia Law Review* 809.
[37] See Horwitz, *The Transformation of American Law 1870–1960*, pp. 185–212.

difficult cases. In the same line of analysis, Ronald Dworkin's approach, in terms first of the "right answer thesis" and later with the "interpretive approach", could be seen as offering a way of legitimising the apparently political nature of the Warren Court's jurisprudence in the United States, at a time when the decisions of that court were attacked as "anti-democratic".[38]

The critics seem to be arguing that theories of interpretation merely decorate and legitimise the choices made by judges, while hiding the real reasons (motivations) for the decisions, and that few decisions are actually determined (or precluded) by the theoretical prescriptions (*e.g.* "neutral principles",[39] "the grand style of judging"[40] or "the judicial virtues"[41]) judges are told to follow.

Dworkin has responded to attempted "debunkings" of this type by claiming that they are irrelevant to his project. Why does it matter, he asks, that there might be historical, psychological or sociological explanations for why a particular theory was put forward or why it was well received?[42] Even if it can be proven that theory serves the interests of a certain class or group at the expense of others, or that the theory expresses the *Zeitgeist* of its era of origin, why should this matter? In the end, the question is whether the theory is right, or whether it is at least better than alternative theories. Historical, psychological and sociological explanations are marginal to investigations into a theory's correctness.

Debunking explanations may not be completely irrelevant, in that we can rightly be suspicious of philosophical positions —whether these be ethical theories, social theories or legal theories—that match the theorist's self-interest or that theorist's particular prejudices regarding how the world should be. However, suspicion is not proof, and as long as argument about the merits of a theory can be conducted on neutral grounds (according to criteria accepted by the participants in the field regarding what

---

[38] See Peter Gabel, Book Review (1977) 91 *Harvard Law Review* 302.

[39] Herbert Wechsler, "Toward Neutral Principles in Constitutional Law" (1959) 73 *Harvard Law Review* 15.

[40] Karl Llewellyn, *The Common Law Tradition: Deciding Appeals* (Little Brown & Co., 1960).

[41] Hart, *The Concept of Law,* p. 200.

[42] See, *e.g.* Dworkin, *Law's Empire,* pp. 271–274 (discussing critical legal studies).

makes for stronger and weaker arguments and for better and worse theories[43]), then the "debunking" arguments can work only to justify beginning a debate about the theory in question; the eventual judgment about its merits will be based on other grounds.

---

[43] The sceptic might argue that there are no "neutral grounds": all criteria already express the interests or the preconceptions of certain groups. I do not have time to consider this argument now, but the matter is related to topics discussed in Chaps. 17 and 19.

PART C

Implications and Applications

There are issues in legal philosophy that are not comfortably constrained within the discussion of particular legal theorists or jurisprudential movements, and which seem to have repercussions simultaneously at different levels of concern. That is, issues like the obligation to obey the law and the problem of legal mistake can be understood and considered both at a level of practical concern about what should be done in certain circumstances and as inextricably part of the larger puzzle about how to think about law. There are also themes, like "will versus reason", that seem to recur, in various guises, in a variety of different jurisprudential debates. The following chapters explore some of these issues and themes.

Chapter Ten

Rights and Rights Talk

The discussions on rights exemplify a basic problem in conceptual analysis: the way abstract arguments can become entangled in particular policy views.

One major difficulty in articles about rights is that two different types of questions often go under the same label. First, conceptual questions about the nature of rights: like other conceptual questions, discussions about the (conceptual) nature of rights generally attempt either to offer an arbitrary definition or delimitation for the purpose of clarity or to discover some element distinctive to the social phenomenon expressed in the way we use the term.[1] (One conceptual claim sometimes made is that one can only have rights to something beneficial.[2] This derives from, or at least is supported by, our linguistic intuitions: that it makes sense to say "I have a right that you pay me five dollars", but not to say "I have a right that the state imprison me for five years as punishment for what I have done".)

In contrast to conceptual questions there are policy questions: to what extent *should* this legal system—or all legal systems —protect a certain category of people, activities, places or things? It is easy when reading articles about rights to confuse the conceptual issues and arguments with the issues and arguments about policy matters.

---

[1] See Chap. 4.
[2] See generally Hart, "Legal Rights", pp. 174–188 (discussing Bentham's "Benefit Theory of Rights"); MacCormick, "Rights in Legislation", pp. 202–205.

A common confusion of this type occurs in discussions about abortion, as when someone responds to an argument in favour of legalising abortion by saying "foetuses have rights". This confuses two levels of discussion, two different types of questions. It is compatible to say both "I do not think it makes sense to speak of foetuses as having rights" and "I believe that abortion is wrong and immoral because it involves severely harming foetuses, harm which should not be condoned except in the most extreme circumstances". Similarly, it is compatible to believe both that foetuses are capable of having rights and that abortion should be allowed in most circumstances (because foetuses in fact do not have rights relevant to this situation, or whatever rights they have are overridden by the conflicting rights of the mother).

To put the matter another way, from the statement "Y is capable of having rights", it does not follow that Y has any rights, or at least it does not follow that Y's rights will trump the conflicting legal interests in the matter under consideration.

The confusion in this area is encouraged by the use of rights rhetoric in political discourse (more prevalent in the United States than in most other countries). When people want to say that making sure that no one goes homeless is a worthy and important government objective, they often use the shorthand "human beings have a right to shelter", and when people want to express their belief that abortion should be prohibited, they sometimes choose the shorthand "unborn babies have rights too!"

Because talk of rights—legal rights, natural rights or human rights—is so entwined in political struggles, it is not surprising that many discussions of rights are muddled. Wesley Hohfeld (1879–1918) wrote a pair of famous articles in which he tried to make "rights talk" clearer.[3] First, he argued that the use of the word "right" in legal discourse was often loose, covering four different kinds of legal concepts:

(1) "rights", narrowly understood as claims correlative to other persons' duties;

---

[3] Wesley Hohfeld, "Some Fundamental Legal Conceptions as Applied in Judicial Reasoning" (1913) 23 *Yale Law Journal* 16; Hohfeld, "Fundamental Legal Conceptions as Applied in Judicial Reasoning" (1917) 26 *Yale Law Journal* 710.

(2)   "liberties",[4] meaning at the least that one has no legal duty
       to refrain from the activity in question (the law may
       expressly protect one's ability to partake in the activity in
       question);
(3)   "powers", the ability to change legal relationships (*e.g.*
       through contracts and wills); and
(4)   "immunities", which correlate with disabilities of another
       (as constitutional rights correlate with disabilities of the
       government to act in certain ways).[5]

Secondly, Hohfeld argued that all rights statements ("rights"
here understood either narrowly, in their first sense, as claims
correlative to another party's duty, or broadly, as involving any of
the four legal concepts named) should be reducible to a three-
variable proposition: A has a right against B for X (where A and B
are people or institutions, and X is an object or activity). For
example, "Sarah has a right against John for five dollars" or "I
have a right that Congress not interfere with my publishing this
book".[6]

Among the problems that this kind of analysis avoids is when
someone says "we have a right to education" or "we have a right
to a job", but the speaker is unwilling to say (or thinks it
unnecessary to say) whom this right is against. If one claims to have
a right to a job, is it then the government's obligation to provide
a job, or perhaps the obligation of the largest employer in town, or
perhaps the obligation of anyone with the means to offer employ-
ment? If the claimant is not willing to specify in such cases whom
the right is against, one can suspect that the reference to rights is
merely a form of rhetoric: "we have a right to a job" then becomes
nothing more than a way of saying "we want a job very much" or
"it would be a very good thing were someone to offer us a job".

---

[4] In his article, Hohfeld uses the word "privilege" for this concept, but in the
current legal literature, the concept is usually labelled as "liberty"; "privilege"
has a different set of connotations.
[5] Hohfeld, "Some Fundamental Legal Conceptions as Applied in Judicial Reasoning", pp. 28–58; see also Hohfeld, "Fundamental Legal Conceptions as Applied
in Judicial Reasoning", p. 717; J. W. Harris, *Legal Philosophies* (London: Butterworths, 1980), pp. 76–86.
[6] Hohfeld, "Fundamental Legal Conceptions as Applied in Judicial Reasoning",
pp. 742–766.

There are a number of difficulties and complications regarding a Hohfeldian approach to legal rights that I do not have time to consider here. One question is the extent to which any analysis of legal rights can or should be the basis of a general theory of rights (which would include moral as well as legal rights).[7] A second question is whether there remains a place and a need for a two-variable rights claim ("A has a right to X"), because there are exceptional cases of rights without correlative duties, or because rights may be generative of duties in a case-by-case manner (a judge deciding in a particular case that because the plaintiff has a certain right, a particular duties should be newly imposed on particular defendants).[8]

---

[7] See Joseph Raz, "Legal Rights" (1984) 4 *Oxford Journal of Legal Studies* 1, reprinted in *Ethics in the Public Domain*, pp. 238–260.

[8] See, *e.g.* MacCormick, "Rights in Legislation", pp. 199–202; Harris, *Legal Philosophies*, pp. 81–86.

Chapter Eleven

Boundary Lines in Law

In the jurisprudential literature, from time to time, in quite different contexts, one comes across debates about boundary lines within law.

One such argument surrounds whether the collections of rules and related institutions in a society should warrant the label "law" if the society (and its legal system) was evil. A similar argument is sometimes raised regarding an unjust rule within a particular legal system. This set of issues has been referred to briefly in the discussions earlier about conceptual theories in jurisprudence (Chapter 4), legal positivism and (Chapter 5) natural law theory (both in Chapter 7). One gets a sense in those discussions that the question of whether a particular rule or a particular rule system is given the title "law" or "legal" is not of great intrinsic importance. After all, it is only a name, albeit one that can carry a significant moral or psychological reverberations. It is more that the label theorists give or withhold in these situations reflects (*i.e.* is a symptom of) their general approach to law (*e.g.* natural law theorists using law as an intermediate step in questions about how to act, as contrasted with legal positivists' quasi-scientific approach to law as a social phenomenon to be studied dispassionately).

A very different kind of argument appears to be going on when theorists wonder about which standards that judges are obliged to apply, or which judges in fact do apply or have applied, should carry the label "law" or "legal".[1] Such debates often arise in the

---

[1] The debate between Joseph Raz and Ronald Dworkin on this point appears in Raz, "Legal Principles and the Limits of Law", pp. 73–87; Dworkin, "A Reply by Ronald Dworkin", pp. 260–263; and Raz, *Ethics in the Public Domain*, pp. 179–193.

context of a larger line-drawing question, raised by larger-scale jurisprudential theories. When a theorist claims that a common law judge should always only declare the law that is already present rather than legislate new law, that there is no necessary connection between legal validity and moral value, or that one can always determine the content of a law without recourse to moral evaluation, much can turn on how (and where) one distinguishes law from non-law, legal standards from non-legal standards, and so on.

As was discussed in the chapter on conceptual theory (Chapter 4), drawing boundaries can be a game where all the rules and underlying purposes are hidden or at best vaguely stated. When a theory turns on the relation between two fluid, contested concepts (for example, whether the content of "legal rules" can always be determined without reference to "moral evaluation"), there will always be doubts regarding whether neutral criteria can be found to arbitrate the result, or whether every theory can simply define the terms in the way which supports its own claims.

Sometimes boundary lines are placed in the service of significant political decisions. This may be best exemplified in discussions about the continuity of legal systems—when does one legal system end and another one begin? This apparently abstract discussion has been used as the basis for determining under what circumstances legal rules and legal institutions from a former regime were still valid after that regime had been overthrown.[2] These are difficult political and moral decisions, and the judges may be excused if they search for an abstract and apparently neutral basis for their decisions. (One might even argue that this kind of search is often central to the legal process.) However, the judge's strong reliance on abstract analytical concepts and categories to decide these questions is inappropriate—and the simplest of reasons for that conclusion is that the abstract analytical concepts in question were not created with these moral or political

---

[2] See, *e.g. Madzimbamuto v. Lardner-Burke N.O.* 1968 (2) S.A. 284; *Uganda v. Commissioner of Prisons, ex p. Matovu* [1966] E.A. 514; see generally John Finnis, "Revolutions and Continuity of Law" in *Oxford Essays in Jurisprudence, Second Series* (A. W. B. Simpson ed., Oxford: Oxford University Press, 1973), pp. 44–76; J. M. Eekelaar, "Principles of Revolutionary Legality" in *ibid.* pp. 22–43.

problems in mind.[3] One should be hesitant to base decisions that may cost individuals their freedom or property on a theorist's toying with boundary lines.

On one hand, one is sceptical when purely analytical discussions are appropriated as the grounds for resolving political and moral issues for which the original discussions are not well suited. It almost seems unfair to the original theorists; perhaps they should have been put on notice that their writings might be used as the justifications for actions on particular moral problems, and the theorists could have reconsidered their positions with that information in mind. As it is, some theorists can come off seeming like defenders of tyranny and injustice when that was neither their intentions nor their nature.[4]

On the other hand, one also has doubts about conceptual debates that seem to have no ties either to actual moral and legal problems or to some larger theory. The example that comes to mind is the question of how one "individuates" laws.[5]

For a brief time, a surprisingly active debate was held within the jurisprudential literature regarding the appropriate way to individuate laws. This is a topic that was raised by Jeremy Bentham,[6] and more recently considered by theorists as eminent as Joseph Raz and A. M. Honoré. The basic motivation behind the topic derives from the fact that legal rules seem to derive from a variety of sources, and a particular single source is rarely sufficient to state any given rule. For example, for a criminal law, an offence may be defined in a statute, the sanction may be stated in a separate statute, and certain defenses or excuses may originate in a number of common law decisions (or be codified in a third statute).

---

[3] Another reason for caution is how poorly equipped the judges often are to understand the concepts they are borrowing. Some of the "post-revolution" decisions turn on a badly misunderstood version of Hans Kelsen's remarks on "Change in the Basic Norm". For example, compare *Madzimbamuto*, pp. 314–321, with Hans Kelsen, *General Theory of Law and State* (New York: Russell & Russell, 1945), pp. 117–118, 220–221.

[4] One thinks of the long-standing argument about whether legal positivist theories helped to encourage the growth, or at least the acceptance, of National Socialism in 1930s Germany. See, *e.g.* Paulson, "Lon L. Fuller, Gustav Radbruch, and the 'Positivist' Theses".

[5] See Raz, *The Concept of a Legal System*, pp. 70–92; A. M. Honoré, *Making Law Bind* (Oxford: Clarendon Press, 1987), pp. 69–88.

[6] See Raz, *The Concept of a Legal System*, pp. 71–72 (quoting Bentham).

One can see the philosophical temptation in asking, when we speak about "*a* legal rule", how do we determine what that singular rule is? How does the legal system divide up into individual rules? That noted, it seems a task without further explanatory power or practical interest. (Which is not to say that there might not be some who find pleasure or fulfilment in the pursuit of such questions.)

Finally, on the topic of boundary lines, one might also consider how much often turns on boundary lines within a legal system (however narrowly "law" is defined). Law is divided into its categories (contract, tort, criminal, etc.), and each of the categories has its own internal divisions. The various areas of law come with their own sets of rules, common analytical moves, acceptable argument forms, values and preferences. While in modern life (and it was probably always so) cases can seem to straddle the borderlines between doctrinal areas, their treatment and resolution can vary sharply depending on to which area they are, in the end, "assigned". The most common, and perhaps best-known, examples, are the fact situations that fall on the borderline between contract and tort.[7] To fall on one side or the other may have significant repercussions for determining the scope of the parties' obligations and the level of damages allowed. A narrower example comes from American law on prenuptial agreements: in jurisdictions where such agreements are treated as a sub-category of contract law, the agreement is usually treated deferentially, with a strong presumption of enforcing the agreement as written; however, in jurisdictions where such agreements are treated as a sub-category of family law, courts seems more comfortable being intrusive, refusing enforcement unless there has been procedural fairness in the creation of the agreement and substantive fairness in its terms.[8]

On one hand, one cannot blame a legal system for taking advantage of decades (and often centuries) of accumulated decisions and legal wisdom, rather than considering each case afresh.

---

[7] *e.g.* there are the English cases of negligent misrepresentation where the parties are in a relationship that is similar to, but not identical with, a contractual relationship: see, *e.g. Hedley Byrne & Co. v. Heller & Partners* [1964] A.C. 465.

[8] See, *e.g. Simeone v. Simeone*, 581 A.2d 162 (Penn. 1990) (changing the Pennsylvania courts' approach to prenuptial agreements from a family law style to a contract style).

On the other hand, there is something suspect about the near-essentialist form of analysis, which begins "this novel fact situation falls under contract (tort, family law, freedom of expression, etc.), therefore the following 17 values, requirements and presumptions should apply". The first step is just too sharp a drop-off from considering the moral merits of the situation on a more individualised basis.

Chapter Twelve

Will and Reason

A theme that runs through discussions within law and about law is the contrast of will as against reason. "Will" represents answers which are the product of choice and decision, whether made by individuals, groups, or institutions. "Reason" represents answers which are the product of analysis: answers given because they are "right" rather than because they have been chosen by someone empowered to decide.

The English and American legal systems in practice show many elements of both will and reason. Statutory law and administrative law are primarily "will", the application of choices made by officials in authority. Contract law and estate law are also largely a matter of "will", enforcing the choices made by private parties. On the other side, common law reasoning is to a significant extent a matter of "reason", the elaboration and application of basic principles on a case-by-case basis. Some older cases even justify the conclusion as to the dispute or as to the correct legal principle as an elaboration of what "Reason" (with a capital "R") requires.

These general statements are hedged, and for good reason. For example, statutory interpretation in the courts often involves analysis that looks far more like analysis from general principles than it does like a search for the legislators' choices and intentions. Similarly, modern contract law often involves the legal (judicial) imposition of terms regardless of the parties' intentions, and the application of rules of interpretation that do not always defer to what the parties meant. On the other side, common law decisions sometimes have elements of "will", in that later decisions some-times are said to turn on what an earlier court intended by a particular decision. Also, it was once argued for common law reasoning, as against the codification of legal rules in statutory form, that common law decisions reflect "the popular will", as reflected through custom.[1]

American constitutional law seems to be a continual battle-ground between "will" and "reason", in the ongoing debate regarding whether the general terms and broad prescriptions of the United States Constitution are to be interpreted according to the intentions of those who wrote and ratified the provisions or according to our present-day best understanding of the values and principles mentioned.[2]

Finally, one can see "reason" and "will" as representing the opposite aspects of law that any good legal theory must incorporate, although most theories tend to emphasise one while ignoring or minimising the other. Lon Fuller referred to the poles as "reason" and "fiat"; Morris Cohen referred to them as (on the one hand) the ideal to which all law aspires and (on the other hand) the hard facts that may only partly embody (or seem to defy) the ideal.[3]

LEGAL POSITIVISM AND NATURAL LAW THEORY

As one can divide aspects of law (or even individual legal decisions) according to whether they are matters (primarily) of "will" or of "reason", so can one divide legal theories.[4] Legal positivist theories work best with the "will" aspects of law. The phrase "positive law" is itself a reference to the setting down—by human rule-makers—of legal standards (as contrasted with the discovery of "natural" or "divine" legal standards through the operation of reason).

---

[1] See Horwitz, *The Transformation of American Law 1870–1960*, pp. 117–121.

[2] See, *e.g.* Paul Brest, "The Misconceived Quest for the Original Understanding" (1980) 60 *Boston University Law Review* 204; Richard Kay, "Adherence to the Original Intentions in Constitutional Adjudication: Three Objections and Responses" (1988) 82 *Northwestern University Law Review* 226.

[3] Winston, "The Ideal Element in a Definition of Law", p. 103, citing Morris Cohen, *Law and the Social Order* (New York: Archon Books, 1967), pp. 278 *et seq.*

[4] Roger Shiner's book, *Norm and Nature* (Oxford: Clarendon Press, 1992), is constructed along a similar axis: instead of will and reason, Shiner uses system ("norm") and value ("nature").

By way of example, H.L.A. Hart's "rule of recognition" analysis becomes far more complicated (and less persuasive) when one tries to apply it to law that arises from custom and common law reasoning (the aspects of modern legal systems that most clearly enter the "reason" category).[5] Legal positivism's analysis (whether one chooses the version of Austin, Hart or Kelsen), works best when one can point to an official who creates the legal standard.

There are occasions, especially with customary law and (less often) with common law decisions, when an official purports only to "declare" law which already existed, whose existence was not due exclusively to a prior official's act of law creation. Some theorists treat these kinds of declarations as "legal fictions" or rhetorical devices, stating that the officials in these situations are in fact only making new law. However, to the extent that one wants to take the officials' actions at face value, legal positivist analyses will be awkward (at best) in explaining what occurred, and an analysis based on "reason" will work better than one based on "will".

Natural law theory, by contrast, is best justified by, and most easily applied to, the "reason" aspects of law.[6] As discussed in an earlier chapter, traditional natural law theory (Aquinas' theory and similar) is about the (direct and indirect) derivation of standards from first principles, and using those standards to guide officials and criticise official actions and promulgations that fall short.

However, even within this tradition, there were significant debates (although the significance may be less clear to us than it was to the participants) about whether law was best understood in terms of "reason" or "will": in particular, whether natural law was a product of divine will or divine reason. The debate, which may seem quite dry and "theological", had implications for how one

---

[5] See Hart, *The Concept of Law*, pp. 44–47, 97; Finnis, *Natural Law and Natural Rights*, pp. 238–245.

[6] Though there are will/reason tensions even within natural law theory. In particular, religion-grounded natural law theories, which see natural law and justice as emanations of God's goodness, but discoverable by the exercise of human reasoning or conscience, sometimes face the quandary of whether divine revelation is thus made superfluous (and whether God could change natural law or order something that was contrary to it): see, *e.g.* J. M. Kelly, *A Short History of Western Legal Theory* (Oxford: Clarendon Press, 1992), pp. 102–104; Weinreb, *Natural Law and Justice*, pp. 64–66.

viewed the universe and faith: the view on one side was that the universe was orderly, and thus accessible to human reason, and reason was compatible with faith (as Aquinas attempted to demonstrate), while the opposing view tended towards contrary views about the accessibility of the universe to reason and the compatibility of faith and reason.[7] Echoes of these debates can be seen in the slightly less abstract debates in later centuries about the nature and legitimacy of the modern nation-state. Are the actions and enactments of officials to be followed because they represent the (express or delegated) will of the sovereign, or are these actions and enactments legitimate only to the extent that they are consistent with the natural rights of the people and the natural powers (and limits to power) of government?[8]

"Modern" natural law theory (*e.g.* the theories of Lon Fuller and Ronald Dworkin), involve the "reason" side of the "reason"/ "will" dichotomy in a different way: for these theories hold that the law is not simply what legal officials have ordered, posited or enacted; rather, the application of (moral) reasoning is required to determine what the law requires.

SOCIAL CONTRACTS AND ECONOMIC ANALYSIS

John Rawls' well-known method for deriving or justifying theories of justice, "the original position", can be helpfully analysed through the "will"/"reason" rubric.

For Rawls, principles of justice are whatever principles would be agreed upon in a thought experiment, by hypothetical persons who are ignorant of their strengths and weaknesses and their circumstances within society.[9] First, one can note that the plurality of decision-makers is superfluous: there is no reason to believe that any of the decision-makers ignorant of their nature and circumstances would decide differently from the others; they are but clones of one another.

---

[7] See Weinreb, *Natural Law and Justice*, pp. 64–66; Francis Oakley, "Medieval Theories of Natural Law: William of Ockham and the Significance of the Voluntarist Tradition" (1961) 6 *Natural Law Forum* 65.

[8] See, *e.g.* Weinreb, *Natural Law and Justice*, pp. 67–90; Kelly, *A Short History of Western Legal Theory*, pp. 222–229, 258–271.

[9] Rawls, *A Theory of Justice*, pp. 11–22, 136–142; John Rawls, *Political Liberalism* (New York: Columbia University Press, 1993), pp. 22–28, 307–310.

More importantly, what Rawls has constructed is an analysis from reason, dressed up as an analysis from will. There are no actual persons choosing; only a thought experiment about what a strange variant on a real person might choose. However, the grounds for respecting answers given by choice are quite different from the grounds for respecting answers given by reason.[10]

To some extent, the same claim can be made about many of the social contract approaches in political theory (as can be found, in quite different variations, in Hobbes, Locke and Rousseau).[11] Such approaches portray a government's legitimacy as deriving from an agreement between citizens to establish that authority. The description of that agreement tends to be somewhat vague, and to the extent that it is claimed that there was some such agreement in the distant past, such claims are almost certainly false (in any event, it would be difficult to demonstrate why those now living should be bound by the terms of the ancient agreement[12]). The social contracts referred to in these theories are best understood as ways of discussing what powers reasonable persons *would* agree to delegate to a governing authority, and under what conditions. However, for our purposes, there is a great difference between the terms to which "reasonable" persons "would" agree and terms to which actual persons *have* agreed. The first is an argument of reason, the second an argument of will, and each brings a moral force or legitimacy of a different kind.

A similar disguising of "reason" arguments as "will" arguments can be found in the law and economics movement. In early articles, Richard Posner sought to create a moral justification for his economic ("wealth maximisation") approach to law (a topic that will be discussed in detail in Chapter 18). He argued that choosing more efficient (or more wealth-maximising) institutions, standards and procedures over those that are less efficient is

---

[10] See, *e.g.* Dworkin, *Taking Rights Seriously*, pp. 150–154 (discussing Rawls' "original position").

[11] This is not true for all writers on the social contract, *e.g.* Immanuel Kant expressly stated that talk of an original contract is not historical, but is merely "an idea of reason": see Weinrib, *The Idea of Private Law*, pp. 85–86 (summarising and quoting from Kant).

[12] Such arguments when made are usually in terms of our actions showing our "tacit consent" to the terms of the old agreement. There are many problems with arguments from "tacit consent" as are outlined below in Chap. 16 ("The Obligation to Obey the Law").

consistent with traditional notions of autonomy and consent. He conceded that people frequently did not consent expressly to the more efficient institutions, but that often there was no practical method of eliciting such express consent. In such situations, Posner asserted, it was sufficient, and consistent with "the principle of consent", that we ask the hypothetical question of whether the parties *would have* agreed to those institutions.[13]

The simple reply is that hypothetical consent is different in kind from actual consent. There are times when the two nearly converge, when an individual considers how he or she might have responded to a hypothetical situation in the recent past, or when someone tries to consider how a close friend would have decided some question.[14] However, once we are speaking about judges or commentators discussing how a group of unknown people would choose, any semblance of an exercise of personal, individual will is absent.

Posner offered an interesting response. He wrote:

> "If there is no reliable mechanism for eliciting express consent, it follows, not that we must abandon the principle of consent, but rather that we should be satisfied with implied (or more precisely, perhaps, hypothetical) consent where it exists."[15]

There are two subtle problems with the response. First, while there may be a place to speak of implied or hypothetical consent, there is always the danger that there is a kind of misleading or misrepresentation going on: masking an argument that is largely one of reason to make it appear to be one of will, for readers who

---

[13] Richard Posner, "The Ethical and Political Basis of the Efficiency Norm in Common Law Adjudication" (1980) 8 *Hofstra Law Review* 487 at 494. For criticisms of Posner's consent analysis, see, *e.g.* Jules Coleman, "The Normative Basis of Economic Analysis: A Critical Review of Richard Posner's *The Economics of Justice*" (1982) 34 *Stanford Law Review* 1105 at 1117–1131; Ronald Dworkin, *A Matter of Principle* (Cambridge, Mass.: Harvard University Press, 1985), pp. 275–280.

[14] The latter situation is raised in American law in medical decision-making, where the patient is temporarily or permanently incompetent to decide for herself. A close friend or relative may be asked to consider, taking into account everything known about the patient's values and attitudes, how that patient would have decided had she been competent: see, *e.g. Cruzan v. Director, Missouri Health Dept.*, 497 U.S. 261 at 289–292 (1990) (O'Connor J. concurring).

[15] Richard Posner, *The Economics of Justice* (Cambridge, Mass.: Harvard University Press, 1983), p. 96.

find will-based arguments more persuasive. Secondly, it is not clear why, when "consent" in its fullest form is not available, we *must* offer analysis or seek argument in terms of some hybrid or diluted variation of "consent". Sometimes consent-based (will-based) arguments will simply be out of place, and recourse must be had to arguments of an entirely different kind (most likely reason-based).

Chapter Thirteen

Authority, Finality and Mistake

The American judge and legal commentator Oliver Wendell Holmes (1841–1935) once wrote, "The prophecies of what the courts will do in fact, and nothing more pretentious, are what I mean by law."[1] This comment trades on an ongoing tension in law (and, indeed, in all rule-based decision-making): should one focus on the rules which are purported to be the basis of decisions, or on the decisions themselves?

In the English case *Davis v. Johnson*,[2] the primary issue was the proper interpretation of a statute protecting women from domestic violence, but there was a secondary issue regarding under what circumstances the English Court of Appeal had the authority to refuse to follow its previous decisions. In the Court of Appeal, Sir George Baker suggested that a new category be added to the limited list of exceptional circumstances in which the Court of Appeal was allowed to overrule its previous decisions[3]: where there is "a conflict between a statutory provision and a decision which has completely misinterpreted the recent statute and failed to understand its purpose".[4] He summarised his argument by saying: "The statute is the law—the final authority."[5]

---

[1] Holmes, "The Path of the Law", p. 461. This quotation is also discussed in Chap. 17, ("American Legal Realism").

[2] [1979] A.C. 264.

[3] Among the accepted circumstances for the Court of Appeal to overrule its own prior decisions are when it must choose between prior conflicting decisions, its earlier decisions was expressly or implicitly overruled by the House of Lords, or the prior decision was made *per incuriam*: *Young v. Bristol Aeroplane Co. Ltd.* [1944] K.B. 718.

[4] *Davis v. Johnson*, p. 290.

[5] *ibid.*

On appeal, the House of Lords upheld the Court of Appeal's interpretation of the statute, but rejected that court's attempts to expand its authority to overrule its previous decisions. For present purposes, though, the most interesting comment in the Lords was given as an aside to the main debate. Lord Diplock was stating that his reading of the statute was contrary to that of his four colleagues, but, he added: "This cannot affect the disposition of the instant appeal nor will it affect the application of the Act in subsequent cases; for the section means what a majority of this House declares it means."[6] The comments of Sir George Baker and Lord Diplock represent two contrary views about the nature of law, legal validity and mistake, two views which are always in tension in the way we talk about law.

The first view emphasises fidelity to the authoritative sources of law, treating the decisions of judges (and the actions of police) as attempts to interpret those sources, attempts that can go wrong, and it in turn assumes a hierarchy of sources, where texts, primarily statutes and written constitutions always have priority over statements and actions which purport to be interpretations or applications of those texts.

In a like spirit, Ronald Dworkin wrote (in the context of a discussion of civil disobedience): "A citizen's allegiance is to the law, not to any particular person's view of what the law is",[7] where it is clear from the context that "any particular person's view of the law" included decisions handed down by judges, even sometimes decisions by the highest court in the land.

The second view notes that the decisions of judges (and other officials) are often themselves sources of law, and, in effect if not in theory, can override the actions and choices of other officials (including the legislators who enacted the law being enforced). An American legal theorist, John Chipman Gray, writing early in this century, stated: "The Law of the State or of any organised body of men is composed of the rules which the courts, that is, the judicial organs of that body, lay down for the determination of rights and duties." He continued: "The difference in this matter between contending schools of Jurisprudence arises largely from not

---

[6] *ibid.* p. 323.
[7] Dworkin, *Taking Rights Seriously*, p. 214.

distinguishing between the Law and the Sources of the Law."[8] The above quotation, along with Justice Holmes' earlier quotation, "The prophecies of what the courts will do in fact, and nothing more pretentious, are what I mean by law", have the attractions of both iconoclasm and worldliness, but they have well-known weaknesses as well.

This worldly approach will never suffice, if one believes that judges sometimes act in good faith: that is, if one believes that not all judges merely disguise their own political biases in legal language and that at least some judges perceive their actions as trying to decide "according to law", at least occasionally deciding a case one way even though they personally would rather it come out another.[9] This is not to say that Holmes or Gray thought that judges were always deciding cases according to their personal preferences. However, to explain the actions of judges acting in good faith, we must be able to understand talk of what the law requires which is at least partly independent of how the law is interpreted by judges.

We also need this (partial) conceptual independence to make sense of the idea of legal mistake. If an enactment means whatever a majority of the House of Lords (or the Supreme Court) says it means, how could we make sense of a later court decision overruling the earlier interpretation as mistaken?[10]

In *The Concept of Law*, in the course of a discussion about "formalism and rule-scepticism", Hart mentioned an imagined game called "scorer's discretion", under which "there was no rule for scoring save what the scorer in his discretion chose to apply".[11]

---

[8] John Chipman Gray, *The Nature and Sources of the Law* (New York: Columbia University Press, 1909), p. 82.

[9] That judges, although attempting to decide "according to law", may be strongly affected by unconscious biases, raises a quite different, if still significant, set of problems.

[10] Examples of a country's highest court overruling its own prior decisions include *Board of Education v. Barnette*, 319 U.S. 624 (1943); *Garcia v. San Antonio Metropolitan Transit Authority*, 469 U.S. 528 (1985); *R. v. Shivpuri* [1987] A.C. 1; *Murphy v. Brentwood District Council* [1990] 3 W.L.R. 414. (The first two cases listed are American cases involving the proper interpretation of constitutional texts; the last two are English cases involving the application of common law principles. Overruling on common law matters raises different conceptual questions than does overruling on an interpretation of an authoritative text, but an analysis of these differences is beyond the scope of the present discussion.)

[11] Hart, *The Concept of Law*, p. 139.

The purpose of the reference was to make a point to those whose
discussions about the law over-emphasised the fact that the decisions of officials in the system often had finality, even when the
decisions were mistaken. The decisions may be final, but the
officials are acting under an obligation to make their decisions
through the application of certain rules: thus, it is both right and
wrong to say "the law is what the officials say it is", just as it is both
right and wrong in the context of many games to say "a score occurs
whenever the scorer says it does".[12] It is right, in the sense that the
decision is final (or, in Hart's phrase, "unchallengeable"). It is
wrong, in the sense that it disregards the fact that the officials are
(most of the time) attempting to apply, and be bound by, rules (at
the least, they must purport to be constrained in that manner).

The difference between real games and "scorer's discretion",
and the difference between (most, and probably all) legal systems
and systems where the law can be usefully equated with "what the
judges say it is", is the tension between authority and correctness—a tension that one can see as well in games as one can in law.
The cynical response that "whatever is done is right" or "whatever
is authorised by the officials is right" is counter-balanced by the
way that citizens and officials (even some biased officials) refer to
the rules to justify their decisions, and will use the rules to warrant
a modification of past (allegedly erroneous) decisions.

The tension between authority and correctness has a slightly
different spin in language. It may be that, according to the
appointed and self-appointed experts (including the "authoritative" reference dictionaries), the way most people use certain
words (e.g. "hopefully") is wrong. However, over time, if enough
people use those words in those ways, that meaning (the one now
thought of as "mistaken") *will be* the meaning of those words. The
attachment of meanings to words is arbitrary: one cannot sensibly
talk, over the long run, of *everyone* being wrong about the meaning
of a word. There is a corresponding situation in the law.

While it makes sense to say that some legal officials were
mistaken in their interpretation or application of particular legal
standards, if that "mistake" is reaffirmed often enough by enough

---

[12] *ibid.* pp. 138–139. As pointed out to me by Neal Feigenson, the issues raised in
this discussion can also be seen as trading on the tension between "will" and
"reason", a theme discussed in Chap. 12.

important members of the legal hierarchy, that "mistake" now *is* the ("settled") law of that legal system. As with language, there is something at best quite strange about stating that *all* legal officials have been wrong for a *long time* about what the law is on a particular issue (and very close to absurdity to speak of a whole legal community being wrong about its own legal system[13]). The reason this claim is only strange, and not nonsensical (as it arguably would be in the case of language), is that in law there are authoritative texts, which can always in theory justify a change in even the most settled law.[14]

---

[13] See Marmor, *Interpretation and Legal Theory*, pp. 96–97.

[14] One famous example being the use of the guarantee of equal protection in the United States Constitution to justify overturning the "settled" legal conclusion that racial segregation was constitutionally permitted. Compare *Plessy v. Ferguson*, 163 U.S. 537 (1896) (affirming the constitutionality of racial segregation) with *Brown v. Board of Education*, 349 U.S. 294 (1955) (holding racial segregation to be in violation of constitutional protections).

Chapter Fourteen

Precedent and Statutory Interpretation

Questions of statutory interpretation turn on the relationship between courts and legislatures (keeping in mind that there is no necessary reason that rules be made and applied by separate institutions, although there are many practical advantages to this separation), and between government and citizens: for example, should judges fill in gaps in legislation? In applying rules, what importance should be given to the intentions of the rule-makers and what importance to the expectations of the public?

These and similar controversies are basically political controversies, which may be informed by different theories about institutional competence and institutional behaviour, but it is unlikely that many such questions will be resolved by reference to statements about the nature of law or about the nature of language. This observation may seem obvious, but it is surprising how often it is ignored in the writings of legal theorists.[1]

There sometimes seems to be a sense of denial in discussions of legal interpretation. Consider the context of English statutory interpretation: the English courts say that they are trying to discover Parliament's intention regarding a statute, but until quite recently[2] neither the judges nor the lawyers appearing before them were allowed even to refer to the record of parliamentary debates. The focus instead was (and largely still is) on the "literal" or "plain" meaning of the statute.

---

[1] In Bix, *Law, Language, and Legal Determinacy*, pp. 154–156, 176–177, I make a similar point in response to metaphysically realist approaches to law and legal interpretation.

[2] See *Pepper v. Hart* [1992] 3 W.L.R. 1032 (allowing reference to *Hansard* to aid the interpretation of statutes in certain limited circumstances).

The denial seems to become even stronger—or at least stranger—in the comments judges and academics offer about these practices. Lord Reid explained: "We are seeking the meaning of the words which Parliament used. We are seeking not what Parliament meant but the true meaning of what they said."[3] Though perhaps not optimally phrased, Lord Reid's point seems clear enough. Yet the eminent commentator Sir Rupert Cross wrote about this quotation: "This is not one of Lord Reid's most helpful remarks because if the true meaning of what someone says is not what he intended to say, it is difficult to know what it is."[4]

Sir Rupert seemed to have overlooked the obvious and familiar distinction between the meaning we wish to get across and the meaning our words in fact convey to the reader or listener, a distinction justified by the frequency of misstatements, misunderstandings, cultural differences between speaker and listener, differing assumptions and expectations, etc. At the least, Sir Rupert was asking a great deal of the phrase "the true meaning".

As many commentators have pointed out, there are many subtleties, complications and paradoxes involved when discussing legislative intentions.[5] Some derive from the fact that "intentions" in the context of a group promulgating a rule simply cannot refer to the same things as the same concept ("intention") means when referring to one individual conversing with another. To the extent that individual, conversational intention is partly a function of what the speaker was actually thinking when he or she spoke, there is no readily available analogue in context of a group. Additionally, legislation usually involves an expectation that the rule promulgated will be used as guidance for the indefinite future by persons not known to the legislators—a purpose or set of expectations far different from what one finds most of the time in individual conversations. Legislation is also more likely to involve a variety of different types of intentions: for example, intentions about what a text means, intentions regarding how the text should be interpreted and intentions regarding how it should be applied[6] (*e.g.* the

---

[3] *Black-Clauson International Ltd v. Papierwerke Waldhof-Aschaffenburg A.G.* [1975] 1 All E.R. 810 at 814.

[4] Rupert Cross, *Statutory Interpretation* (London: Butterworths, 1976), pp. 39–40.

[5] I discussed some of these issues in another context in Bix, "Questions in Legal Interpretation", pp. 142–146.

[6] See Marmor, *Interpretation and Legal Theory*, pp. 165–172.

authors of a standard requiring "reasonable" behaviour could believe that a particular type of action would be "unreasonable" under the standard, but might at the same time believe that judgments of reasonableness should be made by judges according to contemporary standards at the time of judging).

The question, therefore, is: what follows from the fact that there are these differences between legislation and individual communication? A variety of responses have been offered: for example, that legislative intentions should only be legally relevant under certain conditions (generally conditions that make those intentions seem more similar to intentions in a conversational context, *e.g.* when all the legislators shared the same intention and when that intention was relatively recent),[7] that legislative intention should play no role in the interpretation of statutes[8] and that legislative intention is best understood as having nothing to do with intention, but is just a shorthand for saying that certain types of facts should be taken into account when constructing the best interpretation of a statute.[9]

Problems about legislative intention, and the related question about the role of authority in law, have been the focus of numerous articles, conferences and books. In these few pages, I can only hope to have hinted at the variety of different questions and problems raised by the area.

WHOSE PLAIN MEANING?

In *Davis v. Johnson* (discussed earlier), Lord Justice Cumming-Bruce in the Court of Appeal supported emphatically the traditional approach to interpreting statutes by stating: "An Act means what the words and phrases selected by the parliamentary draftsmen actually mean, and not what individual members of the two Houses of Parliament may think they mean."[10]

Lord Justice Cumming-Bruce wanted to distinguish what individual legislators *thought about* a text from what the text *actually*

---

[7] See *ibid.* pp. 155–184.

[8] Jeremy Waldron, "Legislators' Intentions and Unintentional Legislation" in *Law and Interpretation* (A. Marmor ed., Oxford: Clarendon Press, 1995), pp. 329–356.

[9] See Dworkin, *Law's Empire*, pp. 313–354.

[10] *Davis v. Johnson* [1979] A.C. 264 at 316.

means; but actual meanings do not announce themselves for all to hear. To be slightly cynical about matters: in actual practice, the choice becomes one between what the legislators thought the text means (as best as this can be cobbled together from the legislative history) and what the judges think the text means. This is not to say that there are not good reasons for preferring the latter to the former; only that the judges are fooling themselves if they think that their access to meaning is different from and better than that of other people—as though one group had direct access to meanings, while other groups could only offer *interpretations* of meanings, interpretations which were particularly vulnerable to mistake.

It seems relatively clear what Justice Cumming-Bruce was getting at: a statute should be interpreted according to the plain or conventional meaning of its text; when there is a conflict, the conventional meaning of the text should take precedence over any more idiosyncratic meaning that the legislators might have attached to the text. There are, however, two unspoken assumptions in the argument. The first is that there *is* a conventional meaning to be found. One could argue regarding particular texts in particular circumstances (and some might offer a similar argument regarding *all* of language *all* of the time) that no consensus or near-consensus in meaning exists; all there is are the different readings of different groups. The second assumption is that the judge will be able to interpret the text in line with its conventional meaning; one could argue (especially in England, where the judiciary is relatively homogeneous in its background and personal characteristics and far from representative of the general population[11]) that judges are at least as likely to succumb to idiosyncratic interpretations as legislators are.

---

[11] See John Griffith, *The Politics of the Judiciary* (London: Fontana, 1985).

Chapter Fifteen

Legal Enforcement of Morality

As many writers have pointed out, the phrase "legal enforcement of morality" is a misleading title for the issues that are usually raised under that label. No one seriously contends that the government should not establish any legal rules that are consistent with, and could be seen as enforcing, moral norms. There is, and has always been, a large overlap between legal and moral standards. If one were to disallow the legal enforcement of moral standards, most of what passes for criminal law (prohibiting murder, robbery, rape, etc.), tort law (requiring compensation for negligently or intentionally inflicted harm), contract law (enforcing promises), and much of the rest of the legal system would thereby be considered improper. Those who are concerned about whether and how the law enforces morality are not considering such a wholesale overhaul of the legal system.

In the reference to "the legal enforcement of morality", a certain sub-set of moral standards is usually indicated, although there is no consensus for the dividing line advocates would draw between moral standards that the law should enforce and those that the law should not enforce.

DIVIDING LINES

The dividing line most often mentioned in discussions of what moral standards the law should and should not enforce is that proposed by John Stuart Mill (1806–1873) in his pamphlet, "On Liberty": "The only purpose for which power can rightfully be exercised over any member of a civilised community against his will is to prevent harm to others."[1] The supporting arguments for this assertion are partly based on assertions about government (what it is well-placed to do and what it is poorly placed to do, or arguments about limits that should be placed on its powers) and partly based on assertions about individuals within society (the central place of liberty and autonomy in our lives, and the likelihood that society will be better off if a great variety of values and approaches to life is tolerated).[2]

The last point may be the one for which Mill is best known. Mill supported "ethical confrontation",[3] the idea that moral progress is more likely to occur when alternative views about morality, politics and how one should live are subject to open discussion, both in the literal sense and in the sense that ways of living based on these alternative values are tolerated and thereby remain open to public view.

The line drawn between actions that harm others and those that do not has strong intuitive appeal to many: "if my actions do not harm anyone else, then they are no one else's business, especially not the State's." However, in societies where insurance is pervasive (and in some circumstances required by law), where governments may either run the health service or provide the health care of last resort, and where the government may provide social services to those left destitute, there may no longer be many actions which are purely self-regarding. For example, if my reckless behaviour leaves me severely injured, the state may end up paying for my medical bills or supporting my children. My action which on the surface seemed only self-regarding had effects on those around me, and repercussions to a wider group through increased taxes and insurance premiums.

Such facts, which of course vary from country to country, undermine some of the persuasive power of Mill's dividing line, but the line retains much of its substantial intuitive appeal.

---

[1] John Stuart Mill, "On Liberty", Chap. 1 in *On Liberty and Utilitarianism* (New York: Bantam, 1993), p. 12. ("On Liberty" was originally published in 1859.)

[2] The arguments are well elaborated in Mill, "On Liberty", and in H. L. A. Hart, *Law, Liberty and Morality* (Oxford: Oxford University Press, 1963).

[3] Here I am borrowing a term, and some analysis, from Jeremy Waldron, *Liberal Rights* (Cambridge: Cambridge University Press, 1993), pp. 120–121.

Topics

Discussions under the title "the legal enforcement of morality" often focus on matters relating to sexuality, for example, homosexuality,[4] pornography,[5] surrogate motherhood[6] and sado-masochism,[7] reflecting the high level of interest and attention that such issues naturally attract. However, one should note that there are a number of issues in this area that are not connected with sexuality: for example, requiring the wearing of helmets while riding a motorcycle or bicycle and the wearing of seat belts while driving or riding in a car, suicide and assisted suicide, certain kinds of illegal drugs (distinguishing the dangers the substances cause only to the user as against the dangers the user might cause others while "under the influence") and other activities that are dangerous but attractive to some (for example, cliff diving). One should also consider the regulation of food, drugs, machinery, etc.: under a Millian approach, consumers should be given the facts they need to make an informed choice about use or consumption, but there would be no restraint on the production or consumption of dangerous items. (Finally, there are also questions which seem to fall within the issue of "the legal enforcement of morality", but which seem unconnected to Mill's proposed demarcation of self-regarding action. For example, should the state create and enforce a legal duty of one citizen to rescue another from danger, when that rescue can be accomplished without endangering the rescuer?[8])

As a number of the above examples might indicate, there is much room for argument, even if one accepts Mill's dividing line of "harm to others". For example, does this harm include "offence to others" (as religious believers would be deeply

---

[4] See, *e.g. Bowers v. Hardwick*, 478 U.S. 186 (1986) (upholding the constitutionality of a criminal law on sodomy as applied to private homosexual conduct).

[5] See, *e.g. American Booksellers Assoc., Inc. v. Hudnut*, 771 F.2d 323 (7th Cir. 1985), *aff'd mem.*, 475 U.S. 1001 (1986) (invalidating as unconstitutional a feminist anti-pornography ordinance).

[6] See, *e.g. Re Baby M.*, 537 A.2d 1227 (N.J. 1988) (finding a surrogacy contract invalid).

[7] See, *e.g. R. v. Brown* [1993] 2 W.L.R. 556 (upholding the application of criminal assault statutes to private, consensual sado-masochistic activity).

[8] See, *e.g.* Ernest Weinrib, "The Case for a Duty to Rescue" (1980) 90 *Yale Law Journal* 247.

offended by blasphemous actions or statements, were such actions or statements to become known)—and should we distinguish between the offence one feels when confronted by the activity or comment and the offence one might feel from the knowledge of what other people are doing or saying in private? H. L. A. Hart, for example, while arguing for a position close to that of Mill, allowed for legal regulation to protect "public decency".[9] However, he refused to go further, to add protections against offence based on what others do in private. He wrote: "a right to be protected from the distress which is inseparable from the bare knowledge that others are acting in ways you think wrong, cannot be acknowledged by anyone who recognises individual liberty as a value."[10]

HART V. DEVLIN

In many places, the discussion of the legal enforcement of morality is too strongly influenced by the exchange between H. L. A. Hart and Lord Patrick Devlin in the 1960s.[11] The exchange was unhelpful in some ways in that it centered on Lord Devlin's somewhat idiosyncratic position (and his less than optimal arguments in its defence).

Before one can understand Lord Devlin's position, and why it is particularly weak, one must first understand the distinction between "critical" and "conventional" morality (the same distinction is sometimes offered using different terminology[12]; the terminology is not important as long as the distinction is clearly understood and applied). A statement of critical morality is an attempt to state what is morally true, while a statement of conventional morality is an attempt to capture what most people *believe* to be morally true.

This is a type of distinction that one finds in areas other than morality: one could say, for example, that while the conventional belief is that Charles Dickens is the greatest English novelist of all time, the better view is that Jane Austen deserves that honour. On

---

[9] Hart, *Law, Liberty, and Morality*, pp. 38–48.
[10] *ibid.* p. 46.
[11] Patrick Devlin, *The Enforcement of Morals* (Oxford: Oxford University Press, 1965); Hart, *Law, Liberty, and Morality.*
[12] Hart refers to the same distinction under the terms "positive" and "critical" morality: see Hart, *Law, Liberty, and Morality*, pp. 17–24.

one side are statements about reality, about the way things really are; on the other side are statements about people's beliefs.[13] To determine the truth in critical morality, one might think long and hard about the arguments on either side of the debate; to determine the truth in conventional morality, one would be better advised to conduct an opinion poll.

This is not to say that there can be no connection between conventional and critical morality. For example, one might believe that there is no such thing as (objective) moral truth; all there is, one believes, are people's biases and preferences. This person might (but need not) add: the proper way to act is however most people think it is proper to act. For someone with this (extreme) view, it could be said that conventional morality and critical morality merge.

Most of Lord Devlin's writings on the legal enforcement of morality support the reading that he believes that law should enforce conventional morality. (I hedge here, because Lord Devlin was not always as careful as he might have been to make sure that his arguments were consistent.) The argument seems to be as follows: society is held together by its shared morality; actions which undermine the shared morality undermine society; so society is justified in protecting itself through using the law to enforce society's conventional morality.[14]

The problem is that beliefs about moral matters change. At any given time in a community, there may be a consensus on some moral questions, while on other questions there will be sharp divisions. Over time, an issue may go from being a matter of consensus to being a matter of controversy, and given enough time, an issue for which there was a consensus one way may eventually be a matter of consensus the other way (examples of

---

[13] Another way to consider the contrast is as follows: it makes perfect sense to say "most people in this society believe X ('that Dickens is the greatest novelist', 'that capital punishment is morally acceptable', or the like), but I do not believe it", while it is either paradoxical or nonsensical to say "it is true (as a matter of critical morality) that adultery is wrong, but I do not believe it".

[14] Devlin, *The Enforcement of Morality*, pp. 9–10. Devlin's views on these matters are related to ideas first put forward by the social theorist Emile Durkheim. For a discussion of Durkheim's views and their relation to the Hart-Devlin debate, see W. John Thomas, "Social Solidarity and the Enforcement of Morality Revisited: Some Thoughts on H. L. A. Hart's Critique of Durkheim" (1994) 32 *American Criminal Law Review* 49.

this last phenomenon may include the issues of slavery and religious tolerance).

How can we know that our laws are enforcing society's moral consensus, rather than just protecting the last generation's prejudices against a consensus forming around another position? Devlin recognised change in conventional moral beliefs only in terms of greater or lesser "tolerance" on certain issues.[15] However, when we are respectful of religious minorities, we do not see ourselves as being "tolerant" regarding deviations from the old rules of persecuting such minorities; we see ourselves as following a new rule that such respect is correct. A similar analysis could be offered about Devlin's own example of homosexuality. Many of those who believe that homosexual acts should not be criminalised do not see themselves as being "lax" about the immorality of homosexuality; they simply do not think it is immoral at all.[16]

The assumption that changes in conventional moral thinking are only changes in our "laxness" about moral matters or in our "tolerance" of deviation indicates the extent to which Lord Devlin confused or conflated conventional and critical morality. He assumed that there was some true moral thinking to which we would always return. At the least, this is just bad moral history and moral sociology. One would not have spoken of the American and English societies of the nineteenth century as having become more lax or tolerant regarding not returning slaves to their masters. The fact is that conventional moral opinion changes, and it can, over time, change radically (and sometimes for the better).

---

[15] Devlin, *The Enforcement of Morality*, p. 18.

[16] This type of question arises in the philosophy of language under the rubric of "rule-following": how do we know that someone is deviating from a particular rule, rather than conforming to a different rule? See Saul Kripke, *Wittgenstein: On Rules and Private Language* (Cambridge, Mass.: Harvard University Press, 1982). Similar questions arise in moral philosophy and in law, *e.g.* a standard type of legal question is, when an insurance policy covers a variety of medical procedures but does not cover pregnancy, is that policy failing to follow (perhaps in a discriminatory way) a general rule ("all medical procedures are covered"), or is it (legitimately) following a different rule which excludes pregnancy from the class of procedures covered? See *Geduldig v. Aiello*, 417 U.S. 484 (1974) (the exclusion of pregnancy from an otherwise comprehensive list of disabilities covered by state disability insurance did not violate constitutional guarantees of equal protection).

There would be many questions one would have to face if one were serious about wanting to enforce conventional, as opposed to critical, morality. The first would be why one was doing so. Lord Devlin stated that a society is held together by its morality, and argued from this that society had an interest in preventing anything that would "undermine" the shared morality, for that would undermine society. Lord Devlin is here creating an argument from a metaphor.

One could just as easily (and I would argue more accurately) say that anything which *changed* the shared morality would thereby change society. More to the point, matters tend also to work in the other direction: it is the society which shapes the (conventional) morality and, when society changes, the (conventional) morality changes with it.

As indicated earlier, if conventional morality of the moment is what matters, there is no reason to enforce the last generation's conventional morality at the cost of this generation's. What complicates matters further is that on many (if not most) moral matters, there is no consensus at all.

A NEW START

For all the reasons given above, Lord Devlin's position is probably not the most formidable opponent for someone advocating a Mill-like libertarian approach to the question of the legal enforcement of morality. More significant arguments have been presented for a position that some have labeled "perfectionism", which entails the view that the government has a legitimate interest in promoting certain views as to what the good life is. (Most of the modern theorists who support legislative enforcement of public morality have at the same time rejected the arguments and positions Devlin offered.[17])

Writing in response to Mill, James Fitzjames Stephen wrote in favour of legislation whose purpose was "to establish, to maintain, and to give power to that which the legislator regards as a good moral system or standard." After further argument, he offered the

---

[17] *e.g.* Robert George, *Making Men Moral* (Oxford: Clarendon Press, 1993), pp. x, 71–82.

conclusion that "the object of promoting virtue and preventing vice must be admitted to be both a good one and one sufficiently intelligible for legislative purposes."[18] (As against the argument that the government was not well placed to reach final conclusions about what is morally worthy and what is not, Stephen wrote: "How can the State or the public be competent to determine any question whatever if it is not competent to decide that gross vice is a bad thing?"[19])

As to liberty, Stephen had little patience with discussion in the abstract. The proper question, he argued, is liberty towards what end, allowing freedom from which restraints?[20] Liberty to live a worthless or evil life he could not see as a matter worthy of great defence or deference:

> "It is one thing however to tolerate vice so long as it is inoffensive, and quite another to give it a legal right not only to exist, but to assert itself in the face of the world as an 'experiment in living' as good as another, and entitled to the same protection from law."[21]

For Stephen, the primary question was one of balance: could significant good be accomplished (by criminalising vice, and thereby, one hopes, reducing its frequency) without being outweighed by the costs—of compulsion, error, infringements of liberty and privacy, and so on?[22]

A similar, "perfectionist" defence of legal enforcement of morality has been more recently offered by Robert George. George's position was that no "norm of justice or political morality" was violated by legislation protecting public morality (although toleration of moral wrongdoing may sometimes be justified on prudential grounds).[23]

---

[18] James Fitzjames Stephen, *Liberty, Equality, Fraternity* (S. Warner ed., Indianapolis: Liberty Fund, 1993), Chap. 4, pp. 96–97 (the book was originally published in 1873).

[19] *ibid.* p. 84.

[20] *ibid.* pp. 115–116.

[21] *ibid.* p. 101.

[22] *ibid.* pp. 91–92, 105–108.

[23] George, *Making Men Moral*, p. viii.

One can be a perfectionist and still support a view similar to that of Mill. Joseph Raz has put forward[24] a connected set of views grounded on two principles:

(1) moral pluralism: that there are a variety of moral goods, and a variety of ways of living a morally good life, but these goods and ways of life are, either in theory or in practice, inconsistent (*e.g.* one cannot be both a monk and a great general; and it is difficult to excel at ballet, chess, and poetry all at the same time); and

(2) the importance of autonomy: autonomy is a pre-eminent value, to be protected and promoted where possible.

Therefore, for Raz, while it is proper for the state to promote good ways of life and to do what it can to make such choices available to its citizens ("perfectionism"), the value of autonomy counts strongly against promoting good forms of life by coercing those who have chosen non-good forms of life.

All of the above is to be distinguished from prudential arguments that the law should refrain from acting for certain kind of moral objectives because the law is not well suited to achieve such objectives. For example, one could argue that the American experiment of Prohibition, when the sale of alcohol was prohibited, was doomed to failure, because people's desire for alcohol is too strong.

One can also put forward a different kind of argument about the incompatibility of law and moral objectives. The argument is that by the nature of things one cannot force someone to act morally through the threat of legal sanctions. Under this view, it is the nature of moral action that one *voluntarily* make the proper choices. Choices coerced through the fear of legal sanctions may outwardly conform with the choices required by an ethical code, but will lack the crucial inner purpose or intention.[25] If someone avoids illegal drugs or homosexual acts or pornography only

---

[24] Joseph Raz, "Autonomy, Toleration, and the Harm Principle" in *Issues in Contemporary Legal Philosophy* (R. Gavison ed., Oxford: Clarendon Press, 1987), pp. 313–333.

[25] *cf.* John Finnis, "Liberalism and Natural Law Theory" (1994) 45 *Mercer Law Review* 687 at 697–698. As Finnis points out in this article, this position is consistent with the view that the state, through its statements and its funding decisions, should favour virtuous choices over immoral choices.

because he or she fears being caught by the authorities, then, this view states, the person should no more get the credit for acting morally than if this course of action was followed only because of the orders of a gunman.

Chapter Sixteen

The Obligation to Obey the Law

The topic of the moral content of law has come up in a number of ways in earlier discussions in this book, both among the discussions of individual theorists (the natural law theorists, like John Finnis, whose analyses of law are tied directly to when and whether the law "binds in conscience"; H. L. A. Hart defining and defending legal positivism on the basis that the description of law must be separated from its evaluation; Lon Fuller writing of the "internal morality" of law; and Ronald Dworkin's assertion that moral evaluation is integral to any proper description ("interpretation") of the law) and under other general headings: for example, the question discussed in the last chapter of the relationship law should have to morality, in terms of which parts of morality should or should not be enforced through the legal system.

The current topic is the other side of the question. Instead of, "from the perspective of law, what is the place of morality?", this chapter will consider "from the perspective of morality, what is the place of law?" In simpler terms, the question is whether there is a moral obligation to obey the law.

One way to think about the problem of the obligation to obey the law is to consider what you would do if you were driving at 3 a.m. and came upon a stop light at an intersection, and you could see that there were no pedestrians and no cars (in particular, no police cars) in sight. Would you stop?

Many people obey the law for prudential reasons: they fear imprisonment or a fine, or they worry that being caught doing something illegal would harm their reputations or their careers. Some people would stop at the stop light at 3 a.m. just out of habit:

it is easier for them simply to obey the law unreflectively, rather than take the trouble on each occasion to calculate all the moral or prudential factors. Such concerns are not what the debate on the obligation to obey the law is all about. The question is whether the legal status of a command, authorisation or prohibition, by itself, without more, adds any moral reasons for doing or not doing the action indicated.

Various types of arguments have been offered to try to justify the conclusion that there is an obligation to obey the law: arguments based on consent, on gratitude (for the benefits the state confers) and on consequences (the value of maintaining a good legal system, or the claim that, however bad the legal system is, lawlessness would be far worse). For all of these arguments, the type of situation described above, coming to an intersection at 3 a.m., will always be the one that gives the most trouble. In this type of situation, disobedience does not seem to risk harming anyone or anything, and the disobedience looks like it would go undetected. This last point is important not only because sanctions for the violator will be avoided, but also because there would not be an argument that our disobedience sets a bad example, and will undermine other people's respect for the legal system.

In the Hart-Fuller debate (discussed in Chapters 5 and 8), Fuller challenged the legal positivists on the following terms: if the validity of a law is one thing, and its moral value something entirely separate, then how can the positivists speak of there being a "moral dilemma" about whether to obey a morally dubious law?[1] If law is just a label for something which may or may not be morally worthy, then there is no reason to believe that just because something is required or prohibited by law, that by itself is a *moral* reason for doing or not doing that action.

Fuller may have thought of his challenge as a knockdown argument, but some later legal positivists have accepted, without shame or apology, that the legal status of a norm may give it no intrinsic moral weight. These theorists do not argue that we should never obey the law, or even that there are never *moral* reasons for doing what the law tells us to; only that the moral reasons must go beyond the simple declaration "because the law says so".

---

[1] Fuller, "Positivism and Fidelity to Law", p. 656: "It is like saying I have to choose between giving food to a starving man and being mimsy with the borogoves."

For Joseph Raz, we have a moral reason to do as the law states, if and when we believe that we are more likely to make the morally best choice by following the law than by making our own judgment of the situation. For example, if the question is whether to use a particular detergent or not, with the issue being that it might damage the environment, we might defer to the legislature's judgment, on the basis that they have acted to allow or prohibit the detergent only after hearing scientific testimony to which we do not have access.

For another kind of example, consider pure problems of co-ordination. These are problems where it does not matter much what is chosen, as long as everyone chooses the same thing: a standard example is the side of the road cars drive on. For such choices, there are reasons for acting as the law states, for the government is sufficiently prominent to make such choices and expect them to be followed by other citizens.

There are also co-ordination situations where some choices might be better than others, but there is great value in everyone making the same choice, even if it is not the optimal choice. An example might be fighting water pollution. As a pollution expert, you might know that the clean-up program the government has chosen is not the best plan, but you also know that the government's plan, enacted in legislation with sanctions for deviation, is the one most likely to be followed by most people, and that everyone co-operating in that scheme is more likely to achieve results than if different persons went off trying to effect different schemes. Under such a situation, you might have good reason to follow the government's plan, even when you know it is not the best.

Of course, the most common situation when one has a moral obligation to act as the law requires is when the action is the moral thing to do whatever the law might say. For most of us, we do not rob or murder because it would be wrong, not because the law tells us not to. In such situations the fact that the law prohibits the action appears to add nothing to the moral calculation that the action ought not be done.

The types of arguments one comes across (in the literature as well as in classroom discussions) on the topic of the obligation to obey the law reflect a constant changing of perspectives and questions. To arguments like Raz's, the objection goes: "how can *you* know that you have a better idea of what is morally right than the legislature has?" or "if everyone made their own choices about how to act, rather than deferring to the legislature, there would be anarchy." There often is a certain "we" versus "them" attitude when discussing the obligation to obey the law, with the unstated assumption being that "we" are looking for the correct attitude for "them" to have. It is probably better if the discussion remains on the level of "us" deciding how "we" ought to act; this maintains the focus on the moral status of law, avoiding the quite different, if equally interesting, questions of practical governance and crowd control.

A. M. Honoré began his discussion of the obligation to obey the law[2] by trying to refute those who claim that not only is there no such obligation, but that we should not be much worried by this fact. Honoré states that the most difficult moral questions, like the most difficult legal questions, are so closely contested that they are likely to turn on where the burden of proof lies. Regarding the obligation to obey the law, if the initial presumption is that the law should be obeyed, then, more often than not, the final moral judgment will be for obedience. However, if, following those theorists who claim that there is no obligation, the initial presumption is that the law need not be obeyed, then, Honoré argued, people will tend more often to disregard the law, leading to an "attitude of disobedience" and the breakdown of the order and co-operation needed for society to function. This sounds like the discussions of leaders about how best to control the masses, or similar.

In any event, one should not confuse:

(1)   the ethical question: what should I do in this situation?
(2)   the meta-ethical question: how do I determine what is the morally correct thing for me to do? and
(3)   the political consideration: from a particular perspective, what is the set of beliefs and attitudes we want or need the public to hold?

This chapter deals only with the first two questions.

---

[2] A. M. Honoré, *Making Law Bind*, pp. 115–138.

Obligation and Consent

One of the standard arguments for the obligation to obey the law is based on consent. The argument goes that, by some action (or inaction), we have implicitly consented to obeying society's law. This action may be voting, accepting government benefits or simply not leaving the country.[3] The first response is usually that it is not proper to understand these activities as constituting consent to the laws or to the state, either because the citizens do not perceive the action in that way, or because the citizens often do not have effective alternatives.

Another interesting response is that even if the action in question could be held to constitute consent, that does not end the question over whether the citizen acting in this way then has an obligation to obey the society's laws.[4] One must remember that the argument here has two steps, and that both steps must be proven for the argument to succeed. The two steps are:

(1) a certain action (say, voting) constitutes "consent" to obeying the society's laws; and
(2) anyone who consents in this way is morally obliged to obey the law.

The second need not follow from the first.

The reason the second conclusion may fail to follow from the first is that, as a moral matter, acts of consent may have limited force. If I agree to paint your fence for $100, most people would conclude that my promise is a consent to undertake the obligation to paint the fence (for the payment named), an obligation I would not have except for my promise. However, the moral evaluation of the situation might change if what I agreed to was to paint your entire house for one dollar, or to kill your father, or to do anything you told me to do over the next month. The mere promise, even taking into consideration the (nominal) exchange payment, is not sufficient to maintain the large moral claim.

---

[3] This last figures both in Plato's *Crito* and in Locke's dicussion of implied consent to government.

[4] The argument that follows derives from some comments made by Joseph Raz in a lecture.

For this particular context, the claim is that the putative act of consent, for example, voting or not leaving, is not sufficient to justify creating the broad obligation to obey *whatever* the government might enact *from that day onward.* As a moral matter, we might conclude that this is too much to place on a single promise (especially here where the "promise" is an action which has other purposes and meanings).

Arguing over what should be called "consent" too often masks the real moral questions: how do we create moral obligations for ourselves, and what are the limits of those obligations?

CONNECTIONS

While the obligation to obey the law is often treated as a separate topic (as it is in this text), in many ways the issue is ill-suited for such treatment. From any discussion of the questions raised by the issue, it becomes clear that one's answer to whether there is an obligation to obey the law will depend on one's conclusions regarding a series of more basic questions: both basic questions of moral theory (*e.g.* what can/does ground our moral duties: benefit, consent, co-operation, necessity or interdependence?) and basic questions of legal theory (how do we determine the existence or validity of a law or legal system?).

For example, if one's starting point is a traditional form of natural law theory, one's conclusion about whether something is "law" (or "law in its fullest sense") will already incorporate much of the answer about whether or to what extent one has an obligation to obey the law (one has such an obligation for just laws, "laws in their fullest sense"; for unjust laws, there may still be a minimal obligation of public compliance so as not to undermine a generally just legal system).[5]

Legal positivism offers no comparable guidance. Its motto that the validity of law is one thing, its merit another, indicates that legal positivists will have to find answers elsewhere, from whatever moral theory they might bring to their deliberations.

---

[5] This is a position of the natural law theorists St Thomas Aquinas and John Finnis, as discussed in Chap. 2.

PART D

Modern Perspectives on Legal Theory

The last set of chapters discusses general approaches to law and legal education that have come to prominence in this century, with all but the first (American legal realism) grounded primarily in the last few decades.

If one thinks of theory as being divided between the "pure philosophy" tendency to ask questions simply to learn ("philosophy" is a Greek word meaning "love of knowledge" or "love of wisdom"), and the belief that inquiry should always be focused on the ethical question of how we should live our lives, the approaches outlined in these chapters can be seen as pulling jurisprudence toward the latter attitude: being concerned primarily with doing justice rather than being concerned primarily with true understanding. These approaches also are, each in its own way, deeply subversive of conventional understandings about law.

Chapter Seventeen

American Legal Realism

"Legal realism" is the label that was given to a group of American legal theorists in the 1920s, 1930s and 1940s, who challenged the ideas about legal reasoning and adjudication dominant in judicial and legal academic writing at the time. Its influence on (American) legal thinking can be summarised by the fact that the phrase, "we are all realists now" has become a kind of legal academic cliché.[1]

Among those writers who described themselves (or who are described by others) as "realists", there was little by way of agreed views, values, subject-matter or methodology. It has become commonplace to note that the differences among those writers were sufficiently significant that it approaches distortion even to refer to "the legal realists" as though it were a coherent movement (one commentator writing recently preferred to refer to legal realism as a "feel" or "mood"[2]). With those disclaimers noted, I will try to give a general outline of American legal realism.

Many of the themes (and much of the tone) of the legal realists can be found in the work of Oliver Wendell Holmes, who (by most ways of delimiting the realist movement) came earlier. In *The Common Law*, published in 1881, he wrote:

> "The life of the law has not been logic: it has been experience. The felt necessities of the time, the prevalent moral and political theories, intuitions of public policy, avowed or unconscious, even the prejudices which judges share with their fellow-men, have had a good deal more to

---

[1] See, *e.g.* Twining, *Karl Llewellyn and the Realist Movement*, p. 382.
[2] Duxbury, *Patterns of American Jurisprudence*, pp. 68, 69.

do than the syllogism in determining the rules by which men should be governed."[3]

In these few sentences one can find (or at least read in) most of the themes for which the American legal realist movement would be remembered.

The "realism" in "legal realism" is the use of that term in its colloquial meaning: "being realistic" as being worldly, somewhat sceptical, looking beyond ideals and appearances for what is "really going on". First, the main focus of this "realism" was on judicial decision-making: that a proper understanding of judicial decision-making would show that it was fact-centered; that judges' decisions were often based (consciously or unconsciously) on personal or political biases or constructed from hunches; and that public policy and social sciences should play a larger role in judicial decisions. Secondly, feeding into this central focus on adjudication was a critique of legal reasoning: that beneath a veneer of scientific and deductive reasoning, legal rules and concepts were in fact often indeterminate and rarely as neutral as they were presented as being. It was the indeterminacy of legal concepts and legal reasoning that led to the need to explain judicial decisions in other terms—hunches and biases—and the opportunity to encourage a different focus for advocacy and judicial reasoning: social sciences and "public policy". Thirdly, the criticisms of legal reasoning and judicial decision-making flowed towards a parallel criticism of legal education, which was said to reflect the same false formalism and neutrality as were present in legal reasoning and judicial decision-making. (These three themes are clearly interconnected, so there is a certain arbitrariness in deciding where one starts the discussion, and even in deciding where one places various sub-issues: *e.g.* the emphasis on the social sciences could be as easily discussed under any of the three themes.)

REALISM AND LEGAL ANALYSIS

The form of legal analysis dominant at the time the realists were writing was criticised as "formalistic", by which it was meant that the argument was presented as if the conclusion followed simply

---

[3] Oliver Wendell Holmes, *The Common Law* (M. D. Howe ed., Boston: Little Brown, 1963), p. 5 (originally published in 1881).

and inexorably from undeniable premises. Once the proper label was found for an object or action ("contract", "property", "trespass", etc.), the legal conclusion soon followed.

The realists argued that the premises lawyers used were open to question, and that labels and categories hid moral and policy assumptions that should be discussed openly. An example of realist analysis can be seen on the losing side of one of the most famous American tort law cases, *Palsgraf v. Long Island Railroad.*[4] In that case, a railroad employee was negligent in his attempt to assist a passenger; as a result of the negligence, the passenger dropped a package, which happened to contain explosives. An explosion occurred, which led to the injury of the plaintiff, who was standing some distance away. The question in the case was whether someone should be liable for all injuries "proximately caused" by that person's negligence. The majority, in an opinion written by Judge (later Justice) Benjamin Cardozo, decided that the plaintiff could not recover, on the basis that the railroad employee had no duty to the plaintiff, and his negligence was an injury only to the passenger he was trying to help. The dissent, written by Judge William Andrews, included a realist attack on the solidity of the concept of "proximate cause":

> "What we do mean by the word 'proximate' is, that because of convenience, of public policy, of a rough sense of justice, the law arbitrarily declines to trace a series of events beyond a certain point. This is not logic. It is practical politics."[5]

In other words, the legal concepts alone do not get us to a decision, and we are fooling ourselves and the public if we claim that they do. The final conclusion regarding whether "proximate cause" exists or not will be based on unstated premises regarding public policy (or perhaps based on unstated biases or prejudices).

REALISM AND THE COURTS

Judicial decision-making at the time was often portrayed (by judges in their opinions as well as by commentators) as being a

---

[4] 248 N.Y. 339, 162 N.E. 99 (1928).
[5] 248 N.Y. 339 at 352; 162 N.E. 99 at 103 (1928) (Andrews J. dissenting).

nearly mechanical, nearly syllogistic move from basic premises to undeniable conclusion. The legal realist response was to argue that judges often have discretion, that judicial decisions were often in practice determined by factors other than the legal rules, and to move the focus of attention from conceptual analysis to policy argument and fact-finding. One can get a sense of legal realism just from the titles of some of its articles: for example, "Are Judges Human?", "What Courts Do In Fact", "Transcendental Nonsense and the Functional Approach" and "The Judgment Intuitive: The Function of the 'Hunch' in Judicial Decision."[6]

The classical perspective of judicial decision-making was that judges decided cases by merely discovering the appropriate legal rule, a process that required the mere application of simple logical deduction from basic principles. Legal realists offered a variety of counter-images of what they thought really went on in decision-making, a number of which are summed up in this half- caricature of realism: "judges in fact follow their instincts in deciding cases, making sham references to rules of law; generally they are themselves unaware of what they are doing, and persist foolishly in believing that they are being obedient to precedent."[7]

There were (at least) two strands to the realist discussion of judicial decision-making: that decisions were strongly underdetermined by legal rules, concepts and precedent (that is, that judges in many or most cases could have, with equal warrant, come out more than one way); and that judges were (and, by some accounts, should be) highly responsive to the facts, and the way the facts were presented, in reaching their decisions.[8] (One commentator has gone so far as to describe the assertion, "in deciding cases, judges respond primarily to the stimulus of the facts of the case", as the "core claim" of American legal realism.[9])

---

[6] Jerome Frank, "Are Judges Human?", Parts I and II (1931) 80 *University of Pennsylvania Law Review* 17; 223 "What Courts Do In Fact", Parts I and II (1932) 26 *Illinois Law Review* 645, 761; Felix Cohen, "Transcendental Nonsense and the Functional Approach" (1935) 35 *Columbia Law Review* 809; Joseph Hutcheson, Jr., "The Judgment Intuitive: The Function of the 'Hunch' in Judicial Decision" (1929) 14 *Cornell Law Quarterly* 274.

[7] Benjamin Kaplan, "Do Intermediate Appellate Courts Have a Lawmaking Function?" (1985) 70 *Massachusetts Law Review* 10 at 10.

[8] On the last point, see, in particular, Jerome Frank, *Courts on Trial* (Princeton: Princeton University Press, 1949).

[9] Leiter, "Legal Realism".

However, the claim that general principles in fact *do not* determine the results of particular cases and the claim that they *can not* are quite distinct.[10] The first is a statement about causation in the world: why judges decide cases the way they do. The second is a statement about logical possibility, the nature of language or the nature of rules: the point being that one cannot derive in a deductive fashion the result in (some, most, all) legal cases from general principles.

The two claims are independent; one can affirm the first without affirming the second. Both themes were present in the writings of the legal realists. Both themes have become embedded in the way modern lawyers and legal academics think about law, and in the way law is taught. If it was once subversive to think that extra-legal factors influence judicial decisions, it now seems naive to doubt it. And it is commonplace to assume, at least for relatively important and difficult cases, that strong legal arguments can be found for both sides.

There are obvious ties with the first theme discussed: the indeterminacy and lack of neutrality of legal concepts, and the inability to derive unique results in particular cases from general legal rules. If that was the state of law in the abstract, then it comes as no surprise that judicial decisions cannot be based solely on these rules and concepts (and judges who claim otherwise were either fooling themselves—or lying).

What was to fill the conceptual gap left when one's faith in the neutrality and determinacy of legal concepts was lost? For many of the realists, the answer was social science, the understanding of how people actually behave, and the way in which legal rules reflect or affect behaviour. This turn to the social sciences can be seen in a number of places, including "The Brandeis Brief", a brief on legal issues that based its legal conclusions on extensive sociological research.

The "Brandeis Brief" was named after Louis Brandeis, a legal reformer who later sat as a Justice on the United States Supreme

---

[10] This paragraph and the next one follow part of the argument presented in Leiter, "Legal Realism".

Court. The term refers in particular to a brief Brandeis co-wrote defending the constitutionality of a state statute limiting the maximum working hours for women[11]:

> "Containing two pages of legal argument and ninety-five pages of sociological and economic data about the conditions of working women's lives in factories, the Brandeis brief, by highlighting social and economic reality, suggested that the trouble with existing law was that it was out of touch with that reality."[12]

This faith in the social sciences can also be seen indirectly through the work many realists did in the American "New Deal", creating administrative agencies and regulations meant to solve various social problems through the law.[13] The weak point of realist thinking in this area was the tendency towards technocracy, the belief that social scientific expertise by itself would be sufficient to lead to right results, missing the point that there is always a need for a moral or political structure within which to present (or to do) the empirical work; there could not be "neutral experts" on how society should be organised.[14]

REALISM AND LEGAL EDUCATION

The approach of the generation of academics prior to the realists was also a target. Christopher Columbus Langdell, Dean of the Harvard Law School and originator of the "case method" of teaching law,[15] famously advocated that law was a science, whose principles and doctrines could be "discovered" in cases, much as

---

[11] *Muller v. Oregon*, 208 U.S. 412 (1908).
[12] Horwitz, *The Transformation of American Law 1870–1960*, p. 209.
[13] See generally *ibid.* pp. 213–246 ("Legal Realism, Bureaucratic State, and Law"). Neil Duxbury cautions against overstating the connection between the "New Deal" and realism in Duxbury, *Patterns of American Jurisprudence*, pp. 153–158.
[14] See Horwitz, *The Transformation of American Law 1870–1960*, pp. 217–246.
[15] In the case method, the subject was learned by reading a series of (appellate court) decisions in the area, analysing closely and critically the argument offered by the courts in their decisions.

biologists discover the principles of their science in their laboratories.[16] One commentator summarised Langdell's approach as follows:

"To Langdell 'science' conjured up the ideas of order, system, simplicity, taxonomy and original sources. The science of law involved the search for a system of general, logically consistent principles, built up from the study of particular instances. Like the scientist, the lawyer should study original sources; like the botanist, he must select, classify and arrange his specimens."[17]

Given the realist analyses and criticisms given above, it is not surprising that they tended to be scornful of Langdell's "science of law", and all aspects of legal education that seemed to follow from it. To the extent that one can speak of "a realist view" on education, it would primarily be one of following through on the implications of other realist views: that legal concepts should be taught in a way which demystified them; and that legal issues should be shown to be often under-determined by legal rules alone, with policy arguments appropriate and necessary for the resolution of many legal disputes.[18]

AN OVERVIEW

The basic misunderstanding of American legal realism by some later writers turned on a confusion regarding the purpose and point of the realists' work. For example, when the realists stated that we should see law from the perspective of a prediction of what judges will do ("the bad man's" perspective[19]), later writers

---

[16] Christopher Columus Langdell, "Preface" in *A Selection of Cases on the Law of Contracts* (1871), p. viii and a speech to commemorate the 250th anniversary of the founding of Harvard College (in 1887), both quoted in Twining, *Karl Llewellyn and the Realist Movement*, pp. 11–12.

[17] Twining, *Karl Llewellyn and the Realist Movement*, p. 12 (footnote omitted). See also Dennis Patterson, "Langdell's Legacy" (1995) 90 *Northwestern University Law Review* 901.

[18] See Duxbury, *Patterns of American Jurisprudence*, pp. 135–149; William Fisher, Morton Horwitz and Thomas Reed eds., *American Legal Realism* (New York: Oxford University Press, 1993), pp. 270–294.

[19] See Holmes, "The Path of the Law", pp. 460–461.

misunderstand the argument when they saw that as a conceptual claim.[20]

As a conceptual claim, it would have obvious weaknesses (for example, how can a judge on the highest court see the law as a prediction of what the judges will do? The highest court is the final word on what the law will mean and there is no other court whose decisions the judges could try to predict[21]). The predictive theory is better understood as an attempt to shake up the overly abstract and formalistic approach many judges and legal scholars used for discussing law. To put the matter another way, the realists wanted people in the legal profession to spend more time thinking about how law appears "on the ground" or (to change the metaphor) "at the sharp end": to citizens for whom the law means only a prediction of what the trial judge will do in their case (or a prediction of how the police will treat them on the street corner).

In various ways, American legal realism can be seen as the forerunner of the perspectives on law to be discussed in the following Chapters: law and economics (Chapter 18),[22] critical legal studies, critical race theory and feminist legal theory (all in Chapter 19). The connection is often indirect: by undermining the confidence in the "science" of law and the ability to deduce unique correct answers from legal principles (as well as questioning the "neutrality" of those legal principles), the realists created a need for a new justification of legal rules and judicial actions, and they offered a set of arguments that could be used to support claims of pervasive bias (against the poor, against women, or against minorities) in the legal system.

---

[20] Compare Hart, *The Concept of Law*, pp. 132–137 (a conceptual reading of the realists) with Leiter, "Legal Realism".

[21] Richard Posner, *The Problems of Jurisprudence* (Cambridge, Mass.: Harvard University Press 1990), p. 224.

[22] One central figure in law and economics disclaims direct influence from legal realism: Richard Posner, *Overcoming Law* (Cambridge, Mass.: Harvard University Press, 1995), p. 3. However, Posner does not consider the argument (first cogently presented by Arthur Leff, and summarised at the beginning of the next chapter) that legal realism led *indirectly* to law and economics, by undermining the more traditional approaches to law, with law and economics then filling the resulting moral (and academic) vacuum.

Chapter Eighteen

Economic Analysis of Law

In 1897, Justice Oliver Wendell Holmes wrote, "For the rational study of the law the black-letter man may be the man of the present, but the man of the future is the man of statistics and the master of economics."[1] Holmes was prescient, though it took over 60 years for this prediction to be fully realised in legal academia.

In America, no approach to law in recent decades has been more influential than the economic analysis of law (also known by the shorthand "law and economics"). It dominates thinking about antitrust law, tort law, and most commercial law areas. Even areas of law which would seem unsuitable for economic analysis, like domestic relations and constitutional law (civil liberties), have had significant contributions made by law and economics analyses. There seems to be no domain free from attempts to apply this approach. Its influence is growing every year in legal academic circles in Britain and in other countries and, in America, the influence has already been felt in judicial decisions (this last development being hastened by the appointment of prominent advocates of economic analysis, including Richard Posner and Frank Easterbrook, to positions as federal appellate court judges).

Part of the concern of the present chapter will be to understand law and economics by tracing its roots—its roots both in economic analysis and in American jurisprudence.

---

[1] Holmes, "The Path of the Law", p. 469. ("Black-letter law" refers to doctrinal law: the basic rules and principles of law which were often placed in bold black letters in law treatises.)

IN SEARCH OF CONSENSUS

One can start with a general question: on what basis can one argue for a court to adopt one standard rather than another, if there are no prior cases requiring a particular outcome? The novel legal issue could be whether a certain type of activity should be governed by a fault standard, or by some form of strict liability, or whether an independent contractor should be treated the same way as an agent or an employee, or the circumstances under which a bystander to an accident should be allowed to recover damages for nervous shock.

The traditional approach had been that a proper understanding of legal reasoning would allow one always to come to the correct answer through analogical reasoning (and subsumption of a specific fact situation under a general rule). However, in large part because of the criticisms of (among others) the American legal realists, the confidence that such neutral means could resolve every legal question, even the most novel or most difficult ones, dissolved.[2] When the judges said they were "deducing" the correct answer through the simple application of logic and legal reasoning, the suspicion grew that the decision in fact turned on moral or political assumptions that the judges were not revealing (and may not even have recognised).

Another basis for choosing one legal result over another is based on a moral judgment. One could argue, for example, that a correct understanding of justice requires that no one be required to pay compensation except on the basis of fault.[3] The problem is that there is no consensus in most societies about moral matters. One would hope to find a basis for legal argument and legal advocacy on which everyone, or nearly everyone, could agree.

---

[2] See Joseph Singer, "Legal Realism Now" (1988) 76 *California Law Review* 465 at 468: "Current debates about legal reasoning are best understood as attempts to answer the central question that the [legal] realists left unresolved: How can we engage in normative legal argument without either reverting to the formalism of the past or reducing all claims to the raw demands of political interest groups?"

[3] Just such an argument is offered in Weinrib, *The Idea of Private Law*

It is in this context that the movement known as law and economics is best understood.[4] Law and economics tries to offer a basis for decision grounded on consensus. The starting point is as follows: different people have different desires, goals and values, but everyone would agree that they would rather have their desires met than not met, and they would rather have this happen more often rather than less often.

In this way (and in a number of other ways, some of which will be discussed later), law and economics tracks the arguments of and the justification for the theory of moral philosophy known as utilitarianism. Briefly, utilitarianism holds that morality requires the doing of whatever would maximise the sum total of pleasure (while minimising the sum total of pain).[5] The idea had been that the seeking of pleasure and the avoiding of pain are the common and universal aspects of all human life, and that since there was no basis to prefer your desires and pleasures to mine or to anyone else's, the proper basis for social choice is to choose the action which maximises the sum total of pleasures (minus the sum total of pain) in society.[6]

Compared to other moral theories, utilitarianism has the advantage of not requiring difficult value judgments between persons or between value systems. However, there are a number of problems with trying to use utilitarianism as a workable system for social decision-making. The most important of these problems for our purposes is the difficulty (if not impossibility) of measuring and "summing" people's pleasures and pain. (There are a number of other problems with utilitarianism, problems that have been

---

[4] Much of the first part of this section derives from (or at least agrees with) Arthur Leff's discussion in "Economic Analysis of Law: Some Realism About Nominalism" (1974) 60 *Virginia Law Review* 451, which remains one of the best discussions of the strengths and weaknesses of law and economics.

[5] "Utilitarianism" has been defined as "[t]he ethical theory... that answers all questions of what to do, what to admire, or how to live, in terms of maximizing utility or happiness": Simon Blackburn, *The Oxford Dictionary of Philosophy* (Oxford: Oxford University Press, 1994), p. 388. (The same text defines "utility" as "[t]he basic unit of desirability": *ibid.*)

[6] I am not going to go into detail in this section about the different variations of utilitarianism that have developed (for example, act utilitarianism as contrasted with rule utilitarianism), or to consider types of consequentialism which have distanced themselves from classic utilitarianism.

discussed at length in moral philosophy,[7] but a discussion of these problems would be well beyond the scope of this chapter).

Law and economics tries to keep the advantages of utilitarianism—avoiding making controversial value judgments—while losing its disadvantage of being unworkable for social decision-making. The transformation occurs by taking utilitarianism's discussion of "fulfilling desires" and putting it into the context of economic action. How do we determine what people want? We look at how they act: for example, given different ways of spending their time and their money, look at the choices the people ultimately make. For example, if someone chooses to work additional (optional) hours every week, we can conclude that this person prefers the additional pay earned to the additional leisure time he or she could have had if he or she had not worked the additional hours. Economics (in general, not just in its application to law) is built on the "basic assumption" that "people are [always] rational maximizers of their satisfaction".[8]

How do we determine the relative intensity of preferences? By how much people are willing to "pay" for something (in the broadest sense of the term "pay", as we "pay" for objects in time and effort and opportunities foregone, as well as more directly with money). In the simple marketplace example, my purchasing a book indicates that I want it. If there is only one copy of a particular book on sale, and I am willing to pay four times as much as you are for the book, it is reasonable to conclude that I want the book more than you do.[9]

Thus, in two simple transformations, utilitarianism has been made into a (more or less) workable approach for analysing daily behaviour. By defining desires by actions, and by defining levels of desire by how much someone is willing to pay, the marketplace

---

[7] See, *e.g.* Samuel Scheffler ed., *Consequentialism and its Critics* (Oxford: Oxford University Press, 1988).

[8] Posner, *The Problems of Jurisprudence*, p. 353.

[9] At least this conclusion is warranted if the two of us have comparable wealth; how much the general approach is undermined by the fact that this assumption is often not true—that wealth inequalities are pervasive, non-trivial, and not always attributable to the subjects' prior actions—is a matter of going controversy: see, *e.g.* Posner, *The Problems of Jurisprudence*, pp. 380–381; Leff, "Economic Analysis of Law: Some Realism About Nominalism", pp. 478–479.

supplies both the evidence we need for determining how to maximise desires and a practical method for doing so.

If I sell you a book for 20 dollars, one would assume that I prefer the 20 dollars to having the book, and you prefer the book to having the 20 dollars. If that were not the case, why would both of us go through with the transaction?[10] Since it is the case, the transaction has made us both better off (and society as a whole better off, if one defines better off as maximising the sum of happiness).

The market transaction is thus the paradigm of a transaction that increases the sum of happiness; phrasing it in a different way, one could also say that it is the paradigm of a just transaction—in the sense that neither party to the transaction would have any right to claim that it was unjust, given that both parties consented to it. Consent or autonomy is thus the other side of, or the other justification for, economic analysis.

When a transfer or other form of transaction leaves at least one person better off and no one worse off, the situation after the transfer or transaction is referred to in economic analysis as being "Pareto superior"[11] to the situation before. Economists also speak of situations as being "Pareto optimal" when no transfer or transaction is "Pareto superior" to the one in question. (Within the possible distribution of a certain set of goods, there may be—and usually is—more than one "Pareto optimal" situation. Thus "Pareto optimal" differs from the normal usage of "optimal" in that there is no implication that the situation described is "the (uniquely) best" among all possible (comparable) situations.)

---

[10] On the imperfect fit between choices, interests and consent in our lives, and the way such facts may undermine standard law and economics analysis, see Robin West, "Authority, Autonomy and Choice: The Role of Consent in the Moral and Political Visions of Franz Kafka and Richard Posner" (1985) 99 *Harvard Law Review* 384; see also Richard Posner, "The Ethical Significant of Free Choice: A Reply to Professor West" (1986) 99 *Harvard Law Review* 1431; Robin West, "Submission, Choice and Ethics: A Rejoinder to Judge Posner" (1986) 99 *Harvard Law Review* 1449.

[11] "Pareto superior" and "Pareto optimal" are named after the economist Vilfredo Pareto (1848–1923).

It is in this sense that Pareto analysis is sometimes compared with analyses derived from Kantian moral philosophy. Kantian moral philosophy, speaking in broad terms, emphasises autonomy and consent.[12] All participants would, by definition, consent to a transaction which left them either better off, or as well off as before. Therefore, a moral analysis based on autonomy and consent would approve of transactions that were Pareto superior. Exchanges in the free market appear to do well under both Pareto analysis and "wealth maximisation", as all voluntary market transactions lead to Pareto-superior states of affairs, almost by definition (at least if there are no negative consequences for third parties).[13]

However, in less abstract terms, if the transaction involved one person getting more of something, and everyone else having the same amount, those whose possessions had not increased might object to the transaction on the basis of equality (or its negative equivalent, envy).[14–15] Thus, in real world terms, it is difficult to find situations where at least one person is better off and everyone else is (in every sense of the word) no worse off than they were before.

Even in a looser construction of Pareto superiority, most governmental (legislative and judicial) actions would not qualify. In most government actions—awarding contracts, assessing legal liability, setting taxes and benefits, etc.—there are winners and losers. There are groups who, by any measure, are worse off than they were before the government action or decision. If governments could only act when no one was made worse off, there would be little that could be done.

---

[12] In their haste to compare economic analysis with Kantian analysis, most law and economics theorists do not stop to note how much narrower Kant's notion of autonomy was than the one they usually employ, *e.g.* Kant would not describe a choice or action caused by one's emotions as an autonomous action. For Kant, autonomous actions are those based on reason: see, *e.g.* John Kemp, *The Philosophy of Kant* (Bristol: Thoemme Press, 1993), pp. 56–69.

[13] See Richard Posner, "Utilitarianism, Economics, and Legal Theory" (1979) 8 *Journal of Legal Studies* 103 at 114.

[14–15] Lawrence Solum, "Constructing an Ideal of Public Reason" (1993) 30 *San Diego Law Review* 729 at 744.

A form of analysis called "Kaldor-Hicks"[16] or "potential Pareto-superior" is sometimes offered by economists that purports to justify government actions even when some parties are left worse off.[17] This analysis is a kind of wealth-maximisation claim, but with a Pareto twist. Pareto analysis, one recalls, does not speak of dollar amounts or the relative value of people's benefits: only to the hard fact (a fact not requiring any further normative evaluation) of preference, that a given party prefers one state of affairs to another. For a Kaldor-Hicks analysis, the question is whether the parties made better off could, if they chose, compensate the parties who were made worse off, and still be better off. For example, if a certain government decision increases the number of television sets I own, while reducing the number of books you own, I am made better off, and you worse off. Without making any value judgments about the relative worth of books and televisions (or the relative worth of desiring books and desiring televisions), one can still ask whether I would be able to compensate you (pay you money, or give you books) so that you would not feel worse off, and afterwards I would still be better off (that is, I am still happier with my situation: for example, if I still have at least one more television than I did prior to the government's action).

The point here is not that the winning parties *actually* compensate the losing parties; if they did, then the combination of the government decision and the compensation would be a fully Pareto-superior move. The point is that this compensation *could* be paid; and thus, there is a basis for concluding, without any apparent need for controversial comparisons of value, that the government's action was justified.

Much of law and economics analysis involves deciding which judicial or legislative decisions are justified under a Kaldor-Hicks analysis. It does not take much consideration, however, to realise that Kaldor-Hicks superiority may not be enough to persuade

---

[16] Named after the theorists who developed the analysis, Nicholas Kaldor (1907–1986) and J. R. Hicks (1904–1989); see Nicholas Kaldor, "Welfare Propositions of Economics and Interpersonal Comparisons of Utility" (1939) 49 *Economics Journal* 549; J. R. Hicks, "The Foundations of Welfare Economics" (1939) 49 *Economics Journal* 696. Hicks shared the 1972 Nobel Prize in economics with Kenneth Arrow.

[17] See generally George Fletcher, *The Basic Concepts of Legal Thought* (New York: Oxford University Press, 1996), pp. 158–162.

everyone: the losing parties in a decision may be little consoled by the fact that those better off *could have—but have not*—compensated them for their losses. How a Kaldor-Hicks approach might be justified, even with such problems, will be discussed later in the chapter. First, though, it is important to add into the mix the other central element of law and economics: the Coase theorem.

RONALD COASE

If a modified, "practical" version of utilitarianism is one part of the foundation of law and economics, the other part comes from the discussion by Ronald Coase (1910–) (who later won the Nobel Prize in economics, in part for his work in this area) on the interaction of the market and the distribution of legal rights.[18]

Coase's work was an attempt to correct what he saw as two flaws in other economists' work. The first problem was specific to the discussion of law and regulation. An economist named Arthur Pigou (1877–1959) had put forward an influential view that, to keep the economy efficient, businesses should be forced, by taxation, regulation or the operation of the tort system, to "internalise" the costs they impose on other activities ("externalities").[19]

Efficiency in the free market is an interaction of supply, demand and costs, leading to an equilibrium (even if a temporary one) at a particular level of supply and price. However, if the cost of making a product is somehow subsidised (most often, by the government), then this equilibrium will be distorted and the eventual result (not going through all the calculations here[20]) will be that more of the product will be produced than would have been the case in a true and fair market. Pigou's argument was based on the idea that the pollution an industry creates is a cost of that industry, and for that cost to be paid for by other people

---

[18] Ronald Coase, "The Problem of Social Cost" (1960) 3 *Journal of Law and Economics* 1, reprinted in Coase, *The Firm, the Market, and the Law* (Chicago: University of Chicago Press, 1988), pp. 95–156.

[19] See A.C. Pigou, *The Economics of Welfare* (4th ed., London: Macmillan and Co., 1932).

[20] For a more detailed discussion (including the type of graphs for which such analysis is known), see, *e.g.* Murphy and Coleman, *Philosophy of Law* (revised ed.), pp. 182–194.

(whether through the extra expense of cleaning clothes dirtied by polluted air or taxes paid so that the government can clean up polluted water) is to create a subsidy for that industry. Therefore, for the market to return to being true and fair, these externalities should be internalised—the industry should have to pay the equivalent of the costs its activity has imposed on others.

Coase, working within the same general framework of ideas —that the efficient distribution of goods depends on a free market where activities respond to prices and costs without the distortion of subsidies—argued that Pigou's approach was badly flawed. As Coase saw it, the source of the problem was Pigou's assumption, an assumption derived from or at least shared with the common law, that where two activities are in conflict (for example, a railway igniting the crops on farmland near the railroad lines), one of the parties is "imposing" costs on the other. That is, the assumption is that we can tell in advance which activity is "at fault".

Coase's contrary position was that where two activities are in conflict, the "costs" or "externalities" are the product of *the combination* of the two activities. It is not merely the case that, without the railway, there would be no fires in the farmer's crops; it is also the case that, if the farmer did not plant crops so close to the railroad tracks, there would similarly be no fires. This is "the reciprocity of causation". Coase writes:

> "In the case of cattle and the crops, it is true that there would be no crop damage without the cattle. It is equally true that there would be no crop damage without the crops. The doctor's work would not have been disturbed if the confectioner had not worked his machinery [in the nearby building]; but the machinery would have disturbed no one if the doctor had not set up his consulting room in that particular place. . . . If we are to discuss the problem in terms of causation, both parties cause the damage. If we are to attain an optimum allocation of resources, it is therefore desirable that both parties should take the harmful effect (the nuisance) into account in deciding on their course of action."[21]

---

[21] Coase, "The Problem of Social Cost" in *The Firm, The Market, and the Law,* p. 112.

The extent of which Coase proved his case[22] (or persuaded his audience) regarding the reciprocity of causation remains in contention.[23]

The second problem Coase addressed was a more general one among economists. Economic theories were often derived from simplified models of the way the world works. One such simplification was that there were no "transaction costs".[24] There is nothing wrong with simplifying assumptions as such. Without such assumptions, little progress might be made: the real world is so complex, with so many factors to take into account, that without simplifying assumptions it would be difficult to come to any conclusions at all. Simplified models of the world are standard, and not only in the social sciences (*e.g.* physics thought experiments often assume a world without friction). The trick is to figure out how one's conclusions may differ in the real world, where the simplified assumptions no longer hold. This was the nature of Coase's second criticism. Many economists had assumed a world without transaction costs, but had not given enough thought to how the real world might work differently, given that transaction costs are present and are pervasive.

---

[22] In Richard Epstein, "A Theory of Tort Liability" (1973) 2 *Journal of Legal Studies* 151 at 164–165, Epstein offers the following argument against the "reciprocity of causation": Coase's position assumes the existence of a (legal or moral) system under which remedies can be imposed on infringing parties. However, if we remove the available remedies, the harm caused is in one direction only, and it *does* make sense to make an initial assessment of blame (on one side) and right or priority (on the other), *e.g.* when cattle belonging to a neighbour eat grass from my fields, it is true that without my property claim to this field there would be no conflict, and it is also true that my bringing a trespass action against my neighbour will damage her. However, the initial situation is her cattle infringing on my land.

[23] After criticising Coase's argument about the reciprocity of causation, George Fletcher wrote: "The Pigovian theorem will continue to reign so long as the bench is staffed by lawyers rather than economists . . . Coase will never succeed in the courts, because his view of efficiency is incompatible with elementary principles of fairness": Fletcher, *The Basic Concepts of Legal Thought*, p. 167.

[24] Transaction costs are all the costs that parties might pay before a transaction that should occur ("should" occur in the sense that there is a willing buyer and a willing seller and a range of prices in which both would be willing to transact). These costs include "information costs" (how one finds out about the other party—newspaper advertisements, the costs of making inquiries among friends, etc.), negotiation costs, and costs of drawing up the contract, relevant sales taxes, etc.

As an initial point, Coase showed an interesting property of the world of the economists' model. In a world *without* transaction costs, contrary to what one might think, the initial distribution of legal rights would *not* affect which activities occur. Consider a simple situation, where a train going through a rural area gives off sparks which set fires in nearby crops. The initial entitlement may lie either with the railway or with the farmers: if with the farmers, then the farmers may be able to enjoin the running of the trains, or at least the railway will be liable to pay damages for any crops burned; if with the railway, then there will be no right of injunction or recovery.

Start with the assumption that the right lies with the farmers. If the benefit to the railway of running the trains is greater than the damage done to the crops, the railway will negotiate with the farmers and pay them (presumably the cost of the damage, or slightly more) for the right to give off the sparks, and the trains will run. On the other hand, if the benefit to the railway is lower than the cost of the damage, no such arrangement will come about, for the railway will not be willing to pay what the farmers ask to give up their right, and the trains will not run. Similarly if the right is initially with the railway: the farmers will pay the railway not to run its trains if (but only if) protecting their crops is worth more to them than running the trains is to the railway.

Even though this is an intermediate step in Coase's analysis, it is probably his best-known insight. The initial distribution of entitlements (legal rights) does not matter, because they will end up with whichever party values them the most. If the right not to have train sparks is initially with the farmers, but the right to give off such sparks is worth more to the railway, the railway, after paying off the farmers, will end up with the right. Thus, if the concern is "efficiency", government action, at least as a question of the initial distribution of entitlements, will be irrelevant; the total value of the conflicting activities will remain the same regardless of which party initially has the entitlement to constrain the other.[25] However, recall, this is only the case in the magical world of no transaction costs.

Less well known is the second part of Coase's analysis. While the initial distribution of entitlements is in many ways irrelevant in a

---

[25] See, *e.g.* Murphy and Coleman, *Philosophy of Law* (revised ed.), pp. 191–194.

world without transaction costs, the initial distribution *is* significant in a world *with* substantial transaction costs, and that is just the sort of world in which we live. Because of transaction costs, an entitlement (legal right) may not end up with the party who values it most, because the extra expense of the transaction costs may make it no longer worth purchasing from its original holder. For example, you hold a right to stop me from polluting a river. The right is worth $80 to you; having the right is worth $100 to me, but effecting an exchange of the right may cost $40. It would be more efficient for the entitlement to be with me (whether initially or by voluntary bargain), but if the right is initially given to you, it will stay with you because it is not worth it to me to pay both your asking price and the transaction costs (a total of $120, as against my valuation of the right at $100).

Coase's response is to suggest several responses to the problem of transaction costs: two ways to try to "raise the value of production" by reducing transaction costs—organisation of the competing activities as components within a single firm, and government regulation—and a third option, leaving things as they are (on the possibility that the administrative costs of a firm or government regulation would be as great or greater than the transaction costs in the market).[26] Coase's summing up on the matter is a cautious refusal to choose dogmatically: "[a]ll solutions have costs", and "problems of welfare economics must ultimately dissolve into a study of aesthetics and morals."[27] (He goes on to suggest further empirical investigation, to determine the relative advantages of handling the problem in different ways.[28])

This final step is where Coase and the law and economics movement diverge.[29] The law and economics response to the existence of significant transaction costs (which prevent market forces from redistributing rights to those that value them the most) is to state that the government (mostly, the judiciary) should act in ways which mimic what the free market would have done

---

[26] Coase, "The Problem of Social Cost" in *The Firm, The Market, and The Law*, pp. 114–119.

[27] *ibid.* pp. 118, 154.

[28] *ibid.* pp. 118–119.

[29] See generally Pierre Schlag, "An Appreciative Comment on Coase's *The Problem of Social Cost*: A View from the Left" (1986) *Wisconsin Law Review* 919 at 931–945.

had there been no transaction costs. Needless to say, there are many steps in the argument between: (1) in certain (ideal) circumstances, the market would redistribute rights in a certain way; and (2) in other (non-ideal) circumstances, the government should mimic the effects of the market. Unfortunately, the intermediate steps are rarely articulated by proponents of law and economics, at least usually not in a convincing way.[30]

ECONOMICS AND JUSTICE

The most influential figure in the law and economics movement is Richard Posner (1939–). In many of his earlier writings,[31] Posner argued that a theory of wealth maximisation served well both as an explanation of the past actions of the common law courts and as a theory of justice, justifying how judges and other officials should act. I will not focus here on the first (descriptive or "positive") claim,[32] looking instead primarily at the second (prescriptive or "normative") claim.

Under wealth maximisation, judges are to decide cases according to the principles which will maximise society's total wealth.[33] (Somewhat counter-intuitively, transferring an object from one owner to another, without more, even if the transfer was involuntary, can be said to increase social wealth, because wealth is measured by what someone has paid or would be willing to pay, and the second owner may be willing to pay more for the item than

---

[30] This is also to put aside the (epistemological) problem of whether it makes sense to speak of people, acting within a context with various transaction costs, knowing what redistributions would have occurred in a hypothetical world where none of those transaction costs existed.

For one account of how the argument from (1) to (2) in the text necessarily misfires, see Fletcher, *The Concepts of Legal Thought*, pp. 167–168.

[31] Posner has since pulled back from his more ambitious claims: see, *e.g.* Posner, *The Problems of Jurisprudence*, pp. 353–392; Posner, *Economic Analysis of Law* (4th ed., Boston: Little, Brown, 1992), pp. 25–27.

[32] On law and economics' positive claim, see, *e.g.* Posner, *The Problems of Jurisprudence*, pp. 353–374; William Landes and Richard Posner, *The Economic Structure of Tort Law* (Cambridge, Mass.: Harvard University Press, 1987) pp. 1–24; Dworkin, *A Matter of Principle*, pp. 263–266.

[33] "The 'wealth' in 'wealth maximization' refers to the sum of all tangible and intangible goods and services, weighted by prices of two sorts: offer prices (what people are willing to pay for goods they do not already own); and asking prices (what people demand to sell what they do own)": Posner, *The Problems of Jurisprudence*, p. 356.

the first owner was. However, Posner would say that a forced transfer would not usually be justified under wealth maximisation principles in such circumstances, because such transfers are only appropriate where high transaction costs make a consensual (market) bargain between the parties impossible, and thereby justify circumventing the market.[34])

On the normative claim, Posner argued that wealth maximisation was the best *compromise* between utility and autonomy, or that it successfully exemplified *both* utility and autonomy.[35] As discussed earlier in this chapter, one can see law and economics' advocacy of wealth maximisation as an attempt to construct a more practical version of utilitarianism. Welfare or happiness (two approximations of what is meant by "utility") are hard to discover or to measure, so judicial and legislative decisions will not be clearly guided by an instruction to "maximize utility".[36] Posner also argued that many conventional virtues (like the work ethic, telling the truth, and keeping promises) can be more easily derived from wealth maximisation than from utilitarianism.[37]

As to autonomy, a moral theory that strongly emphasises that value (Posner mentions Immanuel Kant's theory) might well require that citizens be coerced, or have their property redistributed, only if those citizens have authorised such actions by their choices, by actual consent. However, the problem with such an autonomy-based approach is that it would be unworkable if applied strictly to government decisions (for the same reason that its cognate, a Pareto-superior requirement, would be unworkable). Many government decisions affect a large number of people (not all of whom could even be identified in advance), and therefore requiring actual consent from every person affected would be

---

[34] Posner, "Utilitarianism, Economics, and Legal Theory", pp. 130–131; see also Posner, *The Economics of Justice*, pp. 108–109. A government-imposed (court-imposed) transfer is justified only in such cases because government officials can only imperfectly mimic the market in guessing how different parties value goods; where the market is able to operate without significant transaction costs, voluntary exchanges will naturally bring goods to the parties that value them most.

[35] See, *e.g.* Posner, *The Economics of Justice*, pp. 98, 115.

[36] See Posner, *The Economics of Justice*, pp. 112–113; Posner, "Utilitarianism, Economics, and Legal Theory", pp. 122, 129–130.

[37] See, *e.g.* Posner, "Utilitarianism, Economics, and Legal Theory", pp. 123–126.

clearly impossible.[38] (Similarly, if one put the focus of actual consent not on individual government decisions, but on the form and institutions of government or the mode of decision-making, obtaining actual consent from every person affected—that is, from every citizen—would clearly be impractical, if not impossible).

Wealth maximisation is better than utilitarianism, according to Posner, because money is easier to measure than utility. It is better than an autonomy-based approach because it allows government action even where actual consent by all affected would not be forthcoming or would be impractical.[39] However, the argument goes, because the only actions allowed would be those that maximised social wealth, everyone (or almost everyone) would have consented to this principle if asked, because it is a principle that leaves everyone (or almost everyone) better off.

This consent is not express consent, but a hypothetical or implied consent: what the people would have said had they been asked ahead of time. While someone who had been in an accident would not choose a liability system under which he or she would not recover, if that person were choosing at an earlier time, before the accident, before knowing whether he or she would be a tort plaintiff, a tort defendant or neither, it would be reasonable to choose a system that would increase total wealth (largely because he or she would have no reason for choosing a system with lower total wealth).[40]

There are a number of basic problems with Posner's attempts to equate justice with wealth maximisation[41]; there is only room in the present text to hint at some of them. Problems with Posner's discussion of consent were discussed in Chapter 12. In the paragraphs that follow, I will briefly discuss some other problems of Posner's theory of wealth maximisation with utility and autonomy.

---

[38] Posner, "The Ethical and Political Basis of the Efficiency Norm in Common Law Adjudication", p. 494.

[39] In Chap. 12, I briefly discussed Posner's analysis of consent in the context of the distinction between "will" and "reason".

[40] See Posner, *The Economics of Justice*, pp. 94–99. (I have excluded some of the details and nuances of Posner's analysis here due to limitations of space.)

[41] Posner recently made a partial retreat on the normative claim of wealth maximisation: "as a universal social norm wealth maximization is indeed unsatisfactory, but . . . it is attractive or at least defensible when confined to the common law arena": Posner, *The Problems of Jurisprudence*, p. 373.

In the section that follows, some more detailed substantive criticisms will be outlined.

In the attempt to create a synthesis of the best of utilitarianism and an autonomy-based approach, wealth maximisation arguably loses the benefits of either. The strong point of utilitarian theories is that it is difficult to argue with the position that pleasure and happiness are good, pain and unhappiness are bad, and in nearly every circumstance it is better if those goods can be maximised and the bad things minimised. The problem for utilitarian (and related) theories is to determine when the increased pleasure or happiness or welfare of a few—or even of the vast majority—can justify suffering and sacrifice by the remainder.

By contrast, it is more contestable to say that increasing wealth is always a moral good, and it will be harder to justify the sacrifice and suffering of some on the basis of the increased wealth of others. In the terms of moral philosophy, increased wealth is usually thought of as an instrumental good: it is valuable because it can help one obtain other things which are of intrinsic moral value, like health, physical comfort and recreation. The response may be that wealth is not offered as something good in itself, but only as a proxy for utility or other values.[42] However, while wealth maximisation may be the closest *workable* approximation of utilitarianism or an autonomy-based theorem, the approximation may break down in just the kind of hard cases where we would hope that our theories could give guidance.

THE LIMITS OF LAW AND ECONOMICS

Law and economics can be criticised in an internal way or in an external way. By an internal criticism, I mean one that accepts most of the approach's aims and assumptions; by contrast, external criticisms challenge law and economics at those basic levels.

An example of a recent sharp internal criticism was offered by Jon Hanson and Melissa Hart.[43] Hanson and Hart state that the

---

[42] See, *e.g.* Posner, "Utilitarianism, Economics, and Legal Theory", pp. 121–127; Posner, *The Economics of Justice*, pp. 112–113.

[43] Jon Hanson and Melissa Hart, "Law and Economics" in *A Companion to the Philosophy of Law and Legal Theory* (forthcoming, D. Patterson ed., Oxford: Basil Blackwell, 1996).

argument that certain rules will increase efficiency (in other words, maximise social wealth) usually depends on a series of assumptions. These include assumptions regarding transaction costs, activity levels, administrative costs, risk neutrality of the parties and the parties' legal knowledge, as well as the ability of a judge to make accurate assessments of the costs and benefits (to the parties) of alternative actions. Hart and Hanson argue that the model on which law and economics operates tends to make unrealistic assumptions or to assume fixed values on variables that will in fact vary greatly (in unpredictable and hard-to-measure ways) between parties. For example, Hart and Hanson wrote the following about "activity levels" (pointing out that accident costs are a function not only of the level of care, but also of the level of activity):

"To deter all accidents that could be cost-justified prevented, judges and juries would need to compare the benefits a party obtains from greater participation in the activity to the resulting increase in expected accident costs. Unfortunately, courts tend to ignore activity level considerations, and most scholars believe that, as a practical matter, courts are *unable* to conduct the necessary activity-level calculus, because of the amount of information they would need."[44]

As noted when talking about Coase's theorem, the fact that an analysis incorporates simplifying assumptions is not fatal; however, Hanson and Hart argue that when one tries to adjust the outcomes of this model's calculations and predictions by taking into account how things actually are, the prediction of efficiency is either directly undermined or left in such doubt that one has serious questions about using the model as a justification for changing (or not changing) the law.[45]

One "external" criticism of law and economics is that it is a reductive system, an approach to law and to life that attempts to analyse everything in terms of a single parameter (money, wealth,

---

[44] *ibid.* (citation omitted).,
[45] Arthur Leff made a similar point in more colourful language: "If a state of affairs is the product of *n* variables, and you have knowledge of or control over less than *n* variables, if you think you know what's going to happen when you vary 'your' variables, you're a booby": Leff, "Economic Analysis of Law: Some Realism About Nominalism", p. 476.

willingness to pay). This criticism is an analysis in terms of "commensurability". As explicated by Martha Nussbaum, commensurability regards "all the valuable things under consideration as measurable on a single scale".[46] The inevitable results of such reductions are distortions in both one's descriptions and one's prescriptions.

Beyond some fairly straightforward difficulties with translating all matters into willingness to pay (first, the things we value the most we often speak of things on which "one cannot put a price"[47]; and secondly, sometimes willingness to pay is a function merely of ability to pay, and may have little to do with how highly one values something), there remains the even more basic objection that any attempt to reduce human decisions and actions to a single variable is going to distort them beyond recognition. John Finnis[48] gave examples of the way law and economics did not (because, in Finnis' view, it cannot) draw distinctions between accidental (negligent) behaviour and intentional misdeeds (both foreseeable but unintended accidents and intentional injuries appear in one of Posner's analyses simply as costs ascribable to the party or activity),[49] distinctions which seem both basic and crucial to our moral view of the world.[50]

There are a variety of other "external" criticisms in the literature; for example:

---

[46] Martha Nussbaum, *Poetic Justice* (Boston: Beacon Press, 1995), p. 14. She adds that those who believe that values are commensurable must believe either that "all the valuable things are valuable because they contain some one thing that itself varies only in quantity . . . or [that] despite the plurality of values, there is an argument that shows that a single metric adequately captures what is valuable in them all": *ibid.*

[47] Margaret Radin, "Market-Inalienability" (1987) 100 *Harvard Law Review* 1849.

[48] John Finnis, "Allocating Risks and Suffering: Some Hidden Traps" (1990) 38 *Cleveland State Law Review* 193 at 200–205.

[49] A contrary view, defending the ability of law and economics to draw appropriate distinctions between accidental and intentional action, might be derived from the discussion of intentional wrongdoing in Landes and Posner, *The Economic Structure of Tort Law,* pp. 149–160.

[50] Arthur Leff discussed the way that the reductive analysis in law and economics eradicates psychological and sociological factors (as to the latter, race and class are obvious examples) which are crucial to a proper understanding of modern behaviour: Leff, "Economic Analysis of Law: Some Realism About Nominalism", pp. 469–477.

(1) that wealth should not be maximised because wealth is neither a true value (that is something valued for itself) nor something that is a good stand-in for things we do or should value[51];

(2) that economic analysis has inherent biases towards the rich over the poor, producers over consumers, and the status quo over reform[52];

(3) that the legal way of looking at language and the world is different from the economic way of looking at it, and the law (and this society) would be worse off to the extent that the economic outlook is allowed to take over law[53]; and

(4) that the objectives of efficiency or wealth maximisation are irrelevant to and often incompatible with corrective justice, which is at the essence of, and the only proper objective for, private law.[54]

Even if one accepts (some or all of) the above criticisms as valid and important (and, of course, not everyone does), there still remains much that is of value to economic analysis in the law.

First, there are legal questions that turn (or should turn) on purely economic matters: for example, for the purposes of competition (antitrust) law, whether a particular kind of vertical or horizontal integration of companies supports, hinders or has no effect upon competition in the long term.

Secondly, economic analysis has often served to sharpen the existing, somewhat fuzzy legal thinking in various areas. For some, economics analysis captures in quantitative terms what had only been vaguely described by long-standing common law concepts like "reasonable care", "negligence" and "proximate cause". Also, economic analysis occasionally highlights concerns that had become lost when the questions were posed in traditional ways, in terms of "fairness" and "justice": for example, in considering the

---

[51] See Dworkin, *A Matter of Principle*, pp. 237–266; for Posner's reply, see Posner, *The Economics of Justice*, pp. 107–115.

[52] See, *e.g.* Kelman, *A Guide to Critical Legal Studies*, pp. 151–185; Morton Horwitz, "Law and Economics: Science or Politics?" (1981) 8 *Hofstra Law Review* 905.

[53] See James Boyd White, "Economics and Law: Two Cultures in Tension" (1987) 54 *Tennessee Law Review* 161.

[54] See Weinrib, *The Idea of Private Law*.

rules of bankruptcy/insolvency law, the way legal rules are developed will affect not only the creditors' rights as against the debtor (the traditional focus for analysis), but also the extent to which individual creditors have incentives to act in ways which will shrink the total amount of assets available, thus working against the interests of the creditors as a group (and perhaps against the social interest as well).[55]

Thirdly, even if one believes that efficiency or wealth maximisation is at best one value among many (or an imperfect approximation of one such value), one would still want to know what effects a current legal rule or practice, or a proposed change to a rule or practice, has on efficiency or wealth maximisation.[56] At the least, there are occasions when an accurate (and subtle) delineation of the costs of the alternative rules or actions will influence the eventual (moral) choice between them.[57] This may also be the place to note Posner's argument that while wealth maximisation may be but one of many desirable goals, it is the one that judges are best placed to promote (by contrast, Posner believes that judges are poorly placed to redistribute wealth, on occasions where that would be desirable).[58]

Fourthly, the method of analysis that law and economics promotes reminds us of long-term effects we might not otherwise have considered.[59] A standard example is the landlord who wants to evict the poor, starving tenant for non-payment of rent. While our sympathies may go immediately to the tenant, we should consider the long-term consequences of a rule where the landlord could not evict in such circumstances. What would likely ensue is that landlords would either become reluctant to lease apartments to those who are less well off, or that higher rents would be charged to everyone, to compensate for losses to non-paying tenants who

---

[55] See Posner, *Economic Analysis of Law*, pp. 400–402. I am indebted to Stephen Gilles for this example.

[56] *e.g.* Posner, "Utilitarianism, Economics, and Legal Theory", pp. 109–110.

[57] *e.g. ibid.* p. 109.

[58] See Posner, *The Economics of Justice*, pp. 103–106; Posner, *The Problems of Jurisprudence*, pp. 372–373.

[59] See, *e.g.* Leff, "Economic Analysis of Law: Some Realism About Nominalism", pp. 459–462.

cannot be evicted.[60] Therefore, while the short-term result of ruling for the tenant may be that one impoverished tenant keeps his or her apartment, the long-term effect may be that many other impoverished tenants cannot find (affordable) apartments to rent.

Fifthly, the other analytical move that economic thinking reinforces, sometimes to a fault, is that a person's preferences can be derived from his or her actions, and the (relative) intensity of those preferences can often be derived by asking how much he or she is willing to pay (in currency, or in giving up other things of value) for the items in question. It is hardly a new discovery that a person's statements, and even his or her conscious beliefs, can be belied by his or her actions; however, it is a matter that is too often and too easily forgotten. On the other hand, when one looks *only* to actions and willingness to pay to determine a person's preferences, the analysis can be equally erroneous: especially when the analysis ignores that some things we have, not because we have chosen them (or want them), but because they are the unavoidable side-effects of things we do desire (the international traveller does not desire jet lag, but accepts it as a consequence of getting to the desired place),[61] and that unwillingness to pay a large sum may simply be a function of the inability to pay that amount.

OTHER DIRECTIONS

In recent years, there have been a variety of articles which are clearly descended from or related to the tradition of law and economics (at least in the sense that they share economics' basic assumptions, mentioned at the beginning of the chapter, that "people are rational maximizers of their satisfactions"), but which take a somewhat different perspective. Among these approaches have been public choice theory and game theory.

---

[60] See, *e.g.* Posner, "The Ethical and Political Basis of the Efficiency Norm in Common Law Adjudication", p. 500; Leff, "Economic Analysis of Law: Some Realism About Nominalism", pp. 459–461. A third possibility is that landlords will put clauses into the leases requiring the tenants to waive their rights under the new ruling. If such clauses are later held to be unenforceable (as sometimes occurs with waiver clauses of this type), then the landlords will likely return to one of the other two strategies outlined in the text.

[61] See Finnis, "Allocating Risks and Suffering: Some Hidden Traps", p. 201.

Game theory is (roughly speaking) the creation of models of "situations in which two or more players have a choice of decisions (strategies), where the outcome depends on all the strategies and where each player has a set of preferences defined over the outcomes."[62] Writers have used game theory to consider how legal rules affect people's strategic behaviour, and to try to construct arguments that current legal rules are or are not successful in meeting their proclaimed or assumed purposes (*e.g.* preventing fraud or encouraging an efficient level of accident prevention measures).[63]

A second later development in the law and economics movement is the application of "public choice theory" to law and legal theory. Roughly speaking, public choice theory is the application of certain standard economic models and assumptions to (various aspects of) governmental action.[64] (In 1986, the Nobel Prize in economics went to James Buchanan for his work on public choice theory.) Again in rough terms, public choice theorists try to see how much of official action can be explained—and predicted—on the basis that the officials (legislators, judges, administrators, and so on) are acting to further their individual interests. (Theorists within the tradition vary in how they define self-interest: some in a narrow way, as purely a matter of money or power; others trying to build a more subtle view of self-interest into their model, which, for example, incorporates the officials' ideological beliefs.) The general line of argument is that if legislators are more accurately seen as acting in their narrow self-interests when they legislate, rather than acting "for the public good", there may be reasons to change various aspects of the legal system (for example, the courts might be less deferential in considering legislation, or they might vary the way they approach interpreting ambiguous statutes[65]). Also, this may be an argument for restructuring the way legislatures or administrative agencies work, in an attempt to curb or channel the influence of interest groups on officials.[66]

---

[62] Blackburn, *The Oxford Dictionary of Philosophy*, p. 153.
[63] See generally Douglas Baird, Robert Gertner and Randal Picker, *Game Theory and the Law* (Cambridge, Mass.: Harvard University Press, 1994).
[64] See, *e.g.* Daniel Farber and Philip Frickey, *Law and Public Choice* (Chicago: University of Chicago Press, 1991), Introduction.
[65] See, *e.g. ibid.* pp. 61–115.
[66] See, *e.g. ibid.* pp. 12–37.

Chapter Nineteen

Modern Critical Perspectives

In the last 20 years or so, a series of loosely related critical approaches to law have developed, which have their roots in (among other places) the Civil Rights Movement, American legal realism and European social theory.

In many cases, the advocates placed under a single label—"critical legal studies", "feminist legal theory" or "critical race theory" —share only that (the label), and a certain distance (on some matters) from mainstream legal theory. The point is that, on almost any substantive issue or question of methodology, there will be as much variation or disagreement within those groups as there will be between those groups and other theorists. Nonetheless, these are the categories by which these theories are known and characterised by others—and, to a great extent, this is how they characterise themselves as well. In this chapter, I will offer an overview of some of the themes identified with each of the three critical approaches to the law.

CRITICAL LEGAL STUDIES

The critical legal studies movement is the name given to a group of scholars who wrote about legal theory using ideas associated with Leftist politics or trying to use law (or legal education or writings about the law) to try to effect Leftist results.

Critical legal studies (hereinafter CLS), as a self-defined group, became active in the late 1970s.[1] The vast majority of work being

---

[1] The story of the emergence of the critical legal studies movement is summarised in Duxbury, *Patterns of American Jurisprudence*, pp. 428–509.

done under that label has been done by American scholars, but there are also followers in other countries.[2] While today there are still a number of people who identify themselves with that label, much of the movement's energy has appeared to have been passed on to the affiliated, but narrower, schools of thought, feminist legal theory and critical race theory, about which more later.

CLS theorists saw themselves as extending and elaborating the more radical aspects of the American legal realists' program. Among the more common themes in CLS writing are the following: the political nature of law (the ideological biases inherent in apparently neutral concepts and analyses)—"law as ideology",[3] the radical indeterminacy of the law,[4] the claim that law promotes the interests of the powerful and legitimates injustice[5] and the argument that rights rhetoric works against the common good and against the interests of the groups the rights purport to protect.[6] Among other topics visited by adherents of CLS are the ideological implications of modern legal education,[7] criticisms of the law and economics movement[8] and the uses of radical theory in rethinking radical legal practice.[9] (CLS was also known for, and to some extent known by, its attempt to apply to law the ideas of European literary theorists, social theorists and philosophers.[10]) Obviously, these topics cannot be covered in detail in the short space available; I can only touch on some aspects of a few of them.

---

[2] See, *e.g.* Peter Fitzpatrick and Alan Hunt, *Critical Legal Studies* (Oxford: Blackwell, 1987) (British CLS writers).

[3] See, *e.g.* Lewis Kornhauser, "The Great Image of Authority" (1984) 36 *Stanford Law Review* 349 at 371–387.

[4] See, *e.g.* Duncan Kennedy, "Freedom and Constraint in Adjudication: A Critical Phenomenology" (1986) 36 *Journal of Legal Education* 518.

[5] See, *e.g.* Douglas Hay, Peter Linebaugh, John Rule, E.P. Thompson and Cal Winslow, *Albion's Fatal Tree* (Middlesex, England: Penguin, 1975).

[6] See, *e.g.* Mark Tushnet, "An Essay on Rights" (1984) 62 *Texas Law Review* 1363.

[7] See, *e.g.* Duncan Kennedy, "Legal Education as Training for Hierarchy" in *The Politics of Law* (revised ed., D. Kairys ed., New York: Pantheon, 1990), pp. 38–58.

[8] See, *e.g.* Kelman, *A Guide to Critical Legal Studies*, pp. 114–185.

[9] See, *e.g.* Peter Gabel and Paul Harris, "Building Power and Breaking Images: Critical Legal Theory and the Practice of Law" (1982–83) 11 *New York University Review of Law and Social Change* 369.

[10] Among the thinkers most often discussed or cited are Jacques Derrida, Michel Foucault, Antonio Gramsci, Jürgen Habermas, Ludwig Wittgenstein, Karl Marx and Jacques Lacan.

On the indeterminacy of law, CLS theorists have offered a variety of views as to what they mean by "indeterminacy", what its causes allegedly are and what consequences follow. James Boyle offered the following as a paraphrase of "the strongest version of the indeterminacy thesis ever put forward by anyone associated with CLS":

"Nothing internal to language compels a particular result. In every case the judge *could* produce a wide range of decisions which were formally correct under the canons of legal reasoning. Of course, shared meanings, community expectations, professional customs and so on may make a particular decision seem inevitable (though that happens less than many people think). But even in those cases, it is not the words of the rule that produce the decision, but instead a bevy of factors whose most marked feature is that they are anything but universal, rational or objective. Legal rules are supposed not only to be determinate (after all, decisions based on race prejudice are perfectly determinate), but to produce determinacy through a particular method of interpretation. That method of interpretation alone, however, produces indeterminate results and it cannot be supplemented sufficiently to produce definite results without subverting its supposed qualities of objectivity and political and moral neutrality."[11]

On legal history, CLS theorists have sometimes pointed out the way that apparently neutral rules actually work to the benefit of the powerful. However, the more common theme is the contingency of legal rules and concepts: the way that the rules could have developed other than the way they did. Similarly, the argument goes, the legal rules and concepts as they are now should not be treated as natural or inevitable, but as contingent and subject to change.[12]

An example of CLS's attack on the apparent neutrality of legal

---

[11] James Boyle, "Introduction" in *Critical Legal Studies* (J. Boyle ed., New York: New York University Press, 1994), p. xx.

[12] Among the best known CLS works on legal history are Morton Horwitz, *The Transformation of American Law 1780–1860* (Cambridge, Mass.: Harvard University Press, 1977); Hay, Linebaugh, Rule, Thompson and Winslow, *Albion's Fatal Tree*; and Robert Gordon, "Critical Legal Histories" (1984) 36 *Stanford Law Review* 57.

concepts has been the attack on the public/private distinction.[13] The argument runs roughly as follows: both within and outside the legal system, a great deal is made of the difference between matters which fall within the "public" realm (and thus are properly subject to significant government control) and matters with the "private" realm (a haven from government intrusion). However, coercion and oppression also occur in the "private" realm: in the family, in domestic violence and abuse, and in private economic ordering, where the economically powerful can set oppressive terms for the economically powerless. The distinction between public and private is thus undermined: the private realm is not a haven from the coercion of the public realm. It is the government's refusal to act to protect the weak in "private matters" (domestic relations and contracts) that allows and legitimates the oppression that occurs. Also, CLS theorists, like some of the legal realists, emphasise the extent to which the rules of private law are no more "natural" or "inevitable" than the rules of public law, and no less a product of official policy.[14]

It is hard to be more definitive about what CLS stood for, as the theorists who considered themselves part of the movement (or were considered part of the movement by others) did not all take the same position on issues. It is not merely that different theorists emphasised different issues, but on any given issue—for example, the value of the "rule of law",[15] the value of rights rhetoric and whether law serves the interests of the powerful—different CLS theorists would be on different sides.

As there has been a large number of writers within CLS presenting a variety of views on a wide range of topics, there has

---

[13] See, *e.g.* Frances Olsen, "The Family and the Market: A Study of Ideology and Legal Reform" (1983) 96 *Harvard Law Review* 1497; Morton Horwitz, "The History of the Public/Private Distinction" (1982) 130 *University of Pennsylvania Law Review* 1423. A good rebuttal to the realist/CLS attack on the public/private distinction can be found in Leiter, "Legal Realism".

[14] The legal realist articles on the subject include Robert Hale, "Coercion and Distribution in a Supposedly Non-Coercive State" (1923) 38 *Political Science Quarterly* 470; and Morris Cohen, "Property and Sovereignty" (1927) 13 *Cornell Law Quarterly* 8.

[15] See, *e.g.* Morton Horwitz, "The Rule of Law: An Unqualified Human Good?" (1977) 86 *Yale Law Journal* 561 (arguing against E.P. Thompson's view that the rule of law is always an unqualified good).

been a comparably wide array of critics and topics for criticism. A brief sample of citations is offered in a footnote.[16]

OUTSIDER JURISPRUDENCE

Two approaches to law, feminist legal theory and critical race theory, are combined here under the label "outsider jurisprudence"[17] because, although each could be discussed in detail separately, they can both be seen as emanating from the same core problem: the extent to which the law reflects the perspective of and the values of white males, and the resulting effects on citizens and on members of the legal profession who are not white males.[18]

The problem about bias can be summarised by the following, from an article in a symposium on critical race theory:

"Long ago, empowered actors and speakers enshrined their meanings, preferences, and views of the world into the common culture and language. Now their deliberation within that language, purporting always to be neutral and fair, inexorably produces results that reflect their interests."[19]

The question of difference can be taken in steps:

---

[16] See, *e.g.* Andrew Altman, *Critical Legal Studies: A Liberal Critique* (Princeton, Princeton University Press, 1990); John Finnis, "On 'The Critical Legal Studies Movement' " (1985) 30 *American Journal of Jurisprudence* 21, reprinted in *Oxford Essays in Jurisprudence, Third Series* (J. Eekelaar and J. Bell eds., Oxford: Clarendon Press, 1987), pp. 145–165; Neil MacCormick, "Reconstruction after Deconstruction: A Response to CLS" (1990) 10 *Oxford Journal of Legal Studies* 539; Lawrence Solum, "On the Indeterminacy Crisis: Critiquing Critical Dogma" (1987) 54 *University of Chicago Law Review* 462.

[17] I take the title from Mari Matsuda, "Public Response to Racist Speech: Considering the Victim's Story" (1989) 87 *Michigan Law Review* 2320 at 2323 and n. 15, and Mary Coombs, "Outsider Scholarship: The Law Review Stories" (1992) 63 *University of Colorado Law Review* 683 at 683–684.

[18] See Scott Brewer, "Introduction: Choosing Sides in the Racial Critiques Debate" (1990) 103 *Harvard Law Review* 1844 at 1850–1851 ("Moral Visions of Racial Distinctiveness"); Scott Brewer, "Pragmatism, Oppression, and the Flight to Substance" (1990) 63 *Southern California Law Review* 1753. See generally Martha Minow, *Making All the Difference* (Ithaca, N.Y.: Cornell University Press, 1990).

[19] Richard Delgado and Jean Stefancic, "Hateful Speech, Loving Communities: Why Our Notion of 'A Just Balance' Changes So Slowly" (1994) 82 *California Law Review* 851 at 861.

(1)   Is the difference between the majority or powerful group and the minority or powerless group(s) simply a reflection of the years of oppression, or are the differences inherent?

(2)   If there are inherent differences, how (if at all) should the law reflect or respond to these differences?

It is more common in feminist legal theory than in critical race theory to find writers who suggest that there are inherent differences between the powerful and the powerless: here, that women are different from men, and should be treated differently.

Among the problems that are common in outsider jurisprudence are those that develop from the fact that one is trying to create equality, justice, or reform in or through the legal system, against a societal background in which inequality, discrimination or oppression are still common, if not pervasive. This leads to standard types of dilemmas in proposing reform: is it better to enforce a regime of strict facial neutrality, which might have the effect of merely reinforcing existing social inequalities; or is it better to advocate forms of special treatment, which might help in the short term, but could have the long-term effect of reinforcing the view that the group receiving the special treatment is weak or inferior?

Finally, one might note that outsider jurisprudence, along with CLS, is directly concerned with justice in a way that most of the other approaches to law discussed in this book are not.[20] The argument in all three approaches is basically that the law is unjust because it is systematically distorted or biased (towards men, whites and/or the rich and powerful). However, while the arguments in these areas are often couched in terms of fairness and justice, a full theory of justice or of the common good is rarely articulated.[21]

---

[20] I am grateful to Jack Balkin for pointing this out.

[21] In Jack Balkin, "Transcendental Deconstruction, Transcendent Justice" (1994) 92 *Michigan Law Review* 1131, Balkin argued that the analytical moves and moral claims supported by deconstruction theory undermine any attempt to construct a theory of justice. In conversation, Balkin has argued that a similar critique could be made of outsider jurisprudence.

A way in which outsider jurisprudence differs from most other approaches to law (including CLS) is the regular focus on proposals for reforms (ways of changing the law through legislation or judicial action) which would remove what were perceived to be injustices in the legal system or in society. One example that will be discussed in some detail later in the chapter is a feminist proposal to change the legal treatment of sexually explicit material. This greater focus on reforming the law also indicates further connections with the realists, some of whom had worked hard to reform the law in line with their ideas about how the law should operate.[22]

FEMINIST LEGAL THEORY

Feminist analyses have offered important critiques in a variety of contexts, from broad political analyses of cultural theories to analyses specific to particular academic disciplines. Though certain themes are common to most of what carries the label "feminist"—in particular, a belief that either theory or practice has been distorted towards the perspective or the interests of men—there is a great deal of variety, even within a single discipline, among those writers who call themselves "feminists"—and here, feminists legal theory is no exception. However, to the extent that one can speak of these writers (and these texts) as a group, their impact has been significant in the United States, and is growing in other countries.[23]

As discussed in the above overview of "outsider jurisprudence", part of feminist legal theory is the analysis of the extent to which the legal system reflects and reinforces a male perspective, and

---

[22] See, *e.g.* Zipporah Wiseman, "The Limits of Vision: Karl Llewellyn and the Merchant Rules" (1987) 100 *Harvard Law Review* 465 (on the connection between realist thought and the Uniform Commercial Code).

[23] One sympathetic critic recently wrote: "To a growing extent, a jurisprudence with very little to add about the concerns and innovations of feminism will not have very much interesting to add, period": Matthew Kramer, *Critical Legal Theory and the Challenge of Feminism* (London: Rowman & Littlefield, 1995), p. 265.

part is (the related) analysis of how women's differences from men should or should not be reflected in legal rules, legal institutions and legal education.

Regarding the first aspect, Patricia Smith has argued that what feminist legal theories have in common is an opposition to the patriarchal ideas that dominate society in general and (relevant to feminist legal theory) the legal system in particular.[24] The differences among feminist legal theorists are then seen as reflecting differences in emphasis or perspective in describing the many aspects and effects of patriarchy, differences in which problems to focus upon and differences in strategy for overcoming the problem of patriarchy (for example, those who believe in moderate reforms as against those who believe that only radical restructuring of society will suffice).[25]

As to the second aspect, one could argue that what is common to feminist legal theories is that they are divergent responses to the inherent or socially constructed differences between men and women, responses regarding what these differences should mean about the way we think about law. One feminist response to difference is:

(1)   *there are* intrinsic differences between men and women;

(2)   society and law are organized around a male standard and a male norm, a situation which works both in the short term and in the long term against the interests of women; and

(3)   society and law should therefore be reformed to remove that bias, and to reflect women's experiences as well as men's.

The differences between men and women which are emphasised include differences in values, ways of seeing the world, responding

---

[24] Patricia Smith, "Feminist Jurisprudence and the Nature of Law" in *A Companion to the Philosophy of Law and Legal Theory* (forthcoming, D. Patterson ed., Oxford: Basil Blackwell, 1996).

[25] See *ibid.*

to other people,[26] responding to problems, ways of speaking[27] and so on.

A second feminist response to difference is that there are no (significant) inherent differences between men and women, and that any aspect of the law which assumes the contrary should be changed. This position often includes the view that what differences appear between men and women are the effect of contingent social or cultural forces.

Feminist approaches and perspectives have been applied to a wide variety of topics and issues. Among these are abortion rights,[28] rape law,[29] sexual harassment,[30] surrogate motherhood,[31] pregnancy and maternity leave[32] and (perhaps most controversially) pornography.[33] Although the arguments necessarily vary from article to article and from author to author, the most common theme is that the current law or current approach in these areas exemplifies a male bias or works to the detriment of women as a group.

I will briefly discuss one of the better-known topics within feminist legal theory, the MacKinnon-Dworkin proposed legislation on sexually explicit material, to give some sense of the complexity and difficulty of the issues raised. (I make no claim that this topic is "representative" of the issues raised by feminist theorists; I do not think any issue would be. The issues raised within feminist legal theory are so broad in range and have such

---

[26] Carol Gilligan's work in some ways exemplifies all three: see Carol Gilligan, *In a Different Voice* (Cambridge, Mass.: Harvard University Press, 1982).

[27] See, *e.g.* Deborah Tannen, *You Just Don't Understand* (New York: William Morrow, 1990).

[28] See, *e.g.* Catherine MacKinnon, *Feminism Unmodified* (Cambridge, Mass.: Harvard University Press, 1987), pp. 93–102; Anita Allen, "The Proposed Equal Protection Fix for Abortion Law: Reflections on Citizenship, Gender, and the Constitution" (1995) 18 *Harvard Journal of Law and Public Policy* 419.

[29] See, *e.g.* Panel Discussion, "Men, Women and Rape" (1994) 63 *Fordham Law Review* 125.

[30] See, *e.g.* Catharine MacKinnon, *Sexual Harassment of Working Women* (New Haven: Yale University Press, 1979).

[31] See, *e.g.* Martha Field, "Surrogacy Contracts: Gestational and Traditional: The Argument for Nonenforcement" (1991) 31 *Washburn Law Review* 3.

[32] See, *e.g.* Minow, *Making All the Difference*, pp. 56–60; Herma Hill Kay, "Equality and Difference: The Case of Pregnancy" (1985) 1 *Berkeley Women's Law Journal* 1.

[33] See, *e.g.* MacKinnon, *Feminism Unmodified*, pp. 127–213.

different contours that any search for a "representative" issue would be doomed to failure.)

Catharine MacKinnon (1946–) and Andrea Dworkin (1946–) drafted a model civil rights ordinance to combat certain kinds of sexually explicit speech.[34] Under the ordinance, anyone who had suffered directly or indirectly because of pornography[35] could sue for damages. This model ordinance was proposed (in slightly different forms) in a number of cities and passed in two, but declared void because unconstitutional in both cases.[36]

In the words of one of the authors, "Pornography, in the feminist view, is a form of forced sex, a practice of sexual politics, an institution of gender inequality."[37] The argument is that what is at the core of (the vast majority of) pornographic material is a portrayal of women as subordinate to men, and women as enjoying their subordinate position.[38] Pornography thus has effects beyond questions about whether it should be restricted because it is "immoral" (immoral because sexually explicit). Under the MacKinnon–Dworkin view, pornography works to silence women by reinforcing the subordination of women and the perception by men that women enjoy that subordination.[39]

In the MacKinnon–Dworkin proposal, "pornography" was defined as the "graphic sexually explicit subordination of women" through pictures or words which portray women as enjoying humiliation, pain, or being the victims of rape or other violence. (The constitutional ground for invalidating the ordinance was that under the right of free expression, the government could not

---

[34] Catharine MacKinnon and Andrea Dworkin (no relation to the Ronald Dworkin of Chap. 9) are also well known for their views on heterosexual sex in general, though these views are often misunderstood or mischaracterised. For a sympathetic and subtle summary and analysis of MacKinnon's views on the matter, see Frances Olsen, "Feminist Theory in Grand Style" (book review) (1989) 89 *Columbia Law Review* 1147 at 1154–1160.

[35] Among the categories of injuries listed were "coercion into pornography", "forcing pornography on a person", "assault or physical attack due to pornography", and "defamation through pornography".

[36] See Mary Becker, Cynthia Grant Bowman and Morrison Torrey, *Feminist Jurisprudence: Taking Women Seriously* (St. Paul, Minn.: West Publishing, 1994), pp. 321–322. Portions of MacKinnon and Dworkin's model ordinance are reprinted on pp. 321–324 of that text.

[37] MacKinnon, *Feminism Unmodified*, p. 148.

[38] See, *e.g. ibid.* pp. 148, 160 and 172.

[39] See, *e.g. ibid.* pp. 146–213.

distinguish between material on the basis of viewpoint; thus, a statute that subjects to civil liability sexually explicit material that implies that women enjoy their subordinate position but not similar material that portrays women as not enjoying such treatment was considered an improper government intrusion on freedom of expression.[40])

One sympathetic commentator summarised this analysis as follows, placing the anti-pornography proposal into a context of a more general feminist analysis:

> "MacKinnon argues that men expropriate women's sexuality, that pornography increases the sexual appeal of the subordination of women, and that the subordination of women creates what we perceive and experience as gender differences. She argues that pornography is central to women's subordination, that it makes the subordination of women sexy and constantly reinforces and eroticizes the domination–subordination dynamic. The point of regulating pornography is not to make life a little less pleasant, but it is a step toward a fundamental transformation of the relations between men and women."[41]

It is important to note that on this issue, as on many of the more controversial topics, there have been feminist theorists on both sides of the issue: in the present case, opposing the MacKinnon–Dworkin proposal, and related restrictions on sexually explicit speech, as well as supporting such restrictions.[42] Those opposing the restrictions on pornography offer a variety of arguments, including the claims that pornography helps to undermine conventional sexual morality which oppresses or confines women; that any government regulation would inevitably affect "good" or "liberating" pornography as much as if not more than "bad" or "oppressive" pornography; and that some women enjoy creating or "consuming" pornography, even types of pornography

---

[40] *American Booksellers Assoc., Inc. v. Hudnut*, 771 F. 2d 323 (7th Cir. 1985), *affirmed mem.*, 475 U.S. 1001 (1986).

[41] Olsen, "Feminist Theory in Grand Style", p. 1160 (footnote and page references omitted).

[42] For views opposing restrictions on sexually explicit speech, see, *e.g.* Varda Burstyn ed., *Women Against Censorship* (Vancouver: Douglas & McIntyre, Ltd, 1985); Wendy McElroy, *XXX: A Woman's Right to Pornography* (New York: St Martin's Press, 1995).

that quite expressly show women enjoying pain or subordination (such as sado-masochistic pornography).[43]

Some of the debate for and against proposals like MacKinnon–Dworkin's turned on questions about autonomy and "false consciousness".[44] To the argument by some women that they actually enjoy making or reading the type of sexually explicit material that the MacKinnon–Dworkin ordinance would restrict, a common response is that these women's perceptions of enjoyment are themselves the product of the pervasively oppressive society in which they were brought up (the argument being that women, like slaves generations earlier, find what pleasure they can, and what meaning they can, within their situations, and may even convince themselves that they have chosen their path voluntarily).[45] About here is where one enters troubled and troubling areas.

As to the possibility of "false consciousness": on one hand, we recognise the experience from ourselves, and others we have known well, where a person seems convinced (for some reason) that something was what he or she wanted or was in his or her best interests, when it really was not, and we see the effects of advertisers, politicians, religious leaders and others trying—and sometimes succeeding—to convince us what we "should" want. (If the process of trying to create new perceptions of need and desire never succeeded, then people would have long ago stopped spending the vast amount of time and money now devoted to just such projects.)

On the other hand, the picture of there being a "real me" somewhere beneath all the selves that have been imposed by societal pressures (whether commercial, religious, political or otherwise), is not entirely convincing. And even if in principle one could distinguish between the "real" self and its "real" interests and desires, and the brainwashed person of day-to-day life, how is this determination to be made and (perhaps more important) who is to make it?

---

[43] These arguments are elaborated in the texts cited in the previous footnote.

[44] "False consciousness" is "[a]n inability to see things, especially social relations and relations of exploitation, as they really are": Blackburn, *The Oxford Dictionary of Philosophy*, p. 135.

[45] See, *e.g.* MacKinnon, *Feminism Unmodified*, pp. 218–219; Catharine MacKinnon, *Towards a Feminist Theory of the State* (Cambridge, Mass.: Harvard University Press, 1989), pp. 148–154.

CRITICAL RACE THEORY

By most accounts, critical race theory developed as an offshoot of CLS in the late 1980s,[46] although here, as elsewhere, there is more than one plausible characterisation of a movement's history. One could just as easily state[47] that critical race theory had its roots in the 1970s, as theorists began to consider what had and had not been accomplished by the American Civil Rights Movement.

As with all the other topics in this part of the book (American legal realism, law and economics, CLS and feminist legal theory), it is hard to speak about critical race theory in general, as it is a label that has been accepted by or applied to a wide variety of ideas and analyses. With that disclaimer in mind, there are some things that can be said that seem to apply to much of the area.[48]

Critical race theory can be understood as having two major strands. The first strand is the theme of racism: the claim that racism is pervasive in the legal system and in society, and that it can be uncovered in many allegedly neutral concepts, procedures and analytical approaches.[49] The second strand (related to, but logically separate from, the first) is that persons from minority ethnic groups (or at least those who have suffered because of their identity as a member of one of those groups) have distinctive views, perceptions and experiences which are not properly recognised or fully discussed in mainstream or conventional discussions of the law (whether these discussions occur in courtrooms, law school

---

[46] Angela Harris describes the "first annual Workshop on Critical Race Theory" as having occurred in July 1989 in Madison, Wisconsin: Angela Harris, "The Jurisprudence of Reconstruction" (1994) 82 *California Law Review* 741 at 741.

[47] As a number of commentators have: see, *e.g.* Richard Delgado and Jean Stefancic, "Critical Race Theory: An Annotated Bibliography" (1993) 79 *Virginia Law Review* 461 at 461; Mari Matsuda, Charles Lawrence, Richard Delgado and Kimberlé Crenshaw, "Introduction" in *Words That Wound: Critical Race Theory, Assaultive Speech, and the First Amendment* (Boulder, Colo.: Westview Press, 1993), p. 3.

[48] In their annotated bibliography of critical race theory (cited in the previous footnote), Richard Delgado and Jean Stefancic list 10 "themes" as common to or distinctive of critical race theory. A somewhat different listing of six "defining elements" of critical race theory is given in Matsuda, Lawrence, Delgado and Crenshaw, "Introduction". The portrait of critical race theory offered in the text will cover some of the same ground, but necessarily in a somewhat sketchier way.

[49] See, *e.g.* Harris, "The Jurisprudence of Reconstruction", pp. 770–771.

classrooms, law review articles or newspaper articles that touch on legal matters).[50]

As regards the first strand, critical race theorists often try to show how pervasive racism affects legal scholarship both in areas where race is near the surface[51] and in areas where race would not, to most observers, immediately seem relevant.[52]

One natural focus of critical race scholarship has been affirmative action (also known as "positive discrimination"), favouring candidates for positions on the basis of their being a member of a minority racial or ethnic group.[53] While many writers have sought to defend—and legitimate—such programmes within a context in which merit-based selection is strongly preferred and discrimination based on race or ethnicity usually (and rightfully) criticised, other writers have offered a more ambivalent response to such programmes.[54] The topic of affirmative action brings together aspects of the first strand of critical race theory—the pervasiveness of racism within society (which can serve both as a justification for such programmes, and an explanation why many such programmes, in their current form, may do more harm than good)—with aspects from the second strand—the distinctive and valuable input that minority workers, professionals and academics can bring to their work settings (one of the justifications offered for affirmative action programmes).

As to the second strand, part of the argument is that group identity and experience are so central a part of who we are and so strongly affect how we perceive the world that it is important that

---

[50] See, e.g. Matsuda, Lawrence, Delgado and Crenshaw, "Introduction", p. 6.

[51] See, e.g. Kimberlé Crenshaw, "Race, Reform, and Retrenchment: Transformation and Legitimation in Antidiscrimination Law" (1988) 101 *Harvard Law Review* 1331; Lani Guinier, "The Triumph of Tokenism: The Voting Rights Act and the Theory of Black Electoral Success" (1991) 89 *Michigan Law Review* 1077.

[52] See, e.g. Patricia Williams, "Fetal Fictions: An Exploration of Property Archetypes in Racial and Gendered Contexts" (1990) 42 *Florida Law Review* 81; Stephen Carter, "When Victims Happen to be Black" (1988) 97 *Yale Law Journal* 420.

[53] Affirmative action programmes also often favour women over men, and there is some indication that women (not members of minority groups) have been the primary beneficiary of American affirmative action programmes.

[54] See, e.g. Derrick Bell, "Xerces and the Affirmative Action Mystique" (1989) 57 *George Washington Law Review* 1595; Richard Delgado, "Affirmative Action as a Majoritarian Device: Or, Do You Really Want to be a Role Model" (1991) 89 *Michigan Law Review* 1222; Mari Matsuda, "Affirmative Action and Legal Knowledge: Planting Seeds in Plowed-Up Ground" (1988) 11 *Harvard Women's Law Journal* 1.

there be a variety of perspectives, so that all aspects of a situation are properly seen, and the view of the majority or dominant group is not mistaken for objectivity or universality.[55] While this is sometimes presented as part of a grand "post-modern" theory, it need not be. The claim need be no more ambitious or controversial than that those who have experienced racial discrimination all their life may have a perspective or insights on discrimination that those who are part of the majority would not have. One critical race theorist, Milner Ball, described the articles of his colleagues as, among other things, "teach[ing] us about the felt effects of law and therefore something about its nature: on being an object of property, on being hurt by constitutionally protected speech, on being a minority member of a white law faculty."[56]

Relative to mainstream thought, the claims of critical race theorists vary from what would be perceived as helpful and unsurprising to what would be perceived as radical, divisive or improbable. The unsurprising side of the spectrum would include what has already been mentioned, the claim that members of oppressed minority groups experience the law differently than do privileged members of the majority, and on that basis have distinctive ideas and perspectives to offer. By "experience the law", I mean the dealings with aspects of the legal systems people (other than lawyers and judges) have on a day-to-day basis. For members of minority groups, this may mean bullying or distrust by police officers, or daily moments of discrimination or humiliation by members of the majority (actions which are illegal, but for which, as a practical matter, there is no remedy within the system).[57]

Along similar lines, critical race theorists have argued that since members of minority groups experience life differently from members of a majority, it is valuable to have ethnic diversity

---

[55] See, e.g. Drucilla Cornell, "Loyalty and the Limits of Kantian Impartiality" (book review) (1994) 107 *Harvard Law Review* 2081.

[56] Milner Ball, "The Legal Academy and Minority Scholars" (1990) 103 *Harvard Law Review* 1855 at 1859 (footnote omitted).

[57] Compare *Lynch v. Donnelly*, 465 U.S. 668 at 688–694 (1984) (O'Connor J. concurring) (on the importance of considering the perspective of religious minorities in considering whether a government action constituted an endorsement of (the majority) religion); *Ellison v. Brady*, 924 F2d 872 at 878–879 (9th Cir. 1991) (applying "the perspective of the victim", a "reasonable woman" test, in evaluating a claim of sexual harassment).

in law school classrooms, law school faculties, the police force, the judiciary and so on, for that diversity will tend to bring a healthy diversity of views and ideas. (One commentator summarised the argument as follows: "Just as the servant knows more than the master, those 'on the bottom' of American society see more than those at the top."[58]) As noted earlier, this is part of a standard argument for affirmative action.

The most controversial claims (some of which are just radical reworkings of more accepted positions) would include the view that there are certain truths that are accessible to members of minority groups which are simply not accessible to members of the majority.[59] One theorist, Robin Barnes, wrote:

> "Minority perspectives make explicit the need for fundamental change in the ways we think and construct knowledge. . . . Distinguishing the consciousness of racial minorities requires acknowledgment of the feelings and intangible modes of perception unique to those who have historically been socially, structurally, and intellectually marginalized in the United States."[60]

Another controversial conclusion, based on more moderate premises, is that certain subjects can only be properly or fully discussed by members of particular groups, for example, only members of minority ethnic groups should or can discuss the legal and moral aspects of racism.[61]

Along with the two substantive strands to critical race theory, one can also note that the writings in this movement are often stylistically distinctive. The use of "narrative" or a "storytelling" approach in academic writings, although by no means exclusive to

---

[58] See Harris, "The Jurisprudence of Reconstruction", p. 769 (footnote omitted).

[59] e.g. Mari Matsuda, "Looking to the Bottom: Critical Legal Studies and Reparations" (1987) 22 Harvard Civil Rights—Civil Liberties Law Review 323 at 326 and 346 ("The victims of racial oppression have distinct normative insights"; "Those who are oppressed in the present world can speak most eloquently of a better one").

[60] Robin Barnes, "Race Consciousness: The Thematic Content of Racial Distinctiveness in Critical Race Scholarship" (1990) 103 Harvard Law Review 1864 at 1864 (footnote omitted).

[61] A position criticised in Randall Kennedy, "Racial Critiques of Legal Academia", pp. 1778–1787.

critical race theory,[62] is quite common within the movement's writings.[63] There are at least two alternative purposes for using storytelling in the place of more conventional normative argument[64]: first, a rich narrative can help people from the majority community begin to understand what it is like to experience the legal system as a member of a minority community[65]; secondly, stories and fables can be used to undermine oversimplified views about human motivation.[66]

The argument against narrative as scholarship is that it can encourage or cover up a lack of rigour about facts, correlation or causation, and that narrative, while encouraging empathy, often does so in a one-sided manner (*e.g.* if it shows the plight of the tenant, it may fail to show the perspective of the landlord).[67]

---

[62] See, *e.g.* William Eskridge, Jr., "Gaylegal Narratives" (1994) 46 *Stanford Law Review* 607; Kathryn Abrams, "Hearing the Call of Stories" (1991) 79 *California Law Review* 971.

[63] See, *e.g.* Delgado and Stefancic, "Critical Race Theory: An Annotated Bibliography", p. 462. Narrative has also been important in feminist legal theory for roughly the same reasons it is central to critical race theory: see, *e.g.* Martha Fineman and Nancy Thomadsen eds., *At the Boundaries of Law* (New York: Routledge, 1991), pp. 1–58 ("Perspectives from the Personal").

[64] Harris, "The Jurisprudence of Reconstruction", pp. 755–757.

[65] Some of the best examples of such uses of narrative are in Patricia Williams, *The Alchemy of Race and Rights* (Cambridge, Mass.: Harvard University Press, 1991).

[66] Among the other claims made for "narrative" are that it "serves to create and confirm identity, both individual and collective", and that it helps to "speak to" our emotions and spiritual feelings as well as our rationality: Harris, "The Jurisprudence of Reconstruction", pp. 762, 780–781 (footnote omitted).

[67] See Richard Posner, *Overcoming Law*, pp. 368–384 (reviewing Patricia Williams, *The Alchemy of Race and Rights*).

Suggested Further Readings:

PART A Legal Theory: Problems and Possibilities

Chapter One

OVERVIEW, PURPOSE AND METHODOLOGY

H. L. A. Hart, "Comment", in *Issues in Contemporary Legal Philosophy* 35–42 (R. Gavison, ed., Oxford: Clarendon Press 1987)

—, "Postscript", in *The Concept of Law* 238–248 (revised edition, Oxford: Clarendon Press 1994)

Michael Moore, "Law as a Functional Kind", in *Natural Law Theories* 188–242 (R. George, ed., Oxford: Clarendon Press 1992)

Laura Nader, "The Anthropological Study of Law", 67 *American Anthropologist* 3 (1965)

Laura Nader & Henry Todd, eds., *The Disputing Process—Law in Ten Societies* (New York: Columbia University Press 1978)

Chapter Two

THE POSSIBILITY OF GENERAL JURISPRUDENCE

H. L. A. Hart, "Comment", in *Issues in Contemporary Legal Philosophy* 35–42 (R. Gavison, ed., Oxford: Clarendon Press 1987)

—, "Postscript", in *The Concept of Law* 238–248 (revised edition, Oxford: Clarendon Press 1994)

Michael Moore, "Law as a Functional Kind", in *Natural Law Theories* 188–242 (R. George, ed., Oxford: Clarendon Press 1992)

Laura Nader, "The Anthropological Study of Law", 67 *American Anthropologist* 3 (1965)

Laura Nader & Henry Todd, eds., *The Disputing Process—Law in Ten Societies* (New York: Columbia University Press 1978)

Chapter Three

TRANSFORMING THE QUESTION

Brian Bix, "Questions in Legal Interpretation", in *Law and Interpretation* 137–154 (A. Marmor, ed., Oxford: Clarendon Press 1995)

H. L. A. Hart, *The Concept of Law* 1–17 (Oxford: Clarendon Press 1961)

—, "Definition and Theory in Jurisprudence", 70 *Law Quarterly Review* 37–60 (1954), reprinted in *Essays in Jurisprudence and Philosophy* 21–48 (Oxford: Clarendon Press 1983)

Chapter Four

CONCEPTUAL QUESTIONS AND JURISPRUDENCE

Isaiah Berlin, "The Purpose of Philosophy", in *Concepts and Categories* 1–11 (New York: Penguin 1981)

L. Jonathan Cohen, *The Dialogue of Reason* (Oxford: Clarendon Press 1986)

Thomas Morawetz, *The Philosophy of Law: An Introduction* 11–16 (New York: Macmillan 1980) ("Law and Conceptual Analysis")

Jay Rosenberg, *The Practice of Philosophy* 5–11 (2nd ed., Englewood Cliffs, N.J.: Prentice-Hall 1984)

Philip Soper, "Legal Theory and the Problem of Definition" (book review), 50 *University of Chicago Law Review* 1170 (1983)

Kenneth Winston, "The Ideal Element in a Definition of Law", 5 *Law and Philosophy* 89 (1986)

PART B Individual Theories about the Nature of Law

Chapter Five

H. L. A. HART AND LEGAL POSITIVISM

Michael Bayles, *Hart's Legal Philosophy: An Examination* (Dordrecht: Kluwer Academic Publishers 1992)

Jules Coleman and Brian Leiter, "Legal Positivism", in *A Companion to the Philosophy of Law and Legal Theory* (D. Patterson, ed., forthcoming, Oxford: Blackwell 1996)

Robert George, ed., *The Autonomy of Law: Essays on Legal Positivism* (forthcoming, Oxford: Clarendon Press 1996) (includes essays by many prominent theorists, including Joseph Raz, Neil MacCormick, John Finnis, Frederick Schauer, Jules Coleman, and Philip Soper)

P. M. S. Hacker and Joseph Raz, eds., *Law, Morality, and Society: Essays in Honour of H. L. A. Hart* (Oxford: Clarendon Press 1977)

H. L. A. Hart, *The Concept of Law*, Second Edition (Oxford: Clarendon Press 1994) (the second edition includes a "Postscript", which is a reply to critics)

—, *Essays in Jurisprudence and Philosophy* (Oxford: Clarendon Press 1983)

—, "Positivism and the Separation of Law and Morals", 71 *Harvard Law Review* 593 (1958)

David Lyons, *Moral Aspects of Legal Theory* (Cambridge: Cambridge University Press 1993)

Neil MacCormick, *H. L. A. Hart* (Stanford: Stanford University Press 1981)

Joseph Raz, *The Authority of Law* (Oxford: Clarendon Press 1979)

—, *Ethics in the Public Domain* (Oxford: Clarendon Press 1994)

Chapter Six

HANS KELSEN'S PURE THEORY OF LAW

Hans Kelsen, *General Theory of Norms* (M. Hartney, trans., Oxford: Clarendon Press 1991)

—, *Introduction to the Problems of Legal Theory* (B. L. Paulson & S. L. Paulson, trans., Oxford: Clarendon Press 1992)

—, *Pure Theory of Law* (M. Knight, trans., Berkeley, Cal.: University of California Press 1967)

Stanley L. Paulson, "Continental Normativism and Its British Counterpart: How Different Are They?", 6 *Ratio Juris* 227 (1993)

Stanley L. Paulson, "The Neo-Kantian Dimension of Kelsen's Pure Theory of Law", 12 *Oxford Journal of Legal Studies* 311 (1992)

Richard Tur & William Twining, *Essays on Kelsen* (Oxford: Clarendon Press 1986) (includes contributions by Joseph Raz, Ota Weinberger, J. W. Harris, and Stanley L. Paulson)

Chapter Seven

NATURAL LAW THEORY AND JOHN FINNIS

Thomas Aquinas, *The Treatise on Law* (R. J. Henle, ed., Notre Dame, Ind.: University of Notre Dame Press 1993) (*Summa Theologiae*, Questions 90–97)

John Finnis, *Natural Law and Natural Rights* (Oxford: Clarendon Press, 1980)

John Finnis, ed., *Natural Law*, 2 volumes (New York: New York University Press, 1991) (a wide-ranging collection of law review articles on Natural Law theory)

Robert George, "Recent Criticism of Natural Law Theory" (Book Review), 55 *University of Chicago Law Review* 1271 (1988)

Robert George, ed., *Natural Law Theory* (Oxford: Clarendon Press, 1992) (a collection of recent articles on Natural Law theory)

Lloyd Weinreb, *Natural Law and Justice* (Cambridge, Mass.: Harvard University Press, 1987)

Chapter Eight

UNDERSTANDING LON FULLER

Symposium on Lon Fuller, 13 *Law and Philosophy* 253–418 (1994) (with articles by Kenneth Winston, Jeremy Waldron, Frederick Schauer, Stanley L. Paulson, and Gerald Postema)

Lon Fuller, "Positivism and Fidelity to Law—A Response to Professor Hart", 71 *Harvard Law Review* 630 (1958)

—, *The Morality of Law*, revised edition (New Haven: Yale University Press, 1969) (the revised edition contains a helpful reply to critics)

—, *The Principles of Social Order* (K. I. Winston, ed., Durham, N.C.: Duke University Press 1981) (collected essays with a helpful introduction by Kenneth Winston)

Robert Summers, *Lon L. Fuller* (Stanford, California: Stanford University Press 1984)

Chapter Nine
RONALD DWORKIN'S INTERPRETATIVE APPROACH

M. Cohen, ed., *Ronald Dworkin and Contemporary Jurisprudence* (London: Duckworth 1984) (includes critical essays and a long reply by Dworkin)

Ronald Dworkin, *Law's Empire* (Cambridge, Mass.: Harvard University Press 1986)

—, *A Matter of Principle* (Cambridge, Mass.: Harvard University Press 1985)

—, "My Reply to Stanley Fish (and Walter Benn Michaels): Please don't Talk about Objectivity Any More", in the *Politics of Interpretation*, 287–313 (W. J. T. Mitchell, ed., London: University of Chicago Press 1983)

—, "On Gaps in the Law", in *Controversies about Law's Ontology* 84–90 (P. Amselek and N. MacCormick, eds., Edinburgh: Edinburgh University Press 1991)

—, *Taking Rights Seriously* (London: Duckworth 1977) (contains a "Reply to Critics")

Jurisprudence Symposium, 11 *Georgia Law Review* 969–1424 (1977) (includes discussions of Dworkin's early work by H. L. A. Hart, Kent Greenawalt, Stephen Munzer, and David Richards, amongst others, and a reply by Dworkin)

Andrei Marmor, *Interpretation and Legal Theory* (Oxford: Clarendon Press 1992)

Symposium on *Law's Empire*, 6 *Law and Philosophy* 281–438 (1987)

PART C Implications and Applications

Chapter Ten
RIGHTS AND RIGHTS TALK

Ronald Dworkin, "A Reply to Critics", in *Ronald Dworkin and Contemporary Jurisprudence* 260–263 (M. Cohen, ed., London: Duckworth 1984)

J. M. Eekelaar, "Principles of Revolutionary Legality", in *Oxford Essays in Jurisprudence*, Second Series 22–43 (A. W. B. Simpson, ed., Oxford: Clarendon Press 1973)

John Finnis, "Revolutions and Continuity of Law", in *Oxford Essays in Jurisprudence*, Second Series 44–76 (A. W. B. Simpson, ed., Oxford: Clarendon Press 1973)

Joseph Raz, "Legal Principles and the Limits of Law", in *Ronald Dworkin and Contemporary Jurisprudence* 73–87 (M. Cohen ed., London: Duckworth 1984)

—, *The Concept of a Legal System* (2nd ed., Oxford: Clarendon Press 1980)

—, *Ethics in the Public Domain* 179–193 (Oxford: Clarendon Press 1994)

Chapter Eleven

BOUNDARY LINES IN LAW

Ronald Dworkin, "A Reply to Critics" in *Ronald Dworkin and Contemporary Jurisprudence* 260–263 (M. Cohen, ed., London: Duckworth 1984)

J. M. Eekelaar, "Principles of Revolutionary Legality", in *Oxford Essays in Jurisprudence*, Second Series 22–43 (A. W. B. Simpson, ed., Oxford: Clarendon Press 1973)

John Finnis, "Revolutions and Continuity of Law", in *Oxford Essays in Jurisprudence*, Second Series 44–76 (A. W. B. Simpson, ed., Oxford: Clarendon Press 1973)

Joseph Raz, "Legal Principles and the Limits of Law", in *Ronald Dworkin and Contemporary Jurisprudence* 73–87 (M. Cohen ed., London: Duckworth 1984)

—, *The Concept of a Legal System* (2nd ed., Oxford: Clarendon Press 1980)

—, *Ethics in the Public Domain* 179–193 (Oxford: Clarendon Press 1994)

Chapter Twelve

WILL AND REASON

Francis Oakley, "Medieval Theories of Natural Law: William of Ockham and the Significance of the Voluntarist Tradition", 6 *Natural Law Forum* 65 (1961)

Lloyd Weinreb, *Natural Law and Justice* 63–96 (Cambridge, Mass.: Harvard University Press 1987)

Chapter Thirteen

AUTHORITY, FINALITY AND MISTAKE

Ronald Dworkin, *Law's Empire*, chapter 9 (Cambridge, Mass.: Harvard University Press 1986) ("Statutes")

Andrei Marmor, *Interpretation and Legal Theory*, chapter 8 (Oxford: Clarendon Press 1992) ("Legislative Intent and the Authority of Law")

Andrei Marmor, ed., *Law and Interpretation* (Oxford: Clarendon Press 1995) (containing articles on statutory interpretation by Michael Moore, Joseph Raz, Jeremy Waldron, Larry Alexander, Heidi Hurd and Meir Dan-Cohen)

Joseph Raz, "Intention in Interpretation", in *The Autonomy of Law* (forthcoming, R. George, ed., Oxford: Clarendon Press 1996)

Chapter Fourteen

PRECEDENT AND STATUTORY INTERPRETATION

Ronald Dworkin, *Law's Empire*, chapter 9 (Cambridge, Mass.: Harvard University Press 1986) ("Statutes")

Andrei Marmor, *Interpretation and Legal Theory*, chapter 8 (Oxford: Clarendon Press 1992) ("Legislative Intent and the Authority of Law")

Andrei Marmor, ed., *Law and Interpretation* (Oxford: Clarendon Press 1995) (containing articles on statutory interpretation by Michael Moore, Joseph Raz, Jeremy Waldron, Larry Alexander, Heidi Hurd and Meir Dan-Cohen)

Joseph Raz, "Intention in Interpretation", in *The Autonomy of Law* (R. George, ed., Oxford: Clarendon Press 1996), pp 249–286

Chapter Fifteen

LEGAL ENFORCEMENT OF MORALITY

Larry Alexander, "Harm, Offense, and Morality", 7 *Canadian Journal of Law and Jurisprudence* 199 (1994)

Patrick Devlin, *The Enforcement of Morals* (Oxford: Oxford University Press 1965)

Gerald Dworkin, ed., *Morality, Harm and the Law* (Boulder, Colo.: Westview Press 1994)

Joel Feinberg, *The Moral Limits of the Criminal Law,* volumes 1–4 (Oxford: Oxford University Press 1984–1988)

Robert George, *Making Men Moral* (Oxford: Clarendon Press 1993)

Kent Greenawalt, "Legal Enforcement of Morality", in *A Companion to the Philosophy of Law and Legal Theory* (D. Patterson, ed., forthcoming, Oxford: Blackwell 1996)

H. L. A. Hart, *Law, Liberty, and Morality* (Oxford: Oxford University Press 1963)

John Stuart Mill, "On Liberty", in *On Liberty and Utilitarianism* 1–133 (New York: Bantam Books 1993)

James Fitzjames Stephen, *Liberty, Equality, Fraternity* (Indianapolis: Liberty Fund 1993) (originally published in 1873)

Jeremy Waldron, *Liberal Rights,* chapters 1–8 (Cambridge: Cambridge University Press 1993)

Chapter Sixteen

THE OBLIGATION TO OBEY THE LAW

John Finnis, "The Authority of Law in the Predicament of Contemporary Social Theory", 1 *Notre Dame Journal of Law and Public Policy* 115 (1984)

—, "Law as Co-ordination", 2 *Ratio Juris* 97 (1989)

A. M. Honoré, *Making Law Bind* 115–138 (Oxford: Clarendon Press 1987)

Joseph Raz, *The Authority of the Law* 233–289 (1979)

M. B. E. Smith, "Is There a Prima Facie Obligation to Obey the Law?", 82 *Yale Law Journal* 950 (1973)

M. B. E. Smith, "The Duty to Obey the Law", in *A Companion to the Philosophy of Law and Legal Theory* (forthcoming, D. Patterson, Oxford: Blackwell 1996)

PART D Modern Perspectives on Legal Theory

Chapter Seventeen

AMERICAN LEGAL REALISM

Neil Duxbury, *Patterns of American Jurisprudence* 65–159 (Oxford: Clarendon Press 1995)

William Fisher, Morton Horwitz & Thomas Reed, eds. *American Legal Realism* (New York: Oxford University Press 1993) (this book contains a collection of (excerpts from) many Realist articles, plus a thorough bibliography)

Jerome Frank, *Law and the Modern Mind* (New York: Brentano's 1930)

Brian Leiter, "Legal Realism" in *A Companion to the Philosophy of Law and Legal Theory* (forthcoming, D. Patterson, ed., Oxford: Blackwell 1996)

Karl Llewellyn, "Some Realism and Realism—Responding to Dean Pound", 44 *Harvard Law Review* 1222 (1931)

Roscoe Pound, "The Call for a Realist Jurisprudence, 44 *Harvard Law Review* 697 (1931)

William Twining, *Karl Llewellyn and the Realist Movement* (Norman, Oklahoma: University of Oklahoma Press 1985)

Chapter Eighteen

ECONOMIC ANALYSIS OF LAW

Guido Calabresi & A. Douglas Melamed, "Property Rules, Liability Rules, and Inalienability: One View of the Cathedral", 85 *Harvard Law Review* 1089 (1972)

Ronald Coase, "The Problem of Social Cost", 3 *Journal of Law and Economics* 1 (1960), reprinted in Coase, *The Firm, the Market, and the Law* 95–156 (Chicago: University of Chicago Press 1988)

Jules Coleman, *Markets, Morals and Law,* chapters 3–5 (Cambridge: Cambridge University Press 1988)

Robert Cooter & Thomas Ulen, *Law and Economics* (New York: HarperCollins 1988)

Neil Duxbury, *Patterns of American Jurisprudence* 301–419 (Oxford: Clarendon Press 1995) ("Economics in Law")

Jon Hanson & Melissa Hart, "Law and Economics", in *A Companion to the Philosophy of Law and Legal Theory* (D. Patterson, ed., Oxford: Blackwell 1996)

William Landes & Richard Posner, *The Economic Structure of Tort Law* (Cambridge, Mass.: Harvard University Press 1987)

Arthur Leff, "Economic Analysis of Law: Some Realism About Nominalism", 60 *Virginia Law Review* 451 (1974)

Jeffrie Murphy and Jules Coleman, "Law and Economics", in *Philosophy of Law* 181–234 (rev. ed., Boulder, Colo.: Westview Press 1990)

A. Mitchell Polinsky, *An Introduction to Law and Economics* (2nd ed., Boston: Little, Brown and Co. 1989)

Richard Posner, *Economic Analysis of Law* (4th ed., Boston: Little, Brown and Co. 1992)

—, The *Economics of Justice* (Cambridge, Mass.: Harvard University Press 1983)

Symposium on Efficiency as a Legal Concern, 8 *Hofstra Law Review* 485–770 (1980) (contributors include Richard Posner, Jules Coleman, Guido Calabresi, Ronald Dworkin, Duncan Kennedy and Frank Michelman)

Symposium on Post-Chicago Law and Economics, 65 *Chicago-Kent Law Review* 3–191 (1989) (contributors include Randy Barnett, Robert Ellickson, Richard Posner, Jonathan Macey, Daniel Farber, and Jules Coleman)

Chapter Nineteen
MODERN CRITICAL PERSPECTIVES
CRITICAL LEGAL STUDIES

James Boyle, ed., *Critical Legal Studies* (New York: New York University Press 1994)

Critical Legal Studies Symposium, 36 *Stanford Law Review* 1–674 (1984) (a wide-ranging collection, which includes articles on the history of CLS, and articles critical of it, as well as pieces explaining or applying CLS ideas)

Alan Hunt, "The Theory of Critical Legal Studies", 6 *Oxford Journal of Legal Studies* 1 (1986)

David Kairys, ed., *The Politics of Law* (rev. ed., New York: Pantheon 1990) (twenty-four articles, sharply edited; the authors include Duncan Kennedy, Robert Gordon, Morton Horwitz, Mark Kelman, Peter Gabel, and Frances Olsen)

Kelman, Mark, *A Guide to Critical Legal Studies* (Cambridge, Mass.: Harvard University Press 1987)

Roberto Unger, *The Critical Legal Studies Movement* (Cambridge, Mass.: Harvard University Press 1986)

FEMINIST LEGAL THEORY

Katharine T. Bartlett & Rosanne Kennedy, eds., *Feminist Legal Theory: Readings in Law and Gender* (Boulder, Colorado: Westview Press 1991)

Martha Fineman & Nancy Thomadsen, eds., *At the Boundaries of Law: Feminism and Legal Theory* (New York: Routledge 1991)

Christine Littleton, "Feminist Jurisprudence: The Difference Method Makes", 41 *Stanford Law Review* 751 (1989)

Catharine MacKinnon, *Feminism Unmodified* (Cambridge, Mass.: Harvard University Press 1987)

Patricia Smith, "Feminist Jurisprudence and the Nature of Law" in *A Companion to the Philosophy of Law and Legal Theory* (D. Patterson, ed., forthcoming, Oxford: Basil Blackwell 1996)

Patricia Smith, ed., *Feminist Jurisprudence* (Oxford: Oxford University Press 1993)

D. Kelly Weisberg, ed., *Feminist Legal Theory: Foundations* (Philadelphia: Temple University Press 1993)

CRITICAL RACE THEORY

Derrick Bell, *And We Are Not Saved* (New York: Basic Books 1987)

Kimberlé Crenshaw, Neil Gotanda, Gary Peller, and Kendall Thomas, eds., *Critical Race Theory: The Key Writings That Formed the Movement* (New York: The New Press 1995)

Richard Delgado, "The Imperial Scholar: Reflections on a Review of Civil Rights Literature", 132 *University of Pennsylvania Law Review* 561 (1984)

Richard Delgado, ed., *Critical Race Theory: The Cutting Edge* (Philadelphia: Temple University Press 1995) (containing fifty articles on a wide range of topics from many different authors)

Richard Delgado and Jean Stefancic, "Critical Race Theory: An Annotated Bibliography", 79 *Virginia Law Review* 461 (1993)

Randall Kennedy, "Racial Critiques of Legal Academia, 102 *Harvard Law Review* 1745 (1989)

Symposium: Critical Race Theory, 82 *California Law Review* 741–1125 (1994)

Patricia Williams, *The Alchemy of Race and Rights* (Cambridge, Mass.: Harvard University Press 1991)

Bibliography

Abrams, Kathryn, "Hearing the Call of Stories" (1991) 79 *California Law Review* 971.

Alexander, Larry, "Harm, Offense, and Morality" (1994) 7 *Canadian Journal of Law and Jurisprudence* 199.

Allen, Anita "The Proposed Equal Protection Fix for Abortion Law: Reflections on Citizenship, Gender, and the Constitution" (1995) 18 *Harvard Journal of Law and Public Policy* 419.

Altman, Andrew, *Critical Legal Studies: A Liberal Critique* (Princeton: Princeton University Press, 1990).

Aquinas, St Thomas, *The Treatise on Law* (R. J. Henle trans. and ed., Notre Dame, Indiana: University of Notre Dame Press, 1993).

Aristotle, *The Complete Works of Aristotle* (J. Barnes ed., Princeton: Princeton University Press, 1984), 2 Vols.

Aron, Raymond, *Main Currents in Sociological Thought*, (R. Howard and H. Weaver trans., New York: Anchor Books, 1970), Vols. I and II.

Austin, J.L., *How to Do Things With Words* (J. O. Urmson and M. Sbisa eds., Cambridge, Mass.: Harvard University Press, 1975).

Austin, John, *The Province of Jurisprudence Determined* (H. L. A. Hart ed., London: Weidenfeld & Nicolson, 1955).

Austin, Regina, "Sapphire Bound! (Minority Feminist Scholarship)" (1989) *Wisconsin Law Review* 539.

Baird, Douglas; Gertner, Robert and Picker, Randal, *Game Theory and the Law* (Cambridge, Mass.: Harvard University Press, 1994).

Baker, Gordon, "Defeasibility and Meaning" in *Law, Morality, and Society* (P. M. S. Hacker and J. Raz eds., Oxford: Clarendon Press, 1977), pp. 26–57.

Balkin, Jack, "Transcendental Deconstruction, Transcendent Justice" (1994) 92 *Michigan Law Review* 1131.

Ball, Milner, "The Legal Academy and Minority Scholars" (1990) 103 *Harvard Law Review* 1855.

Barnes, Robin, "Race Consciousness: The Thematic Content of Racial Distinctiveness in Critical Race Scholarship" (1990) 103 *Harvard Law Review* 1864.

Bartlett, Katharine, "Feminist Legal Methods" (1990) 103 *Harvard Law Review* 829.

Bartlett, Katharine and Kennedy, Rosanne, *Feminist Legal Theory: Readings in Law and Gender* (Boulder, Colo.: Westview Press, 1991).

Bayles, Michael, *Hart's Legal Philosophy: An Examination* (Dordrecht: Kluwer Academic Publishers, 1992).

Becker, Mary, Bowman, Cynthia Grant and Torrey, Morrison, *Feminist Jurisprudence: Taking Women Seriously* (St. Paul, Minn.: West Publishing, 1994).

Bell, Derrick, *And We Are Not Saved* (New York: Basic Books, 1987).

——, *Faces at the Bottom of the Well* (New York: Basic Books, 1992).

——, "Xerces and the Affirmative Action Mystique" (1989) 57 *George Washington Law Review* 1595.

Bell, John, "The Acceptability of Legal Arguments" in *The Legal Mind* (N. MacCormick and P. Birks ed., Oxford: Clarendon Press, 1986), pp. 45–65.

——, *Policy Arguments in Judicial Decisions* (Oxford: Clarendon Press, 1983).

Berlin, Isaiah, "The Purpose of Philosophy" in *Concepts and Categories* (New York: Penguin, 1981), pp. 1–11.

Binder, Guyora, "Critical Legal Studies" in *A Companion to the Philosophy of Law and Legal Theory* (forthcoming, D. Patterson ed., Oxford: Basil Blackwell, 1996).

Bix, Brian, "A. D. Woozley and the Concept of Right Answers in Law" (1992) 5 *Ratio Juris* 58, reprinted in modified form in *Law, Language, and Legal Determinacy* (Oxford: Clarendon Press, 1993), pp. 79–88.

——, "Conceptual Questions and Jurisprudence" (1995) 1 *Legal Theory* p. 415.

——, *Law, Language, and Legal Determinacy* (Oxford: Clarendon Press, 1993).

——, "Natural Law Theory" in *A Companion to the Philosophy of Law and Legal Theory* (forthcoming, D. Patterson ed., Oxford: Basil Blackwell, 1996).

——, "Questions in Legal Interpretation" in *Law and Interpretation* (A. Marmor ed., Oxford: Clarendon Press, 1995), pp. 137–154.

——, "Questions in Legal Interpretation" (1994) 18 *Tel Aviv Law Review* 463.

Blackburn, Simon, *The Oxford Dictionary of Philosophy* (Oxford: Oxford University Press, 1994).

Blackstone, William, *Commentaries on the Law of England* (Oxford: Clarendon Press, 1765–1769), 4 Vols.

Brest, Paul, "The Misconceived Quest for the Original Understanding" (1980) 60 *Boston University Law Review* 204.

Brewer, Scott, "Introduction: Choosing Sides in the Racial Critiques Debate" (1990) 103 *Harvard Law Review* 1844.

Brewer, Scott, "Pragmatism, Oppression, and the Flight to Substance" (1990) 63 *Southern California Law Review* 1753.

Boyle, James, "Introduction" in *Critical Legal Studies* (J. Boyle ed., New York: New York University Press, 1994), pp. xiii–liii.

Boyle, James ed., *Critical Legal Studies* (New York: New York University Press, 1994).

Burstyn, Varda ed., *Women Against Censorship* (Vancouver: Douglas & McIntyre, Ltd., 1985).

Burton, Steven, "Reaffirming Legal Reasoning: The Challenge from the Left" (1986) 36 *Journal of Legal Education* 358.

Calabresi, Guido and Melamed, A. Douglas, "Property Rules, Liability Rules, and Inalienability: One View of the Cathedral" (1972) 85 *Harvard Law Review* 1089.

Cardozo, Benjamin, *The Nature of the Judicial Process* (New Haven: Yale University Press, 1921).

Carter, Stephen, "When Victims Happen to be Black" (1988) 97 *Yale Law Journal* 420.

Christie, George and Martin, Patrick eds., *Jurisprudence: Text and Readings on the Philosophy of Law* (2nd ed. St. Paul, Minn.: West Publishing, 1995).

Cicero, Marcus Tullius, *De Re Publica; De Legibus* (C. W. Keyes trans., Cambridge, Mass.: Harvard University Press, 1988).

Coase, Ronald, "The Problem of Social Cost" (1960) 3 *Journal of Law and Economics* 1, reprinted in *The Firm, the Market and the Law* (Chicago: University of Chicago Press, 1988), pp. 95–156.

Cohen, Felix, "Transcendental Nonsense and the Functional Approach" (1935) 35 *Columbia Law Review* 809.

Cohen, L. Jonathan, *The Dialogue of Reason* (Oxford: Clarendon Press, 1986).

Cohen, Marshall ed., *Ronald Dworkin and Contemporary Jurisprudence* (London: Duckworth, 1984).

Cohen, Morris, "The Basis of Contract" (1933) 46 *Harvard Law Review* 553.

——, *Law and the Social Order* (New York: Archon Books, 1967; original edition 1933).

——, "Property and Sovereignty" (1927) 13 *Cornell Law Quarterly* 8.

——, *Reason and Law* (Glencoe, Ill.: The Free Press, 1950).

——, *Reason and Nature* (New York: Harcourt, Brace, 1983).

Coleman, Jules, "Authority and Reason" in *The Autonomy of Law* (R. George ed., Oxford: Oxford University Press, 1996), pp. 287–319.

——, *Markets, Morals and the Law* (Cambridge: Cambridge University Press, 1988).

Coleman, Jules, "Negative and Positive Positivism" (1982) 11 *Journal of Legal Studies* 139.

——, "The Normative Basis of Economic Analysis: A Critical Review of Richard Posner's *The Economics of Justice*" (1982) 34 *Stanford Law Review* 1105.

——, "Truth and Objectivity in Law" (1995) 1 *Legal Theory* 33.

Coleman, Jules and Leiter, Brian, "Legal Positivism" in *A Companion to the Philosophy of Law and Legal Theory* (forthcoming, D. Patterson ed., Oxford: Basil Blackwell, 1996).

Colloquy, "Responses to Randall Kennedy's *Racial Critiques of Legal Academia*" (1990) 103 *Harvard Law Review* 1844.

Cook, Walter Wheeler, "The Logical and Legal Bases of the Conflict of Laws" (1924) 33 *Yale Law Journal* 457.

Coombs, Mary, "Outsider Jurisprudence: The Law Review Stories" (1992) 63 *University of Colorado Law Review* 683.

Cooter, Robert and Ulen, Thomas, *Law and Economics* (New York: Harper Collins, 1988).

Cornell, Drucilla, "Loyalty and the Limits of Kantian Impartiality" (book review) (1994) 107 *Harvard Law Review* 2081.

Cotterrell, Roger, *The Politics of Jurisprudence* (London: Butterworths, 1989).

Crenshaw, Kimberlé, "Race, Reform, and Retrenchment: Transformation and Legitimation in Antidiscrimination Law" (1988) 101 *Harvard Law Review* 1331.

Crenshaw, Kimberlé, Gotanda, Neil, Peller, Gary and Thomas, Kendall eds., *Critical Race Theory: The Key Writings That Formed the Movement* (New York: The New Press, 1995).

Critical Legal Studies Symposium (1984) 36 *Stanford Law Review* 1–674.

Cross, Rupert, *Statutory Interpretation* (London: Butterworths, 1976).

Davidson, Donald, *Inquiries into Truth and Interpretation* (Oxford: Clarendon Press, 1984).

Dawson, John, "Economic Duress—An Essay in Perspective" (1947) 45 *Michigan Law Review* 253.

DeBow, Michael and Lee, Dwight, "Understanding (and Misunderstanding) Public Choice: A Response to Farber and Frickey" (1988) 66 *Texas Law Review* 993.

Delgado, Richard, "Affirmative Action as a Majoritarian Device: Or, Do You Really Want to be a Role Model" (1991) 89 *Michigan Law Review* 1222.

——, "Brewer's Plea: Critical Thoughts on Common Cause" (1991) 44 *Vanderbilt Law Review* 1.

——, "The Imperial Scholar: Reflections on a Review of Civil Rights Literature" (1984) 132 *University of Pennsylvania Law Review* 561.

Delgado, Richard, "Storytelling for Oppositionists and Others: A Plea for Narrative" (1989) 87 *Michigan Law Review* 2411.

——, "When a Story is Just a Story: Does Voice Really Matter?" (1990) 76 *Virginia Law Review* 95.

Delgado, Richard ed., *Critical Race Theory: The Cutting Edge* (Philadelphia: Temple University Press, 1995).

Delgado, Richard and Stefancic, Jean, "Critical Race Theory: An Annotated Bibliography" (1993) 79 *Virginia Law Review* 461.

——, "Hateful Speech, Loving Communities: Why Our Notion of 'A Just Balance' Changes So Slowly" (1994) 82 *California Law Review* 851.

Devlin, Patrick, *The Enforcement of Morals* (Oxford: Oxford University Press, 1965).

Dewey, John, "Logical Method and the Law" (1924) 10 *Cornell Law Quarterly* 17.

Dupré, John, "Natural Kinds and Biological Taxa" (1981) 90 *Philosophical Review* 66.

Duxbury, Neil, *Patterns of American Jurisprudence* (Oxford: Clarendon Press, 1995).

——, "Post-Realism and Legal Process" in *A Companion to the Philosophy of Law and Legal Theory* (forthcoming, D. Patterson ed., Oxford: Basil Blackwell, 1996).

Dworkin, Gerald ed., *Morality, Harm and the Law* (Boulder, Colo.: Westview Press, 1994).

Dworkin, Ronald, *Law's Empire* (Cambridge, Mass.: Harvard University Press, 1986).

——, "Legal Theory and the Problem of Sense" in *Issues in Contemporary Legal Philosophy* (R. Gavison ed., Oxford: Claraendon Press, 1987), pp. 9–20.

——, *A Matter of Principle* (Cambridge, Mass.: Harvard University Press, 1985).

——, "My Reply to Stanley Fish (and Walter Benn Michaels): Please don't Talk about Objectivity Any More" in *The Politics of Interpretation* (W. J. T. Mitchell ed., London: University of Chicago Press, 1983), pp. 287–313.

——, " 'Natural' Law Revisited" (1982) 34 *University of Florida Law Review* 165.

——, "On Gaps in the Law" in *Controversies about Law's Ontology* (P. Amselek and N. MacCormick eds., Edinburgh: Edinburgh University Press, 1991), pp. 84–90.

——, "Pragmatism, Right Answers and True Banality" in *Pragmatism in Law and Society* (Boulder, Colo.: Westview Press, 1991), pp. 359–388.

——, "A Reply to Critics" in *Ronald Dworkin and Contemporary Jurisprudence* (M. Cohen ed., London: Duckworth, 1984), pp. 247–300.

Dworkin, Ronald, *Taking Rights Seriously* (London: Duckworth, 1977).

Eekelaar, J.M., "Principles of Revolutionary Legality" in *Oxford Essays in Jurisprudence, Second Series* (Oxford: Clarendon Press, 1973), pp. 22–43.

Epstein, Richard, "A Theory of Strict Liability" (1973) 2 *Journal of Legal Studies* 151.

Eskridge, William, "Gaylegal Narratives" (1994) 46 *Stanford Law Review* 607.

Estrich, Susan, *Real Rape* (Cambridge, Mass.: Harvard University Press, 1987).

Farber, Daniel and Frickey, Philip, *Law and Public Choice* (Chicago: University of Chicago Press, 1991).

Feinberg, Joel. *The Moral Limits of the Criminal Law* (Oxford: Oxford University Press, 1984–1988), Vols. 1–4.

Field, Martha, "Surrogacy Contracts: Gestational and Traditional: The Argument for Nonenforcement" (1991) 31 *Washburn Law Review* 3.

Fineman, Martha, "Feminist Theory and Law" (1995) 18 *Harvard Journal of Law and Public Policy* 349.

Fineman, Martha and Thomadsen, Nancy eds., *At the Boundaries of Law: Feminism and Legal Theory* (New York: Routledge, 1991).

Finnis, John, "Allocating Risks and Suffering: Some Hidden Traps" (1990) 38 *Cleveland State Law Review* 193.

——, "The Authority of Law in the Predicament of Contemporary Social Theory" (1984) 1 *Notre Dame Journal of Law, Ethics and Public Policy* 115.

——, "Concluding Reflections" (1990) 38 *Cleveland State Law Review* 231.

——, "Comment" in *Issues in Contemporary Legal Philosophy* (R. Gavison ed., Oxford: Clarendon Press, 1987), pp. 62–75.

——, "Law as Co-ordination" (1989) 2 *Ratio Juris* 97.

——, "Natural Law and Legal Reasoning" (1990) 38 *Cleveland State Law Review* 1, reprinted in modified form in *Natural Law Theory* (R. George ed., Oxford: Clarendon Press, 1992), pp. 134–157.

——, *Natural Law and Natural Rights* (Oxford: Clarendon Press, 1980).

——, "The 'Natural Law Tradition' " (1986) 36 *Journal of Legal Education* 492.

——, "On 'Positivism' and 'Legal Rational Authority' " (1985) 5 *Oxford Journal of Legal Studies* 74.

——, "On Reason and Authority in *Law's Empire*" (book review) (1987) 6 *Law and Philosophy* 357.

Finnis, John, "On 'The Critical Studies Movement' " (1985) 30 *American Journal of Jurisprudence* 21, reprinted in *Oxford Essays in Jurisprudence, Third Series* (J. Eekelaar and J. Bell eds., Oxford: Clarendon Press, 1987), pp. 145–165.

——, "Revolutions and Continuity of Law" in *Oxford Essays in Jurisprudence, Second Series* (Oxford: Clarendon Press, 1973), pp. 44–76.

——, "The Truth in Legal Positivism" in *The Autonomy of Law* (R. George ed., Oxford: Clarendon Press, 1996) pp. 195–214.

Finnis, John ed., *Natural Law* (New York: New York University Press, 1991), 2 Vols.

Fischl, Richard, "Some Realism about Critical Legal Studies" (1987) 41 *University of Miami Law Review* 505.

Fisher, William, Horwitz, Morton and Reed, Thomas eds., *American Legal Realism* (New York: Oxford University Press, 1993).

Fitzpatrick, Peter and Hunt, Alan eds., *Critical Legal Studies* (Oxford: Basil Blackwell, 1987).

Fletcher, George, *Basic Concepts of Legal Thought* (New York: Oxford University Press, 1996).

Foot, Philippa, "Moral Arguments" (1958) 67 *Mind* 502.

Frank, Jerome, "Are Judges Human?", Parts I and II (1931) 80 *University of Pennsylvania Law Review* 17, 233.

——, *Courts on Trial* (Princeton: Princeton University Press, 1949).

——, *Law and the Modern Mind* (New York: Brentano's 1930).

——, "What Courts Do In Fact", Parts I and II (1932) 26 *Illinois Law Review* 645, 761.

Fuller, Lon, "American Legal Realism" (1934) 82 *University of Pennsylvania Law Review* 429.

——, "The Forms and Limits of Adjudication" (1978) 92 *Harvard Law Review* 353.

——, *The Morality of Law* (revised ed., New Haven: Yale University Press, 1969).

——, "Positivism and Fidelity to Law—A Reply to Professor Hart" (1958) 71 *Harvard Law Review* 630.

——, *The Principles of Social Order* (K. I. Winston ed., Durham, N.C.: Duke University Press, 1981).

Gabel, Peter, Book Review (1977) 91 *Harvard Law Review* 302.

Gabel, Peter and Harris, Paul, "Building Power and Breaking Images: Critical Legal Theory and the Practice of Law" (1982–83) 11 *New York University Review of Law and Social Change* 369.

George, Robert, *Making Men Moral* (Oxford: Clarendon Press, 1993).

——, "Recent Criticism of Natural Law Theory" (book review) (1988) 55 *University of Chicago Law Review* 1271.

George, Robert ed. *The Autonomy of Law: Essays on Legal Positivism* (Oxford: Clarendon Press, 1996).

——, *Natural Law Theory* (Oxford: Clarendon Press, 1992).

Gilligan, Carol, *In a Different Voice: Psychological Theory and Women's Development* (Cambridge, Mass.: Harvard University Press, 1982).

Golding, Martin, "Jurisprudence and Legal Philosophy in Twentieth-Century America—Major Themes and Developments" (1986) 36 *Journal of Legal Education* 441.

Gordon, Robert, "Critical Legal Histories" (1984) 36 *Stanford Law Review* 57.

Gray, John Chipman, *The Nature and Sources of the Law* (New York: Columbia University Press, 1909).

Greenawalt, Kent, *Conflicts of Law and Morality* (New York: Oxford University Press, 1987).

——, "Legal Enforcement of Morality" in *A Companion to the Philosophy of Law and Legal Theory* (forthcoming, D. Patterson ed., Oxford: Blackwell, 1996).

Griffith, John, *The Politics of the Judiciary* (London: Fontana, 1985).

Guinier, Lani, "The Triumph of Tokenism: The Voting Rights Act and the Theory of Black Electoral Success" (1991) 89 *Michigan Law Review* 1077.

Hacker, P.M.S., "Hart's Philosophy of Law" in *Law, Morality and Society: Essays in Honour of H. L. A. Hart* (P. M. S. Hacker and J. Raz eds., Oxford: Clarendon Press, 1977), pp. 1–25.

Hacker, P.M.S. and Raz, Joseph eds., *Law, Morality and Society: Essays in Honour of H. L. A. Hart* (Oxford: Clarendon Press, 1977).

Hale, Robert, "Bargaining, Duress, and Economic Liberty" (1943) 43 *Columbia Law Review* 603.

——, "Coercion and Distribution in a Supposedly Non-Coercive State" (1923) 38 *Political Science Quarterly* 470.

Hanson, Jon and Hart, Melissa, "Law and Economics" in *A Companion to the Philosophy of Law and Legal Theory* (forthcoming, D. Patterson ed., Oxford: Basil Blackwell, 1996).

Harris, Angela, "Foreword: The Jurisprudence of Reconstruction" (1994) 82 *California Law Review* 741.

——, "Race and Essentialism in Feminist Legal Theory" (1990) 42 *Stanford Law Review* 581.

Harris, J.W., *Law and Legal Science* (Oxford: Clarendon Press, 1979).

——, *Legal Philosophies* (London: Butterworths, 1980).

Hart, H.L.A., "Comment" in *Issues in Contemporary Legal Philosophy* (R. Gavison ed., Oxford: Clarendon Press, 1987), pp. 35–42.

——, *The Concept of Law* (Oxford: Clarendon Press, 1961; revised edition, 1994).

Hart, H.L.A., "Definition and Theory in Jurisprudence" (1954) 70 *Law Quarterly Review* 37–60, reprinted in *Essays in Jurisprudence and Philosophy* (Oxford: Clarendon Press, 1983), pp. 21–48.

——, *Essays in Jurisprudence and Philosophy* (Oxford: Clarendon Press, 1983).

——, *Essays on Bentham: Jurisprudence and Political Theory* (Oxford: Clarendon Press, 1982).

——, "Introduction" in *Essays in Jurisprudence and Philosophy* (Oxford: Clarendon Press, 1983), pp. 1–18.

——, *Law, Liberty and Morality* (Oxford: Oxford University Press, 1963).

——, "Legal Rights" in *Essays on Bentham* (Oxford: Clarendon Press, 1982), pp. 162–193.

——, "Positivism and the Separation of Law and Morals" (1958) 71 *Harvard Law Review* 593, reprinted in *Essays in Jurisprudence and Philosophy* (Oxford: Clarendon Press, 1983), pp. 49–87.

——, "Postscript" in *The Concept of Law* (revised ed., Oxford: Clarendon Press, 1994), pp. 238–276.

Hart, Henry and Sacks, Albert, *The Legal Process: Basic Problems in the Making and Application of Law* (W. Eskridge and P. Frickey eds., Westbury, N.Y.: Foundation Press, 1994).

Hartney, Michael, "Introduction" and "Appendix: Bibliography of Kelsen's Publications in English" in Hans Kelsen, *General Theory of Norms* (M. Hartney trans. and ed., Oxford: Clarendon Press, 1991), pp. ix–liii, 440–454.

Hay, Douglas, Linebaugh, Peter, Rule, John, Thompson, E.P and Winslow, Cal, *Albion's Fatal Tree* (Middlesex, England: Penguin, 1975).

Hicks, J.R., "The Foundations of Welfare Economics" (1939) 49 *Economics Journal* 696.

Hill, H.H., "H. L. A. Hart's Hermeneutic Positivism: On Some Methodological Difficulties in *The Concept of Law*" (January 1990) 3 *Canadian Journal of Law and Jurisprudence* 113.

Hohfeld, Wesley, "Fundamental Legal Conceptions as Applied in Judicial Reasoning" (1917) 26 *Yale Law Journal* 710.

——, "Some Fundamental Conceptions as Applied in Judicial Reasoning" (1913) 23 *Yale Law Journal* 16.

Holmes, Oliver Wendell, *The Common Law* (M. D. Howe ed., Boston: Little, Brown, 1963).

——, "The Path of the Law" (1897) 10 *Harvard Law Review* 457.

——, "Privilege, Malice and Intent" (1894) 8 *Harvard Law Review* 1.

Honoré, A.M., "The Dependence of Morality on Law" (1993) 13 *Oxford Journal of Legal Studies* 1.

——, *Making Law Bind* (Oxford: Clarendon Press, 1987).

Honoré, A.M., "A Theory of Coercion" (1990) 10 *Oxford Journal of Legal Studies* 94.

Horwitz, Morton, "The History of the Public/Private Distinction" (1982) 130 *University of Pennsylvania Law Review* 1423,

——, "Law and Economics: Science or Politics?" (1981) 8 *Hofstra Law Review* 905.

——, "The Rule of Law: An Unqualified Human Good?" (1977) 86 *Yale Law Journal* 561.

——, *The Transformation of American Law 1780–1860* (Cambridge, Mass.: Harvard University Press, 1977).

——, *The Transformation of American Law 1870–1960: The Crisis in Legal Orthodoxy* (Oxford: Oxford University Press, 1992).

Hunt, Alan, "The Theory of Critical Legal Studies" (1986) 6 *Oxford Journal of Legal Studies* 1.

Hurley, Susan, *Natural Reasons* (Oxford: Oxford University Press, 1989).

Hutcheson, Joseph, "The Judgment Intuitive: The Function of the 'Hunch' in Judicial Decision" (1929) 14 *Cornell Law Review* 274.

Jurisprudence Symposium (1977) 11 *Georgia Law Review* 969–1424.

Kairys, David ed., *The Politics of Law* (revised ed., New York: Pantheon, 1990).

Kaldor, Nicholas, "Welfare Propositions of Economics and Interpersonal Comparisons of Utility" (1939) 49 *Economics Journal* 549.

Kaplan, Benjamin, "Do Intermediate Appellate Court Have a Lawmaking Function?" (1985) 70 *Massachusetts Law Review* 10.

Kay, Herma Hill, "Equality and Difference: The Case of Pregnancy" (1985) 1 *Berkeley Women's Law Journal* 1.

Kay, Richard, "Adherence to the Original Intentions in Constitutional Adjudication: Three Objections and Responses" (1988) 82 *Northwestern University Law Review* 226.

Kelly, J.M., *A Short History of Western Legal Theory* (Oxford: Clarendon Press, 1992).

Kelman, Mark, *A Guide to Critical Legal Studies* (Cambridge, Mass.: Harvard University Press, 1987).

Kelsen, Hans, "The Concept of the Legal Order" (1982) 27 *American Journal of Jurisprudence* 64 (trans. S. L. Paulson).

——, *General Theory of Law and State* (New York: Russell & Russell, 1945).

——, *General Theory of Norms* (M. Hartney trans. and ed., Oxford: Clarendon Press, 1991).

——, *Introduction to the Problems of Legal Theory* (B. L. Paulson and S. L. Paulson trans., Oxford: Clarendon Press, 1992).

——, "On the Basis of Legal Validity" (1981) 26 *American Journal of Jurisprudence* 178 (trans. S. L. Paulson).

Kelsen, Hans, "On the Theory of Interpretation" (1990) 10 *Legal Studies* 127 (trans. S. L. Paulson).

——, *The Pure Theory of Law* (M. Knight trans., Berkeley, Calif.: University of California Press, 1967).

Kemp, John, *The Philosophy of Kant* (Bristol: Thoemme Press, 1993).

Kennedy, Duncan, "Freedom and Constraint in Adjudication: A Critical Phenomenology" (1986) 36 *Journal of Legal Education* 518.

——, "Legal Education as Training for Hierarchy" in *The Politics of Law* (rev. ed., D. Kairys ed., New York: Pantheon, 1990), pp. 38–58.

Kennedy, Randall, "Racial Critiques of Legal Academia" (1989) 102 *Harvard Law Review* 1745.

Kornblith, Hilary, *Naturalizing Epistemology* (2nd ed., Cambridge, Mass: MIT Press, 1994).

Kornhauser, Lewis, "The Great Image of Authority" (1984) 36 *Stanford Law Review* 349.

Kramer, Matthew, *Critical Legal Theory and the Challenge of Feminism* (London: Rowman & Littlefield, 1995).

Kress, Ken, "Legal Indeterminacy" (1989) 77 *California Law Review* 283.

Kretzmann, Norman, "*Lex Iniusta Non Est Lex*: Laws on Trial in Aquinas' Court of Conscience" (1988) 33 *American Journal of Jurisprudence* 99.

Kripke, Saul, *Wittgenstein on Rules and Private Language* (Cambridge, Mass.: Harvard University Press, 1982).

Landes, William and Posner, Richard, *The Economic Structure of Tort Law* (Cambridge, Mass.: Harvard University Press, 1987).

Leff, Arthur, "Economic Analysis of Law: Some Realism About Nominalism" (1974) 60 *Virginia Law Review* 451.

Leiter, Brian, "Legal Realism" in *A Companion to the Philosophy of Law and Legal Theory* (forthcoming, D. Patterson ed., Oxford: Basil Blackwell, 1986).

——, "Objectivity and the Problems of Jurisprudence" (book review) (1993) 72 *Texas Law Review* 187.

Limerick, Patricia Nelson, "More Than Just Beads and Feathers" (book review), *New York Times Book Review,* January 8, 1995.

Littleton, Christine, "Feminist Jurisprudence: The Difference Method Makes" (1989) 41 *Stanford Law Review* 751.

Llewellyn, Karl, *The Bramble Bush* (New York: Oceana, 1930).

——, *The Common Law Tradition: Deciding Appeals* (Boston: Little, Brown & Co., 1960).

——, "A Realistic Jurisprudence—The Next Step" (1930) 30 *Columbia Law Review* 431.

——, "Some Realism about Realism" (1931) 44 *Harvard Law Review* 1222.

Lloyd, Lord and Freeman, M.D.A., *Lloyd's Introduction to Jurisprudence* (6th ed., London: Sweet & Maxwell, 1995).

Lyons, David, *Ethics and the Rule of Law* (Cambridge: Cambridge University Press, 1984).

——, *Moral Aspects of Legal Theory* (Cambridge: Cambridge University Press, 1993).

MacCormick, Neil, *H. L. A. Hart* (Stanford, Calif.: Stanford University Press, 1981).

——, *Legal Reasoning and Legal Theory* (Oxford: Clarendon Press, 1978).

——, "A Moralistic Case for A-Moralistic Law?" (1985) 20 *Valparaiso University Law Review* 1.

——, "On 'Open Texture' in Law" in *Controversies about Law's Ontology* (P. Amselek and N. MacCormick eds., Edinburgh: Edinburgh University Press, 1991), pp. 73–83.

——, "Reconstruction after Deconstruction: A Response to CLS" (1990) 10 *Oxford Journal of Legal Studies* 539.

——, "Rights in Legislation" in *Law, Morality and Society* (P. M. S. Hacker and J. Raz eds., Oxford: Clarendon Press, 1977), pp. 189–209.

McElroy, Wendy, *XXX: A Woman's Right to Pornography* (New York: St. Martin's Press, 1995).

McGinn, Colin, *Wittgenstein on Meaning* (Oxford: Basil Blackwell, 1984).

Mackie, John, "The Third Theory of Law" (1977) 7 *Philosophy and Public Affairs* 3, reprinted in *Ronald Dworkin and Contemporary Jurisprudence* (M. Cohen ed., London: Duckworth, 1984), pp. 161–170.

MacKinnon, Catharine, *Feminism Unmodified* (Cambridge, Mass.: Harvard University Press, 1987).

——, "Reflections on Sex Equality Under Law" (1991) 100 *Yale Law Journal* 1281.

——, *Sexual Harassment of Working Women* (New Haven: Yale University Press, 1979).

——, *Towards a Feminist Theory of the State* (Cambridge, Mass.: Harvard University Press, 1989).

Marmor, Andrei, *Interpretation and Legal Theory* (Oxford: Clarendon Press, 1992).

Marmor, Andrei ed., *Law and Interpretation* (Oxford: Clarendon Press, 1995).

Matsuda, Mari, "Affirmative Action and Legal Knowledge: Planting Seeds in Plowed-Up Ground" (1988) 11 *Harvard Women's Law Journal* 1.

——, "Looking to the Bottom: Critical Legal Studies and Reparations" (1987) 22 *Harvard Civil Rights-Civil Liberties Law Review* 323.

Matsuda, Mari, Lawrence, Charles, Delgado, Richard and Crenshaw, Kimberlé, "Introduction" in *Words that Wound: Critical Race Theory,*

Assaultive Speech and the First Amendment (Boulder, Colo.: Westview Press, 1993), pp. 1–15.

Mill, John Stuart, "On Liberty" in *On Liberty and Utilitarianism* (New York: Bantam, 1993).

Minow, Martha, *Making All the Difference* (Ithaca: Cornell University Press, 1990).

Moore, Michael, "The Interpretive Turn in Modern Theory: A Turn for the Worse?" (1989) 41 *Stanford Law Review* 871.

——, "Law as a Functional Kind" in *Natural Law Theories* (R. George ed., Oxford: Clarendon Press, 1992), pp. 188–242.

——, "Metaphysics, Epistemology and Legal Theory" (book review) (1987) 60 *Southern California Law Review* 453.

Moore, Underhill, "Rational Basis of Legal Institutions" (1923) 23 *Columbia Law Review* 609.

Morawetz, Thomas, *The Philosophy of Law: An Introduction* (New York: Macmillan, 1980).

Morrison, W. L., *John Austin* (London: Edward Arnold, 1982).

Mueller, Ingo, *Hitler's Justice: The Courts of the Third Reich* (D. L. Schneider trans., Cambridge, Mass.: Harvard University Press, 1991).

Murphy, Jeffrie and Coleman, Jules, *Philosophy of Law: An Introduction to Jurisprudence* (rev. ed., Boulder, Colo.: Westview Press, 1990).

Nader, Laura, "The Anthropological Study of Law" (1965) 67 *American Anthropologist* 3.

Nader, Laura and Todd, Henry eds., *The Disputing Process—Law in Ten Societies* (New York: Columbia University Press, 1978).

Nozick, Robert, *Philosophical Explanations* (Cambridge, Mass.: Harvard University Press, 1981).

Nussbaum, Martha, *Poetic Justice* (Boston: Beacon Press, 1995).

——, "Skepticism about Practical Reason in Literature and the Law" (1994) 107 *Harvard Law Review* 714.

——, "The Use and Abuse of Philosophy in Legal Education" (1993) 45 *Stanford Law Review* 1627.

Oakley, Francis, "Medieval Theories of Natural Law: William of Ockham and the Significance of the Voluntarist Tradition" (1961) 6 *Natural Law Forum* 65.

Olivecrona, Karl, *Law as Fact* (London: Stevens & Sons, 1971).

Olsen, Frances, "Constitutional Law: Feminist Critiques of the Public/Private Distinction" (1993) 10 *Constitutional Commentary* 319.

——, "The Family and the Market: A Study in Ideology and Legal Reform" (1983) 96 *Harvard Law Review* 1497.

Panel Discussion, "Men, Women and Rape" (1994) 63 *Fordham Law Review* 125.

Patterson, Dennis, "Langdell's Legacy" (1995) 90 *Northwestern University Law Review* 901.

Paulson, Stanley L., "Continental Normativism and Its British Counterpart: How Different Are They?" (1993) 6 *Ratio Juris* 227.

———, "Kelsen on Legal Interpretation" (1990) 10 *Legal Studies* 136.

———, "Kelsen's Legal Theory: The Final Round" (1992) 12 *Oxford Journal of Legal Studies* 265.

———, "Lon L. Fuller, Gustav Radbruch, and the 'Positivist' Theses" (1994) 13 *Law and Philosophy* 313.

———, "Material and Formal Authorisation in Kelsen's Pure Theory" (1980) 39 *Cambridge Law Journal* 172.

———, "The Neo-Kantian Dimension of Kelsen's Pure Theory of Law" (1992) 12 *Oxford Journal of Legal Studies* 311.

———, "On Ideal Form, Empowering Norms, and 'Normative Functions' " (1990) 3 *Ratio Juris* 84.

———, "Towards a Periodization of the Pure Theory of Law" in *Hans Kelsen's Legal Theory* (L. Gianformaggio ed., Torino: G. Giappichelli, 1990), pp. 11–47.

Peller, Gary, "The Metaphysics of American Law" (1985) 73 *California Law Review* 1151.

Perry, Stephen, "Interpretation and Methodology in Legal Theory" in *Law and Interpretation* (A. Marmor ed., Oxford: Clarendon Press, 1995), pp. 97–135.

Pigou, A.C., *The Economics of Welfare* (4th ed., London: Macmillan and Co., 1932).

Plato, *The Complete Dialogues of Plato* (E. Hamilton and H. Cairns eds., Princeton: Princeton University Press, 1961).

Polinsky, A.M., *An Introduction to Law and Economics* (2nd ed., Boston: Little, Brown and Co., 1989).

Posner, Richard, *Economic Analysis of Law* (4th ed., Boston: Little, Brown, 1992).

———, *The Economics of Justice* (Cambridge, Mass.: Harvard University Press, 1983).

———, "The Ethical and Political Basis of the Efficiency Norm in Common Law Adjudication" (1980) 8 *Hofstra Law Review* 487, reprinted in modified form in *The Economics of Justice* (Cambridge, Mass.: Harvard University Press, 1983), pp. 88–115.

———, "The Ethical Significance of Free Choice: A Reply to Professor West" (1986) 99 *Harvard Law Review.*

———, *Law and Literature: A Misunderstood Relation* (Cambridge, Mass.: Harvard University Press, 1988).

———, *Overcoming Law* (Cambridge, Mass.: Harvard University Press, 1995).

Posner, Richard, *The Problems of Jurisprudence* (Cambridge, Mass.: Harvard University Press, 1990).

——, *Sex and Reason* (Cambridge, Mass.: Harvard University Press, 1992).

——, "Utilitarianism, Economics, and Legal Theory" (1979) 8 *Journal of Legal Studies* 103.

Postema, Gerald, "Coordination and Convention at the Foundations of Law" (1982) 11 *Journal of Legal Studies* 165.

——, "Implicit Law" (1994) 13 *Law and Philosophy* 361.

——, "The Normativity of Law" in *Issues in Contemporary Legal Philosophy* (Ruth Gavison ed., Oxford: Clarendon Press, 1987), pp. 81–113.

——, " 'Protestant' Interpretation and Social Practices" (1987) 6 *Law and Philosophy* 283.

Pound, Roscoe, "The Call for a Realist Jurisprudence" (1931) 44 *Harvard Law Review* 697.

——, "Mechanical Jurisprudence" (1908) 8 *Columbia Law Review* 605.

Putnam, Hilary, "The Meaning of 'Meaning' " in *Mind, Language and Reality* (New York: Cambridge University Press, 1975), pp. 215–271.

Radin, Margaret, "Market- Inalienability" (1987) 100 *Harvard Law Review* 189.

——, "Reconsidering the Rule of Law" (1989) 69 *Boston University Law Review* 781.

Radin, Max, "Statutory Interpretation" (1930) 43 *Harvard Law Review* 863.

——, "The Theory of Judicial Decision: or How Judges Think" (1925) 11 *American Bar Association Journal* 357.

Rawls, John, *Political Liberalism* (New York: Columbia University Press, 1993).

——, *A Theory of Justice* (Cambridge, Mass.: Harvard University Press, 1971).

Raz, Joseph, *The Authority of Law* (Oxford: Clarendon Press, 1979).

——, "Autonomy, Toleration, and the Harm Principle" in *Issues in Contemporary Legal Philosophy* (R. Gavison ed., Oxford: Clarendon Press, 1987), pp. 313–333.

——, *The Concept of a Legal System* (2nd ed., Oxford: Clarendon Press, 1980).

——, "Critical Study: Kelsen's General Theory of Norms" (1976) 6 *Philosophia* 495.

——, "Dworkin: A New Link in the Chain" (book review) (1986) 74 *California Law Review* 1103.

——, *Ethics in the Public Domain* (Oxford: Clarendon Press, 1994).

——, "Facing Up" (1989) 62 *Southern California Law Review* 1153.

Raz, Joseph, "Intention in Interpretation" in *The Autonomy of Law* (R. George ed., Oxford: Clarendon Press, 1996) pp. 249–286.

——, "Legal Rights" (1984) 4 *Oxford Journal of Legal Studies* 1, reprinted in *Ethics in the Public Domain* (Oxford: Clarendon Press, 1995), pp. 238–260.

——, "Legal Principles and the Limits of Law" in *Ronald Dworkin and Contemporary Jurisprudence* (M. Cohen ed., London: Duckworth, 1984), pp. 73–87.

——, *The Morality of Freedom* (Oxford: Clarendon Press, 1986).

——, *Practical Reason and Norms* (2nd ed., Princeton: Princeton University Press, 1990).

Rhode, Debra, *Justice and Gender* (Cambridge, Mass.: Harvard University Press, 1989).

Roberts, Simon, *Order and Dispute* (Middlesex, England: Penguin, 1979).

Rosenberg, Jay, *The Practice of Philosophy* (2nd ed., Englewood Cliffs, N.J.: Prentice-Hall, 1984).

Scales-Trent, Judith, "Black Women and the Constitution: Finding Our Place, Asserting Our Rights" (1989) 24 *Harvard Civil Rights-Civil Liberties Law Review* 9.

Schauer, Frederick, Critical Notice (reviewing R. Shiner, *Norm and Nature* (1992)) (1994) 24 *Canadian Journal of Philosophy* 495.

——, "Fuller's Internal Point of View" (1994) 13 *Law and Philosophy* 285.

——, *Playing by the Rules* (Oxford: Oxford University Press, 1991).

——, "Positivism as Pariah" in *The Autonomy of Law: Essays in Legal Positivism* (R. George ed., Oxford: Clarendon Press, 1996) pp. 31–55.

Scheffler, Samuel ed., *Consequentialism and its Critics* (Oxford: Oxford University Press, 1988).

Schlag, Pierre, "An Appreciative Comment on Coase's *The Problem of Social Cost*: A View from the Left" (1986) *Wisconsin Law Review* 919.

Schlegel, John Henry, "American Legal Realism and Empirical Social Science: From the Yale Experience" (1979) 28 *Buffalo Law Review* 459.

——, "American Legal Realism and Empirical Social Science: The Singular Case of Underhill Moore" (1980) 29 *Buffalo Law Review* 195.

——, "The Ten Thousand Dollar Question" (book review) (1989) 41 *Stanford Law Review* 435.

Shiner, Roger, *Norm and Nature: The Movements of Legal Thought* (Oxford: Clarendon Press, 1992).

Simmonds, N.E., *Central Issues in Jurisprudence: Justice, Law and Rights* (London: Sweet & Maxwell, 1986).

Singer, Joseph, "Legal Realism Now" (1988) 76 *California Law Review* 465.

Smith, M.B.E., "The Duty to Obey the Law" in *A Companion to the Philosophy of Law and Legal Theory* (forthcoming, D. Patterson ed., Oxford: Basil Blackwell, 1996).

——, "Is There a Prima Facie Obligation to Obey the Law?" (1973) 82 *Yale Law Journal* 950.

Smith, Patricia, "Feminist Jurisprudence and the Nature of Law" in *A Companion to the Philosophy of Law and Legal Theory* (forthcoming, D. Patterson ed., Oxford: Basil Blackwell, 1996).

Smith, Patricia ed., *Feminist Jurisprudence* (Oxford: Oxford University Press, 1993).

Solum, Lawrence, "On the Indeterminacy Crisis: Critiquing Critical Dogma" (1987) 54 *University of Chicago Law Review* 462.

Soper, Philip, "Legal Theory and the Problem of Definition" (book review) (1983) 50 *University of Chicago Law Review* 1170.

——, "Some Natural Confusions About Natural Law" (1992) 90 *Michigan Law Review* 2393.

Sophocles, "Antigone" in *Sophocles I* (E. Wyckoff trans., Chicago: University of Chicago Press, 1954), pp. 157–204.

Stephen, James Fitzjames, *Liberty, Equality, Fraternity* (Indianapolis: Liberty Fund, 1993).

Summers, Robert, *Lon L. Fuller* (Stanford: Stanford University Press, 1984).

Symposium on Critical Race Theory (1994) 82 *California Law Review* 741–1125.

Symposium on Efficiency as a Legal Concern (1980) 8 *Hofstra Law Review* 485–770.

Symposium on *Law's Empire* (1987) 6 *Law and Philosophy* 281–438.

Symposium on Lon Fuller (1994) 13 *Law and Philosophy* 253–418.

Symposium on Post-Chicago Law and Economics (1989) 65 *Chicago-Kent Law Review* 3–191.

Tannen, Deborah, *You Just Don't Understand* (New York: William Morrow, 1990).

Taylor, Charles, *Philosophy and the Human Sciences* (Cambridge: Cambridge University Press, 1985).

Thomas, W. John, "Social Solidarity and the Enforcement of Morality Revisited: Some Thoughts on H. L. A. Hart's Critique of Durkheim" (1994) 32 *American Criminal Law Review* 49.

Tur, Richard and Twining, William, eds., *Essays on Kelsen* (Oxford: Clarendon Press, 1986).

Tushnet, Mark, "Critical Legal Studies: An Introduction to its Origins and Underpinnings" (1986) 36 *Journal of Legal Education* 505.

——, "An Essay on Rights" (1984) 62 *Texas Law Review* 1363.

Tushnet, Mark, "Following the Rules Laid Down: A Critique of Interpretation and Neutral Principles" (1983) 96 *Harvard Law Review* 781.

Twining, William, "Academic Law and Legal Philosophy: The Significance of Herbert Hart" (1979) 95 *Law Quarterly Review* 557.

——, "The Bad Man Revisited" (1973) 58 *Cornell Law Review* 275.

——, *Karl Llewellyn and the Realist Movement* (Norman, Oklahoma: University of Oklahoma Press, 1985).

Unger, Roberto, *The Critical Legal Studies Movement* (Cambridge, Mass.: Harvard University Press, 1986).

von Wright, Georg Henrik, *Norm and Action* (London: Routledge & Kegan Paul, 1963).

Waldron, Jeremy, "Legislators' Intentions and Unintentional Legislation" in *Law and Interpretation* (A. Marmor ed., Oxford: Clarendon Press, 1995), pp. 329–356.

——, *Liberal Rights* (Cambridge: Cambridge University Press, 1993).

——, "Why Law—Efficacy, Freedom, or Fidelity?" (1994) 13 *Law and Philosophy* 259.

Waluchow, Wil, *Inclusive Legal Positivism* (Oxford: Clarendon Press, 1994).

Weber, Max, *The Methodology of the Social Sciences* (E. Shils and H. Finch eds., New York: Free Press, 1949).

——, " 'Objectivity' in Social Science and Social Policy" in *The Methodology of the Social Sciences* (E. Shils and H. Finch eds., New York: Free Press, 1949), pp. 50–112.

——, *The Protestant Ethic and the Spirit of Capitalism* (T. Parsons trans., New York: Scribner, 1976).

Wechsler, Herbert, "Toward Neutral Principles in Constitutional Law" (1959) 73 *Harvard Law Review* 15.

Weinreb, Lloyd, *Natural Law and Justice* (Cambridge, Mass.: Harvard University Press, 1987).

——, "The Natural Law Tradition: Comments on Finnis" (1986) 36 *Journal of Legal Education* 501.

Weinrib, Ernest, "The Case for a Duty of Rescue" (1980) 90 *Yale Law Journal* 247.

——, *The Idea of Private Law* (Cambridge, Mass.: Harvard University Press, 1995).

Weisberg, D. Kelly ed., *Feminist Legal Theory: Foundations* (Philadelphia: Temple University Press, 1993).

West, Robin, "Authority, Autonomy and Choice: The Role of Consent in the Moral and Political Visions of Franz Kafka and Richard Posner" (1985) 99 *Harvard Law Review* 384.

West, Robin, "Jurisprudence and Gender" (1988) 55 *University of Chicago Law Review* 1.

West Robin, "Submission, Choice, and Ethics: A Rejoinder to Judge Posner" (1986) 99 *Harvard Law Review* 1449.

White, James Boyd, "Economics and Law: Two Cultures in Tension" (1987) 54 *Tennessee Law Review* 161.

Williams, Bernard, *Ethics and the Limit of Philosophy* (Cambridge, Mass.: Harvard University Press, 1985).

Williams, Patricia, *The Alchemy of Race and Rights* (Cambridge, Mass.: Harvard University Press, 1991).

——, "Fetal Fictions: An Exploration of Property Archetypes in Racial and Gendered Contexts" (1990) 42 *Florida Law Review* 81.

Winch, Peter, *The Idea of a Social Science* (London: Routledge, 1958).

Winston, Kenneth, "The Ideal Element in a Definition of Law" (1986) 5 *Law and Philosophy* 89.

——, "Introduction" in Lon Fuller, *The Principles of Social Order* (K. Winston ed., Durham, N.C.: Duke University Press, 1981), pp. 11–44.

——, "Legislators and Liberty" (1994) 13 *Law and Philosophy* 389.

Wiseman, Zipporah, "The Limits of Vision: Karl Llewellyn and the Merchant Rules" (1987) 100 *Harvard Law Review* 465.

Wittgenstein, Ludwig, *Philosophical Investigations* (3rd ed., G. E. M. Anscombe trans., New York: Macmillan, 1968).

Index